COMMUNICATION AND DEMOCRACY
Exploring the Intellectual Frontiers
in Agenda-Setting Theory

LEA's COMMUNICATION SERIES
Jennings Bryant/Dolf Zillmann, General Editors

Select titles in Journalism (Maxwell McCombs, Advisory Editor) include:

For a complete list of other titles in LEA's Communication Series, please contact Lawrence Erlbaum Associates, Publishers

COMMUNICATION AND DEMOCRACY
Exploring the Intellectual Frontiers
in Agenda-Setting Theory

Edited by
Maxwell McCombs
University of Texas at Austin
Donald L. Shaw
University of North Carolina at Chapel Hill
David Weaver
Indiana University

LEA LAWRENCE ERLBAUM ASSOCIATES, PUBLISHERS
1997 Mahwah, New Jersey   London

Lawrence Erlbaum Associates, Inc., Publishers
10 Industrial Avenue
Mahwah, New Jersey 07430

Library of Congress Cataloging-in-Publication Data

Communication and democracy : exploring the intellectual
frontiers in agenda-setting theory / edited by Maxwell
McCombs / Donald L. Shaw / David Weaver.
          p.   cm.
     Includes bibliographical references and index.
     ISBN 0-8058-2554-1 (c : alk. paper). — ISBN 0-8058-
2555-X (p : alk. paper)
     1. Mass media—Political aspects. 2. Press and poli-
tics. 3. Mass media and public opinion. I. McCombs,
Maxwell E. II. Shaw, Donald Lewis. III. Weaver, David
H. (David Hugh), 1946– .
P95.8.C559 1997
302.23—dc20   97-12616
                                                   CIP

Printed in the United States of America
10 9 8 7 6 5 4 3 2 1

Contents

Prologue:
"The Game Is Afoot"

Exciting intellectual frontiers are open for exploration as agenda-setting theory moves beyond its 25th anniversary. *Communication and Democracy* offers an intriguing set of maps to guide this exploration over the near future, calling to scholars as Sherlock Holmes did to Dr. Watson when a new case arose, "Come, Watson, come! The game is afoot."

By way of preface, this is not the first book that anyone should read about the agenda-setting role of mass communication. This is a book for those who already are reasonably well read in the research literature that has accumulated in the 25 years since publication of McCombs and Shaw's original 1972 *Public Opinion Quarterly* article, a literature documenting the influence of the news media agenda on the public agenda in a wide variety of geographic and social settings, elaborating the characteristics of audiences and media that enhance or diminish those agenda-setting effects, and cataloging those exogenous factors explaining who sets the media's agenda. For those acquainted with that literature, this is the book to read. An exciting set of maps for explicating new levels of agenda-setting theory have been sketched here by a new generation of young scholars, launching an enterprise that has significant implications both for theoretical research and for the day-to-day role of mass communication in democratic societies.

Prominent among these maps of the new frontiers are those detailing what recently has come to be called the second level of agenda-setting theory. Most of the research in the 25 years subsequent to the original Chapel Hill study closely followed its lead. Taking the metaphor of agenda almost literally, the emphasis was on the agenda of issues found in the news media and among the general public. Although a few investigators probed other kinds of agendas and agenda items—such as Weaver, Graber, McCombs, and Eyal's (1981) investigations of the salience of political interest and candidate images on personal agendas during the 1976 U.S. presidential campaign—the vast majority followed the traditions of public opinion research and tracked issues.

In the abstract, most of these studies, whether they examined issues, political interest, the slate of contenders during the presidential primaries, or whatever, focused on an agenda of objects. Explicitly stating the focus of the theory in this way, an agenda of objects, immediately suggests a second level of attention. Objects have attributes. When the news media report on public issues, political candidates, the presidential campaign, or any other object, they describe that object. In these descriptions some attributes are very prominent and frequently mentioned, some are given passing notice, and others are omitted. In short, news reports also define an agenda of attributes that vary considerably in their salience. Similarly, when people talk about and think about these objects—public issues, presidential candidates, or whatever—the attributes ascribed to these objects also vary considerably in their salience. These agendas of attributes are the second level of agenda setting. The core theoretical idea is the same for agendas of attributes as it is for agendas of objects: The salience of elements, objects or attributes, on the media agenda influences the salience of those elements on the public agenda (McCombs, 1992; McCombs & Evatt, 1995). By extension, of course, we can talk about the transfer of salience from any agenda to another, the president of the United States to the news media, the *New York Times* to other newspapers, and so forth.

At the first level of agenda setting are agendas of objects. This is the traditional domain of agenda-setting research, represented by an accumulation of hundreds of studies over the past quarter-century. At the second level of agenda setting are agendas of attributes. This second level is one of the new theoretical frontiers whose aspects are discussed in detail in the opening chapters of *Communication and Democracy*. Other chapters offer maps of yet other theoretical frontiers. Among the frontiers mapped by these chapters are political advertising agendas and their impact on behavior, the framing of various agendas in the mass media and the differential impact of print and TV, the theoretical role of individual differences in the agenda-setting influence of the news media on the public agenda, methodological advances for determining cause and effect roles in agenda setting, and the application of agenda-setting theory to historical analysis.

There is an overview in Fig. P.1 of these frontier territories that are mapped by the chapters of *Communication and Democracy*. At the top of the diagram are the familiar elements of the agenda-setting idea, the media agenda, and the public agenda. This diagram has been expanded to call explicit attention to the two levels of agenda setting, the influence of object salience in the news media on object salience among the public (Level 1) and the influence of attribute salience in the news media on attribute salience among the public (Level 2).

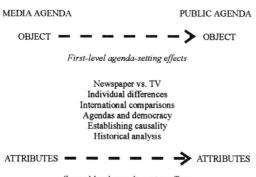

MEDIA AGENDA   PUBLIC AGENDA

OBJECT ➤ OBJECT

First-level agenda-setting effects

Newspaper vs. TV
Individual differences
International comparisons
Agendas and democracy
Establishing causality
Historical analysis

ATTRIBUTES ➤ ATTRIBUTES

Second-level agenda-setting effects

Framing the agenda   Impact on opinions
Political advertising   Impact on behavior

FIG. P. 1. Topics discussed in the various chapters are displayed here as first- or second-level agenda-setting effects.

Centered under the first level are summary labels for a variety of theoretical maps presented in the book. Of course, these research expeditions also can be pursued at the second level of agenda setting. Listed first under the second level is a summary label for the opening chapters of *Communication and Democracy*. Also at the second level are additional theoretical topics listed under either the media agenda or the public agenda. It is a rich array of topics.

Drawing further on the Sherlock Holmes tradition, Arthur Conan Doyle described life at 221B Baker Street as consisting of periods of intense excitement when a case was afoot that were interspersed among lengthy periods of intellectual torpor, punctuated by pistol practice on the living room wall or other efforts at arousal. This may be overdone as an analogue of life in social science research, but in the intellectual life of agenda-setting research most certainly there have been periods of intense excitement over the exploration of new ideas interspersed among more quiescent, conservative periods of careful extension and explication. At times, scholars have been explorers like Lewis and Clark, whose journals sketched the outlines of a vast new territory. At other times, the role of scholars has been more like those anonymous surveyors who painstakingly mapped the routes for the transcontinental railroads. We are now entering a new period of creative exploration in agenda-setting research. The chapters of this book have been prepared by early explorers for the benefit of other scholars who would join them in mapping new theoretical territories over the next few years.

AN INTERNATIONAL EXPEDITION

The editors of this book—Maxwell McCombs, Donald Shaw, and David Weaver—represent the established generation of agenda-setting scholars. McCombs and Shaw, of course, carried out the original Chapel Hill study.

Weaver joined in the very next project, a panel study of the 1972 U.S. presidential election reported in *The Emergence of American Political Issues* (Shaw & McCombs, 1977) and was the lead author of *Media Agenda-Setting in a Presidential Election* (Weaver et al., 1981), a year-long panel study of the 1976 U.S. presidential election. All three have continued to contribute to agenda-setting research, but a new generation of young scholars also has made important contributions to the evolution of agenda-setting theory. So in the fall of 1994, the three editors invited 14 young scholars to prepare theoretical essays outlining the priority areas that should be pursued in agenda-setting research in the coming years. For purposes of this invitation, "young scholars" were defined as persons who had finished graduate school in the last 5 or 6 years and who had published agenda-setting research.

Nearly all of these persons have some direct personal link with one of the three editors, most commonly as a graduate student who studied with one of the editors for his or her PhD, but sometimes the role is faculty colleague or research collaborator. This network of scholars constitutes a loosely linked invisible college, too loosely linked in the view of the editors because with few exceptions the links are to a single senior editor without direct connections among the young scholars themselves. The international scatter of this college—from Europe across the United States to Asia—is an inadequate explanation for the dispersion of this college in a time of e-mail, fax, and frequent international conferences.

In view of this situation as agenda-setting theory moves into a new era, the goals of this book are threefold:

- To introduce a broad set of ideas about agenda setting.
- To enrich the exploration of these ideas by enhancing scholarly dialogue among the members of this invisible college.
- To enhance the discussion of agenda-setting research in seminars and research groups around the world. Above all, this book is an invitation to others to become active members of the invisible college of agenda-setting scholarship.

COMMUNICATION AND DEMOCRACY

Communication is central to democracy. Whether the simple face-to-face dialogues of the Greek agora or the complex dialogues mixing conversations, narrowcasting, and mass media in contemporary democracies, communication is what democracy is about. This is a time of great change both for democracy as a general political model and for the underlying communication patterns. On the international stage, there are more than a dozen emerging democracies, with particularly strong, concurrent trends in East Asia, Eastern Europe, and South America. But the surge of democracy is literally worldwide. In all these countries, and even more so in the established democracies, there has been a revolution in the techniques of politics and political communication in the latter half of this century. A deluge of public opinion polling and the preeminence of television—both its news programming and its reach as an advertising medium—are only the most visible aspects of the changes in democratic politics. More fundamental than these obtrusive changes in the nature of political campaigns is a shift in the very dynamics of democratic politics, a shift with particular implications for journalism as a profession and for political communication as a civic process. Summing up this situation in *Politics, Media, and Modern Democracy*, Swanson and Mancini (1996) noted:

> In many countries, the presumed importance of mass media, especially television news, as a conduit to citizens whose voting decisions reflect momentary opinions rather than historical allegiances has led to a struggle between politicians and a more or less independent media establishment over who shall control the agendas of campaigns. (p. 252)

In short, understanding the dynamics of agenda setting is central to understanding the dynamics of contemporary democracy. This book's set of theoretical essays, grounded in the accumulated literature of agenda-setting theory and in the creative insights of young scholars, will help lead the way toward that understanding. Agenda setting has remained a vital and productive area of communication research over a quarter-century because it has continued to introduce new research questions into the marketplace of ideas and to integrate this work with other theoretical concepts and perspectives about journalism and mass communication.

Each new generation writes its own history of the world because it comes of age under new formative circumstances, wrote Protess and McCombs (1991) in introducing their anthology of agenda-setting research. Although they had in mind the influence of the mass media on the general public, this observation is no less true for the specialized population of communication scholars represented in *Communication and Democracy*. A new generation of scholars has begun the task of writing its own history of mass communication. The game is afoot!

I

THE PICTURES
IN OUR HEADS

1

Filling in the Tapestry:
The Second Level of Agenda Setting

Salma Ghanem

More than two decades have passed since the original agenda-setting hypothesis was stated by McCombs and Shaw (1972), and scholars have published more than 200 articles weaving agenda-setting research into a rich theory (Rogers, Dearing, & Bregman, 1993). Over these years this research has detailed the patterns in the transfer of issue salience from the media to the public, the contingent conditions for agenda setting, and influences on the media agenda. The underlying assumption for all three areas is that what is covered in the media affects what the public thinks about.

Agenda setting is now detailing a second level of effects that examines how media coverage affects both what the public thinks about and how the public thinks about it. This second level of agenda setting deals with the specific attributes of a topic and how this agenda of attributes also influences public opinion (McCombs & Evatt, 1995).

In the abstract, every agenda consists of a set of objects. In turn, each of these objects possesses a set of attributes. For example, the agenda of issues examined in the original Chapel Hill study—and in numerous subsequent studies—is, in the abstract, a set of objects. In contrast, Benton and Frazier's (1976) examination of one object on the issue agenda, the economy, probed two sets of attributes: the specific problems, causes, and proposed solutions associated with this general issue; and the pro and con rationales for economic policies. Agenda setting is about more than issue or object salience.

This shift in emphasis does not negate the basic agenda-setting hypothesis, but rather builds on what already exists. It is one highway linking up with another major thoroughfare. The first level of agenda setting deals with the transfer of object salience from the media to the public agenda, whereas the second level of agenda setting involves two major hypotheses about attribute salience:

1. The way an issue or other object is covered in the media (the attributes emphasized in the news) affects the way the public thinks about that object.
2. The way an issue or other object is covered in the media (the attributes emphasized in the news) affects the salience of that object on the public agenda.

Figure 1.1 shows the difference between the two levels of agenda setting and also illustrates the two hypotheses about second-level agenda-setting effects.

For both the first and second levels of agenda setting, the independent and dependent variables are the same: There is a media agenda and a public agenda. The theoretical difference between the two levels is in the details of the way that the variables are conceptualized and operationalized.

For first-level agenda setting, the independent variable is considered in terms of objects, the topics or issues discussed on the media agenda. For the second level, the media agenda (the same independent variable as at the first level) is considered in terms of attributes or perspectives. The dependent variable for both levels of agenda setting still remains the public agenda. However, in the case of the first level, the public agenda is operationalized in terms of issue or topic salience, whereas at the second level the salience of the attributes of the issue or topic are measured.

These two levels of agenda-setting effects are represented by the two horizontal arrows in Fig. 1.1. The top arrow illustrates the influence of issue or topic salience. This is the original agenda-setting hypothesis. The bottom arrow illlustrates the influence of attribute salience on how people think about an object on the agenda. This is the initial second-level agenda-setting hypothesis stated earlier. The diagonal arrow represents the second hypothesis stated earlier, the influence of particular attributes or perspectives in news coverage on the salience of an issue or topic on the public agenda. Some of the attributes of an object presented in the media can have striking influence on the salience of that object on the public agenda. This influence of attributes or frames from the second level of the media agenda on the salience of objects on the first level of the public agenda defines "compelling arguments" in the media message (McCombs, 1996).

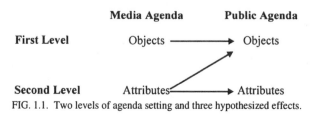

FIG. 1.1. Two levels of agenda setting and three hypothesized effects.

The agenda of objects and the agenda of attributes can be looked at as two concentric circles with the agenda of issues being the outer circle and the agenda of attributes imbedded within that circle. Kosicki (1993) referred to agenda setting as the "shell of the topic." The shell of the topic can be compared to the issues or other objects examined, whereas the attributes are an exploration of what is inside the shell. Noelle-Neumann and Mathes (1987) suggested that media content can be examined at three levels: agenda setting, focusing, and evaluation. Agenda setting deals with the importance of issues and problems; focusing deals with the definition of issues; and problems and evaluation deals with the creation of a climate of opinion. We can easily replace their term agenda setting with the first level of agenda setting and their second and third levels by the second level of agenda setting.

The link between the two levels of agenda setting takes us back to Lippmann's (1922) idea of pictures in our heads. By examining the attributes of an issue, we get a more detailed examination of that picture. The examination of attributes is similar to the examination of an issue or other object under a magnifying lens, whereas the agenda of issues deals with examination by the naked eye. The attributes of an object are the set of perspectives or frames that journalists and the public employ to think about each object. How news frames impact the public agenda is the emerging second level of agenda setting.

A recent study on the coverage of crime in the news media (Ghanem, 1996) examined both levels of agenda setting and introduced the concept of compelling arguments, which is represented by Hypothesis 2 earlier and by the diagonal arrow in Fig. 1.1. Replicating first-level agenda-setting effects, salience of crime on the media agenda correlated positively (.73) with salience of crime on the public agenda over a period of several years. Supporting Hypothesis 2 about compelling arguments, 13 attributes of this coverage that were examined also correlated positively with the salience of crime on the public agenda. In this particular study, the salience of crime on the public agenda was not affected by actual crime rates, which had been decreasing during the years examined. Hypothesis 1 about second-level effects was not tested in this study.

Several studies did explore this second level of agenda setting even before explicit theorizing had begun. During the 1976 presidential election, Weaver, Graber, McCombs, and Eyal (1981) conducted a nine-wave panel study that looked at the agenda of attributes in the descriptions of presidential candidates in the news and the agenda of attributes in voters' descriptions of the candidates. A strong cross-lagged correlation was found between the media agenda and the public agenda. Becker and McCombs (1978) looked at the 1976 presidential primaries and found considerable correspondence between the agenda of attributes in *Newsweek* and the agenda of attributes in New York Democrats' descriptions of the contenders.

Outside the setting of presidential elections, Benton and Frazier (1976) examined the issue of the economy at three levels of information holding. Level 1 included general issue names, the economy in this case; Level 2 consisted of subissues, including problems, causes, and solutions; and Level 3 contained more specific information about the subissues. Levels 2 and 3 are similar to the focusing level mentioned by Noelle-Neumann and Mathes (1987). Once again significant correspondence between the media and the public agenda was found. Iyengar and Simon's (1993) research on the coverage of the Persian Gulf crisis provides another example that illustrates the difference between the two levels. When respondents state that the Gulf crisis is the most important problem facing the nation, we are dealing with the first level. When respondents describe the crisis in terms of military or diplomatic options, we are dealing with the second level.

Many researchers, including Iyengar and Simon (1993), have distinguished between the first and second levels of agenda setting by labeling the attributes *frames*. No discussion of the second level of agenda setting is complete without an extensive examination of media frames. The principal difference between the research literature on frames and on the second level of agenda setting is that the latter examines the impact of news frames on the public agenda, whereas many framing studies have focused solely on the frames themselves.

DEFINITIONS OF FRAMES

Researchers from a variety of social sciences have defined frames, some in terms of their effects on the audience, and others by focusing on what a frame is. Frames, according to Entman (1993), "call attention to some aspects of reality while obscuring other elements, which might lead audiences to have different reactions" (p. 55). The way a problem is framed might determine how people understand and evaluate the issue. Framing is the selection of a perceived reality "in such a way as to promote a particular problem definition, causal interpretation, moral evaluation, and/or treatment recommendation for the item described" (p. 52). Entman (1989) also argued that "news slant significantly influences public opinion" (p. 75).

According to Gamson and Modigliani (1989), every policy issue has a culture where the discourse evolves and changes over time and provides interpretive interpretations or packages: "A package has an internal structure. At its core is a central organizing idea, or frame, for making sense of relevant events, suggesting what is at issue" (p. 3). Hackett (1984) linked frames to ideology, which is defined as "a system of ideas, values, and propositions which is characteristic of a particular social class..." (p. 261). According to Gitlin (1980), "Media frames are persistent patterns of cognition, interpretation, and presentation, of selection, emphasis and exclusion, by which symbol-handlers routinely organize discourse" (p. 7). Goffman (1974) referred to frames as strips that are the principles of organization that form the definition of a situation.

Tankard, Hendrickson, Silberman, Bliss, and Ghanem (1991) described a media frame as "the central organizing idea for news content that supplies a context and suggests what the issue is through the use of selection, emphasis, exclusion and elaboration" (p. 3). A story angle or story line "which transforms an occurrence into a news event, and that, in turn, into a news report, is a frame" (Mendelsohn, 1993, p. 150). The essence of news judgment, according to Tiffen (1989), are story frames or angles. Framing is defined in cognitive psychology "as the function that specifies the relations that hold among the arguments comprising a particular conceptual bundle at a particular level of abstraction" (Friedman, 1979, p. 321).

How options are framed affects decision making. Studies have shown that the wording of examples leads people to choose differently (Machina, 1990). If a situation is presented to a person in terms of losses, the decision is very different than if it is presented to that person in terms of gains (Elster, 1990). The perception of problems and evaluation of probabilities produce predictable shifts of preference depending on how the problem is framed (Tversky & Kahneman, 1981, 1990).

Social scientists have long discussed the importance of word choice in survey questionnaires. For example, Fine (1992) conducted a study on the impact of issue framing on public opinion toward affirmative action programs. He concluded that the way questions are framed affects how people perceive issues. The same logic can be applied to the coverage of issues in the media: Depending on how an issue is presented or framed in the media, the public will think about that issue in a particular way. Media coverage of issues in the media has been linked to public opinion where the salience of issues in the media agenda leads to the salience of issues in the public agenda. How the media covers an issue, argue researchers, also can have a cognitive influence on how the public thinks about the issue. This transference of the salience of attributes is the core of the second level of agenda setting.

Framing and Other Mass Communication Theories

One of the ways to understand the concept of framing is to examine the concept in light of other theories and concepts in the field of communication, including agenda setting, schema, priming, bias, indexing, and cultivation.

Agenda Setting. As mentioned earlier, frames and attributes can be used interchangeably when we are dealing with the second level of agenda setting. Price and Tewksbury (1995), on the other hand, saw agenda setting as one variant of priming or framing. They did not differ, however, from other scholars in their definitions of both concepts. Agenda setting looks on story selection as a determinant of public perceptions of issue importance and, indirectly through priming, evaluations of political leaders. Framing focuses not on which topics or issues are selected for coverage by the news media, but instead on the particular ways those issues are presented, on the ways public problems are formulated for the media audience.

Wanta, Williams, and Hu (1991) regarded story frames as contingent conditions in the agenda-setting process. They examined the agenda-setting effect of international stories and observed that some types of international story frames have a stronger agenda-setting impact on the public than other frames. Patterson (1993a) also made the distinction between agenda setting and framing and said that every news story has a theme or a frame that functions as the central organizing idea, but that the topic is the summary label of the domain of social experiences covered by a story.

Another way to look at the relationship between agenda setting and framing is that traditional agenda setting posits that the media tell us what to think about, and framing deals with the issue of the media telling us how to think about an issue. Framing "shares with agenda-setting research a focus on the public policy issues in the news and in voters' minds. However, it expands beyond what people talk or think about by examining how they think and talk " (Patterson, 1993b, p. 70).

Basically, the first level of agenda setting deals with the selection of issues by the news media and its impact on the public agenda. Framing deals with the selection of elements within a particular issue. The second level of agenda setting deals with the influence of the particular elements of an issue on the public's agenda of attributes.

Schema.   A concept closely linked to framing is schema. Schemas are the cognitive structures that organize a person's thinking (Entman, 1989). These cognitive structures are based on prior knowledge (Fiske & Linville, 1980). A schema as defined by Fiske and Taylor (1991) is "a cognitive structure that represents knowledge about a concept or type of stimulus, including its attributes and the relations among those attributes" (p. 98). This cognitive structure according to McLeod, Sun, Chi, and Pan (1990) reduces complicated information into a manageable number of frames, and they refer to frames as the architecture of cognition. According to Graber (1988), people use schematic thinking to handle information. They extract only those limited amounts of information from news stories that they consider important for incorporation into their schemata. She added that the media make major contributions to this schema formation.

Perceptions, according to Fiske and Taylor (1991), involve the interplay between what is out there and what a person brings to it. Schemas deal with what a person brings with him or her when examining an issue. The focus of framing at the second level of agenda setting deals predominantly with what is out there (at least in terms of its representation in the media) and not what an individual brings to it and not how it came about psychologically.

Framing in this instance deals with the manifest content of media messages. Some, however, do use the terms frames and schemas interchangeably when referring to media content. Hagen (1995), for example, stated, "The term news schema refers to the typical narrative structure of news items, or in other words, to the overall organization of global topics a news item is about" (p. 5).

Priming.   Priming, on the other hand, is the process by which schemas are activated (McLeod et al., 1990). According to Iyengar and Kinder (1987), priming is a psychological process whereby media emphasis on particular issues activates in people's memories previously acquired information. Price and Tewksbury (1995) took a narrower approach to priming and stated that priming is the effect of the media's agenda on the public's evaluations of political leaders. They refer to priming as "the tendency of audience members to evaluate their political leaders on the basis of those particular events and issues given attention in recent news reports" (p. 5). Framing, on the other hand, deals with story presentation and thus framing is the "ability of media reports to alter the kinds of considerations people use in forming their opinions" (p. 6).

Bias.   Framing is a form of bias, not an ideological bias, but rather a structural bias. It is a bias that results from the selection process that takes place in the news. Framing can be looked at as a sociological bias that refers to a "systematic (non-random) measurement error, which can be found almost anywhere, including the media" (Lotz, 1991, p. 67). Referring to bias in the media, Lotz stated:

> Whenever reporters have to compress a multifarious reality into a few paragraphs, distortion inevitably results, particularly when some parts are deliberately highlighted and others completely left out, which happens in every news story written. Therefore, in the sociological sense, communication biases are ever present. (p. 67)

Frames are not necessarily positions for or against some policy measures (Gamson, 1988), but rather the criteria by which the policy measures might be evaluated. One could argue that the selection process or adopted frames should not be labeled *bias* because of the pejorative nature of the term. According to Hackett (1984), bias is not a useful construct because language is not neutral and cannot be removed from values or viewpoints.

Indexing.   The indexing hypothesis states that the media tend to index the range of viewpoints expressed in government debate (Bennett, 1990). Both framing and indexing deal with the parameters of an issue or of a debate. The difference between the two is that indexing links the range of options available in the media to official sources (Althaus, Edy, Entman, & Phalen, 1995), whereas the range of meaning in framing is not confined by a particular source, but is left wide open.

Cultivation.   According to Gerbner and his colleagues (Gerbner, Gross, Morgan, & Signorielli, 1994), one of the media's possible effects is cultivation, the adoption of a particular point of view that is more in line with media presentation than with reality. These researchers pointed out that presentation of crime and law enforcement in the entertainment media is by far a distorted representation of reality.

Because of this distortion, people who watch more television are more likely to view the world as mean and are more like to perceive themselves as potential victims of violence than those who watch less television. Cultivation studies have focused on the entertainment media. Framing, on the other hand, deals with the idea that the news media may also be presenting a worldview construed in a particular way that does not necessarily mesh with reality. Because of the framing that takes place in the news, the question becomes: What are the effects of these frames on the public? One way to conceptualize framing is to look at it as an example of cultivation theory that deals with the news media rather than the entertainment media.

THE DIMENSIONS OF FRAMES

To examine the frames or the attributes of an issue, a multidimensional approach is required to capture the complexities of this concept. According to Hendrickson (1995), "characterizing all media content, or even one story on a particular topic or issue with any one frame overlooks a great deal of complexity and subtlety" (p. 3). Perhaps the simplest way to understand the multidimensional aspect of frames is to look at some of the metaphors used to describe this concept. Bateson (1972) used the picture frame analogy in his book, *Steps to an Ecology of Mind*. According to Bateson, a frame delimits a class or set of messages. Patterson (1993b) equated a frame to "a 'cognitive window' through which a news story is 'seen'" (p. 59).

Tankard et al. (1991) reviewed the literature on framing and noted that the framing metaphor can be examined from several different angles. One way is to think of a picture frame that includes some slice of reality, excluding other portions. A picture frame not only determines what is included, but also sets the tone of the picture. An ornate picture frame sets a very different tone for a painting than a simple rustic frame. Other aspects of this picture frame metaphor are the location and size of the frame. A large frame placed in the entryway of a home will be noticed more than a small picture frame placed at an obscure angle on the wall. The same holds true for the type of picture that is framed. A Picasso painting might or might not be as noticed as a van Gogh.

The metaphor of a picture frame is very useful in helping us conceptualize frames and attributes. Media frames can be broken into four major dimensions:

- The topic of a news item (what is included in the frame).
- Presentation (size and placement).
- Cognitive attributes (details of what is included in the frame).
- Affective attributes (tone of the picture).

This breakdown reflects to a certain extent Gamson and Modigliani's (1989) discussion of framing devices and reasoning devices. The latter two dimensions also reflect McCombs' (1992) assertion that news messages are both cognitive and affective.

These four dimensions (see Fig. 1.2) can help in the development of frames for analyzing a variety of issues and topics. One of the weaknesses of most framing studies is that the attributes of the issue or topic are not generalizable across issues, so even though the specific subdimensions are not generalizable, these four larger dimensions could be the basis of comparisons across many different agendas.

Subtopics

Attributes, which are the independent variable at the second level of agenda setting, are the subtopics within a particular issue. Brosius and Eps (1994) examined the coverage of attacks against foreigners and asylum seekers in Germany and came up with subtopics such as trials, foreigners, assaults and political action. Examining the agenda-setting process for AIDS, Rogers, Dearing, and Chang (1991) identified 13 distinct subissues ranging from government policy to ethics. Takeshita and Mikami (1995) divided their agenda-setting study into general-issue salience and subissue salience. They found evidence of second-level agenda-setting effects for both television and newspapers.

In terms of theory building, the weakness of studies that just focus on subtopics is that the researcher usually comes up with a list of topic-specific frames based on his or her perceptions and then proceeds to content analyze the material on hand. The problem then becomes the lack of distinction between content analysis in general and the examination of frames. Coming up with a list of frames for each issue is similar to—and shares the weaknesses of—the dictionary approach of computerized content analysis where separate diction-aries are developed for specific discourse (Krippendorff, 1980).

Framing Mechanisms

The second thing that needs to be considered when examining media frames deals with the emphasis given to topics in the media, such as placement and size as well as other elements that influence the prominence of a news item.

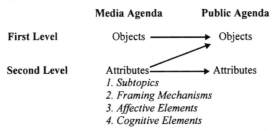

FIG. 1.2. Describing agenda attributes: four dimensions of framing.

Photographs, pull quotes, subheads, and so on, all serve to give a story in a newspaper more prominence. This aspect of salience needs to be examined when we are looking at the relationship between the salience of items on the media agenda and the salience of those items on the public agenda. Tankard et al. (1991) referred to these focal points of news presentations and labeled them "framing mechanisms" (p. 15).

Agenda-setting studies have focused on how frequently an issue is mentioned in the media. The frequency with which a topic is mentioned probably has a more powerful influence than any particular framing mechanism, but framing mechanisms could serve as catalysts to frequency in terms of agenda setting.

Affective Dimension

Bearing in mind that the news communicates much more than facts (McCombs, 1992; Patterson, 1993b), this dimension examines the affective aspect of the news. The affective dimension deals with the public's emotional response that may result from media coverage. One of the ways that the media exerts this affective response is through the narrative structure of the news. Koch (1990) went as far as to equate framing with the narrative itself. The way a news story is structured focuses and thus limits the causes and outcomes of the issue (Schulman, 1990). Schudson (1982) argued that the power of the media lies in the forms in which declarations appear. The narrative is the link among the components of who, what, where, why, how, and when (Bennett & Edelman, 1985) that form the content of the message. Here we are looking at the journalist as story teller (Barkin, 1984).

Researchers distinguish between two forms of narrative, the chronicle and the story. The chronicle relies more on an inverted pyramid style that provides a record that something noteworthy has happened. The story, on the other hand, engages the reader because of its style. Donohew (1983), for example, suggested that narrative or chronologically ordered stories tend to produce significantly greater physiological arousal for readers than the traditional summary style.

Two other elements that may cause concern among the public are based on news values. Proximity and human interest are possible news values that might make a reader or a viewer identify more closely with what is being reported. Such news values are a cultural as well as an institutional product (Hall, 1981). Price and Tewksbury (1995) argued that news values help determine which angles to take in writing the news and which details need to be emphasized.

According to Elliott (1988), in a study of the hijacking of an airline, political causes of the hijackers are too complex to cover and thus the media focus on human elements of the story by focusing on friends and families of hostages. Not only are the political causes too complex, but the human element can easily become the focus of a story with a beginning, middle, and end. The human element in much of the coverage is akin to the tendency of the media to personalize stories in the press: "Happenings (or fantasies) involving individual persons stand a high chance of becoming news stories" (Fowler, 1991, p. 91). According to Hall (1981), the personalization of the news isolates the person from relevant social and institutional context. Bringing a story to such a personal level might help the reader identify with the happenings in the story and thus feel more concern for what is going on.

Cognitive Dimension

This dimension deals with general cognitive categories that might shed light on whether the media and the audience are thinking about the problem in the same way. Cognitive categories could move us from topical categories by identifying meaning in topics regardless of what the topic is. Edelstein, Ito, and Kepplinger (1989) came up with the *problematic situation*, which could address the issue of generalizable frames. Although they did not use the term *framing*, their concept is very much applicable to framing.

Edelstein (1993) argued that the problematic situation sheds light on meaning equivalence between the media and the audience. For example, if the media present news about a condition of conflict and the audience also perceives conflict, then both the media and the audience are in accord. Edelstein et al. (1989) conducted a comparative cultural study in the United States, Germany, Japan, and Hong Kong. Using the problematic situation as a conceptual tool for their comparison, they focused on two major elements of their theory, which are the problem and the steps taken to address the problem.

Hendrickson (1995) also used general categories and examined the coverage of child maltreatment using an ecological framework. This framework consists of five dimensions: the individual, the microsystem, the mesosystem, the exosystem, and the macrosystem. The similarity between the ecological framework and the problematic situation is the distinction the researchers make on whether the problem is identified from the individual or the social perspective. The ecological framework is more detailed than the problematic situation.

Iyengar (1991) used the general categories of thematic and episodic frames to examine news coverage. The episodic news frame focuses on specific events or cases, whereas the thematic frame places the issue in some general context. Similar to the thematic and episodic frames are Yagade and Dozier's (1990) division of coverage into abstract or concrete categories. They equated concrete issues with visual and easy to understand issues.

Focusing on causes and solutions, Klandermans and Sidney (1988) examined social movements and argued that a social movement has an ideology that contains a diagnosis (causes and agents responsible), a prognosis (what must be done), and a rationale (who must do the job and arguments that action needs to be taken). According to Rucinski (1992), the social construction of reality deals with attributions of causes and solutions. Maher (1995) looked at the causes of a pollution problem in Austin, Texas. He examined the causes mentioned in the local newspaper and found a perfect correspondence with the perception of the causes held by the public.

A recent study by Ghanem (1996) examined operational definitions for all four dimensions—subtopics, framing mechanisms, affective elements, and cognitive elements—for media coverage of crime. She found correspondence between the four dimensions and public concern about crime.

CONCLUSION

This extensive overview of attributes was undertaken to explain the independent variable at the second level of agenda setting. The emergence of the second level of agenda setting incorporates many aspects of framing studies, and thus we are able to meet the criticism that our theories are not cumulative. At this juncture of agenda-setting research, it is useful to examine agenda setting as a theory. The evaluation of a theory includes four basic standards: scope, parsimony, precision of prediction, and accuracy of explanation (Hage, 1972). Agenda setting meets the criteria for all four standards. Agenda setting is wide in scope and yet is extremely parsimonious. The basic hypothesis can be summarized in one sentence. Is it wide in scope? The many research projects based on the first level of agenda setting and the emergence of the second level of agenda setting that incorporates several dimensions are testimony to the theory's scope. The scope and parsimonious aspects of agenda setting have been a direct result of the theory's precision of prediction as well as its accuracy of explanation. With the emergence of the second level of agenda setting, the theory gains even more credibility. The second level links agenda setting with several other theories in our field, and thus the tapestry of communication studies grows richer and the texture of the field becomes even more refined.

2

Exploring the Media's Roles in Defining Reality: *From Issue-Agenda Setting to Attribute-Agenda Setting*

Toshio Takeshita

As Lippmann (1922) pointed out more than 70 years ago, "we can see how indirectly we know the environment in which nevertheless we live" (p. 4). It is not only a matter of geographical distance. In a Great Society like ours, the social structure has grown tremendously in size and in complexity. The institutional activities as a whole are hardly visible to an average citizen. Therefore it is one of the principal functions of the media to mediate between "the world outside" and "the pictures in our heads." The media provide information that is a major component of our "pictures"—Lippmann also termed this a *pseudo-environment*. This function of the media has significant implications for politics: In a contemporary mass democracy, it is people's cognitions and choices based on them that determine the main direction of a polity in the long run.

The question of how the media mediate between the external objective reality and our social reality (our belief of what the world is like) has been one of the most fundamental themes in mass communication research. However, despite the argument advanced by Lippmann as early as the 1920s, and despite the fact that scientific study of media effects began in the 1930s, it has been just two decades or so since this question of reality definition has become a central focus in mass communication research.

For example, the cultivation analysis advanced by Gerbner and his associates has investigated how and to what degree TV portrayal of reality (mostly in fictional content such as dramas and movies) influences and homogenizes the viewers' conceptions of social reality (see Gerbner, Gross, Morgan, & Signorielli, 1994). Based on the work in phenomenological sociology, Adoni and Mane (1984) developed a tripolar model composed of objective social reality, symbolic social reality, and subjective social reality with which the media's role in the process of the social construction of reality should be explored. Scholars in the sociology of news work in England and the United States have studied how the media select and create news and what the likely effects are (e.g., Cohen, 1981; Cohen & Young, 1973; Tuchman, 1978).

Agenda-setting perspectives also share with the just named researchers an interest in "definition" research (we use this summary label for convenience). As far as media effects are concerned, it seems that agenda setting has been a most productive and fruitful perspective in definition research. The aim of this chapter is to sketch out what agenda-setting research has contributed to definition research and what its problems are. I also discuss what a recent development in agenda setting—the study of attribute-agenda setting—is expected to add to this line of inquiry.

DEFINITION RESEARCH BEFORE AGENDA SETTING

Study of Unwitting Bias

In the beginning of scientific research on the process and effects of mass communication, few scholars dealt with Lippmann's interest in the reality-definition function of the press. The dominant research paradigm from the 1930s to the 1950s was that of persuasive communication, which put an emphasis on attitude changes induced by media messages. Katz (1987) argued that some historical conditions helped shape the trend of media research: (a) There was an expectation among the intellectuals of the role of broadcasting (radio) to enlighten the mass public, and (b) the government and the military were concerned with wartime propaganda. These social demands (and intentions of funding agencies) more or less influenced the direction of the research.

An exception in this period was the study by Lang and Lang. In the event called MacArthur Day conducted on April 26, 1951 in Chicago, Lang and Lang attempted to compare the welcome parade for General Douglas MacArthur experienced through live television with the parade experienced on the spot (Lang & Lang, 1953, 1984). The parade experienced by the observers on the spot was far from enthusiastic, rather a dull event. On the other hand, the parade watched on TV looked like indeed a dramatic ceremony, with the general located in the center of the screen surrounded by cheering crowds of citizens.

What made this striking difference between the impressions gained on the spot and on TV? Lang and Lang attributed the reason to some technical factors involved with making the program. In making a live show, they explained, TV producers applied a perspective that was based on what the producers assumed to be the viewers' expectation of the event, and restructured the event by the camera and audio. Thus, the TV image had a kind of "unwitting bias" in it.

Lang and Lang published another study of unwitting bias. It dealt with how the networks portrayed the Democratic convention in July 1952 (Lang & Lang, 1955, 1984). In this convention, the images of the official proceedings were provided by pool coverage. Each network added its own commentaries and complementary visuals by its own camera crew. During the period analyzed, most of the images were from the pool, which meant the monitors of each network watched almost identical images. Their impressions of the event, however, were found to be quite different depending on the network they watched. By assigning the same visuals different explanations and interpretations by its commentator, each network defined the event in quite a different way, which might lead its viewers to draw a different inference. It was not the amount of information and the particular facts reported, but the manner in which any given episode was linked to prior or outside events that produced differential viewing effects from network to network. Lang and Lang (1984) supposed that differences in the definitions of the event by each network resulted from news people's assumptions about what information was salient at any moment and through their choice of themes to depict the mood of the convention. It is a little surprising that their theoretical framework was very similar to that of framing research, a recent focus of scholarly attention.

The case studies of the MacArthur Day and of the 1952 Democratic convention had a flaw in external validity, because they employed just a small number of observers or monitors (graduate students) and made comparisons among their impressions of the event in question. However, their work should be highly evaluated for its creativity and because it pioneered a new perspective in media effects research. Despite the high reputation given to them (the MacArthur Day study won the 1952 Edward L. Bernays Award from the American Sociological Association), however, few followed their unwitting bias perspective. The unwitting bias study was off the dominant paradigm of mass communication research in the United States at that time. Interestingly, we can find a similar approach in news research in the British cultural studies rather than in the United States (e.g., Halloran, Elliott, & Murdock, 1970).

Pseudo-Environment Theory in Japan

It is also interesting that Lippmann's interest in the reality-definition function of the press revived about 30 years after the publication of his book, *Public Opinion*, in a Far East country—Japan. In his diagnosis of modern society, Shimizu (1951) advanced a theory of dominance of the copy. By the words *the copy*, he meant the media's portrayal of reality or the mediated realities, with *the original* corresponding to reality.

Shimizu (1951) argued that, in a modern society, people have to depend on the copy provided by the media so that they can adapt to the enlarged environment. It is almost impossible for ordinary people to check the copy against the reality, but they are forced to depend on the copy at the risk of their fate. If the copy reflects the original with complete fidelity, there would be no problem, however, it is unlikely, Shimizu said. He pointed out the conditions that cause some distortion in the copy. When a commercial company runs the media, they tend to produce copy leaning toward "primitive interests"—interests in sex, crime, conflict, and so on—that everyone shares, hoping to maximize profit. On the other hand, when the government owns the media, the copy tends to be propaganda to achieve some political goals. Shimizu concluded that, in either case, the copy will not help people adapt to the environment in a rational way, but is likely to impose irrationality on people.

The theory Shimizu proposed was not an empirically testable hypothesis, but a kind of "grand theory." However, it encouraged many younger scholars in their inquiry into the media's role from an epistemological point of view.

The work of Shimizu gave rise to a new theoretical perspective called *pseudo-environment theory* in Japanese mass communication research. One of the most elaborate works in this tradition is Fujitake (1968). Fujitake used the word *pseudo-environment* as the key concept and discussed how people accept the media's portrayal of reality as a legitimate surrogate for reality and why.

First of all, Fujitake distinguished between pseudo-environment in the broad sense and pseudo-environment in the narrow sense. The former means a subjective image of the environment, which corresponds to the way Lippmann used this word, that is the pictures in our heads; the latter denotes the media's portrayal of reality. Fujitake himself used the word pseudo-environment in the narrow sense. A pseudo-environment is no more than a representation of a real environment, a fiction constructed by media personnel. However, a person would equate this fiction with the real environment. It is likely that the media's definition of reality moves to that of the audience members' without being questioned.

Fujitake explained why this process works as follows. First, in a modern society, a person has to depend on the mass media for information about what is going on in the world outside direct experience. Second, because information from the media could be shared by almost everyone, it is expected to work as a coin of social exchange. A pseudo-environment provided by the media is assumed to serve as a "common world"—a socially recognized area of subjects. Third, the journalism activity of the media has a periodicity, which means a pseudo-environment is updated periodically. This nature of periodicity helps the media keep public attention on ever-changing pseudo-environments. Due to these conditions together, Fujitake concluded, pseudo-environment in the narrow sense is likely to become a legitimatized part of pseudo-environment in the broad sense.

The conception of the pseudo-environment theory by Fujitake has much in common with that of agenda-setting research. Unfortunately, it failed to develop into as large a research tradition as agenda setting did. As Ito (1987) criticized, the method of the pseudo-environment theory was mainly descriptive with anecdotal evidence. No testable hypothesis was formulated. Other researchers probably found it a little difficult to follow and to test the theory empirically.[1] It is still noteworthy that there existed a research perspective that belonged to definition research in the 1950s and 1960s in Japan.

AGENDA SETTING AS DEFINITION RESEARCH

Journalistic Paradigm and Agenda Setting

In the 1970s, there occurred a paradigm change in the field of mass communication research, especially in political communication research. Chaffee (1980) termed it the change from a persuasional paradigm to a journalistic paradigm: The former would evaluate communication practices in terms of their effectiveness in mobilizing people; the latter would see the role of the media as providing people with information needed to make informed choices on public affairs.

It was a new generation of researchers that facilitated the paradigm change. In the 1960s, a number of scholars who graduated from newly established graduate schools of journalism and mass communication made their debut in the academic world. They were trained in social science methodology, but unlike the preceding researchers from sociology, psychology, and political science, they were likely to have research interests rooted in journalism: They thought that the primary role of the media was not persuading people but providing people with information (Chaffee & Hochheimer, 1985). Thus they oriented themselves to the effects at the cognitive level rather than those at the attitude level. No one would argue that the agenda-setting perspective does not embody the journalistic paradigm. Lowery and DeFleur (1988) evaluated agenda setting as follows:

> The study of agenda-setting is made to order for the communication researcher who looks back to the great traditions of journalism rather than to the founders honored by social and behavioral scientists. Agenda-setting focuses on the classical topics. ... These were the issues of James Bryce and Walter Lippmann, not those of the founders of sociology and psychology. In short, the study of agenda-setting may represent a major turning point in the scientific study of the effects of mass communication. (p. 351)

The concept of agenda setting revived Lippmann's conception of how the media contribute to the shaping of the pictures in our heads. McCombs and Shaw (1972) hypothesized that the issues emphasized in the news media

---

[1]Another reason why the pseudo-environmental theory failed to develop into a research tradition would be that Fujitake then worked for NHK Broadcasting Research Institute, a branch of NHK, the public broadcasting corporation in Japan. Unlike colleges and universities, he had no students to follow his theory.

influence the issues the voters regard important. In other words, the media agenda determines, to some degree, the audience (public) agenda. Determining what to select for attention and what to ignore among a number of existing issues means determining the perspective you apply to view the political world as a whole. Agenda setting is indeed another expression of the reality definition function of the media.

Two contributions of agenda setting to definition research were that it set the issue of reality-definition by the media as a central focus of attention in the scientific study of mass communication, and second, it formulated the issue into an empirically testable hypothesis and presented a standard procedure for measurement, which encouraged researchers to replicate the findings and enabled the research to develop cumulatively and systematically.

Agenda setting appeared as a "middle-range theory" (Merton, 1957). Since the seminal study by McCombs and Shaw (1972), it has developed steadily (for recent reviews, see McCombs & Shaw, 1993; Rogers & Dearing, 1988). Dearing and Rogers (1996) noted that, from 1972 to 1994, there were some 350 publications.

Issue-Centered Bias

At the most general level, agenda setting means the transference of salience from the media to the audience members. Agenda-setting researchers define the word *agenda* as objects accorded saliency in the media content or in people's consciousness. Agenda can be operationalized at various levels. As early as 1977, McCombs argued the possibility of expanding the conceptual domains of agenda beyond the original notion of an agenda of issues (McCombs, 1977a). That is, one could think of an agenda of attributes of a particular issue, an agenda of attributes of a political candidate, an agenda of political candidates—this would be related to the perception of which candidate is the most viable in an election, and a larger social agenda where politics is only one topic, as measured by level of political interest. The notion of agendas of attributes was quite intriguing, as it suggested that agenda setting has some common ground with traditional inquiries into image making and stereotyping.

Despite such an important suggestion, however, we cannot help saying that agenda-setting research has had a kind of issue-centered bias—that is, the great majority of agenda-setting studies published thus far chose to adopt the same concept of an agenda of general issues as the original McCombs and Shaw (1972) study did. In a sense, a criticism made by Kosicki (1993) seems to the point that the dominant agenda-setting research has not examined the substance of an issue, but dealt with only the *shell* of the topic.

What caused the issue-centered bias? McCombs (1992) assumed that, first, there is a powerful normative tradition among social scientists that emphasizes the importance of issues to informed public opinion, and, second, public issues provide a strong link between mass communication research and public opinion research. Anyway, clinging to the concept of agendas of issues must have benefits of its own. In addition to the points McCombs advanced earlier, there might be three points of benefit.

1. Links to behavioral outcomes. Many agenda-setting studies have been conducted in the context of election campaigns, and have hypothesized that the media determine the main issues of the election. Voting studies in the 1970s, coincidentally, began to pay close attention to issues as a determinant of voting choices in contrast to the declining power of party identification (Nie, Verba, & Petrocik, 1976). Thus, issues imply a link between the cognitive effects of the media and their behavioral consequences.

2. Links to political process. In the 1970s, another perspective in political science emerged with the key concept of agenda—the agenda-building perspective (Cobb & Elder, 1972; Cobb, Ross, & Ross, 1976). *Agenda building* is defined as the process in which demands of various groups in society become an item of legitimate attention by public officials. Cobb et al. investigated the conditions under which a particular issue is included or excluded from the policy agenda. The encounter of agenda setting with the agenda-building perspective suggested another frontier of media research—how the media agenda is related to the policy agenda. In other words, how do the media influence or how are they influenced by the decision makers? Agenda building also provides an opportunity to conceive of a wider theoretical framework—for example, a tripolar model of the media agenda, the public agenda, and the policy agenda (Manheim, 1987; Rogers & Dearing, 1988). In such a model, the agenda of issues would serve as a key concept.

3. MIP data as resources. The Most Important Problem (MIP) measure, a standard measure for the public agenda in agenda-setting research, is a very familiar one in public opinion polls in the United States. For example, the Gallup Poll has been using the question "What do you think is the most important problem facing the country?" since the late 1940s (Smith, 1980). Polls by other organizations and by universities also have adopted the same or a similar measure. Thus there exists a vast collection of MIP data available to researchers for secondary analysis and a validity check of their own data. This might be another reason why the issue-centered approach has attracted researchers.

ATTRIBUTE-AGENDA SETTING
AND FRAMING RESEARCH

Existing Studies of Attribute-Agenda Setting

Despite the issue-centered bias, some published studies have attempted to extend the conceptual domain of agenda. Here, for convenience, the model using the agenda of issues is termed *issue-agenda setting*, whereas the model using the agenda of attributes of an issue or a public figure is called *attribute-agenda setting*. McCombs (1994) called the former the "first dimension" of agenda setting, and the latter the "second dimension." Whereas issue-agenda setting deals with transmission of issue (object) salience, attribute-agenda setting means transmission of attribute salience from the media to the audience members.

The study that best fits the word *attribute* must be that of candidate images by Weaver, Graber, McCombs, and Eyal (1981). They defined a candidate image as an array of perceived attributes with varying saliency. Because most of the voters have little direct contact with the presidential candidates, the image they have of a candidate will be dependent on how the media portray the candidate—that is, which attributes are emphasized and which attributes are not referred to in media content. Weaver and his associates tested this hypothesis in the 1976 U.S. presidential campaign. They found some evidence that the attribute agenda of the newspaper influenced that of the voters.

An issue can be seen as comprised of various aspects or subissues, which can be treated as attributes.[2] Benton and Frazier (1976) focused on a general issue—the economy—and examined agenda setting effects at some "lower" levels. One level of analysis was that of subissue, which included problems, causes, and proposed solutions. Another level contained specific information about subissues such as rationales for proposed solutions. For example, Benton and Frazier (1976) found that the solutions to economic problems that were salient to the public (such proposals as tax rebate and oil tax) corresponded, to a certain degree, with solutions emphasized in the newspaper.

Takeshita and Mikami (1995) examined both issue-agenda setting and attribute-agenda setting in the 1993 general election in Japan. The latter was tested with political reform, the main issue of the election. The content analysis showed that in the political-reform debates in the election reports, the system-related subissues (electoral system reform) dominated over ethics-related subissues (such as imposing legal controls on politicians, and tightening discipline among politicians). The survey revealed that attentiveness to political news was associated with the salience of system-related subissues, but not with ethics-related salience, among the respondents. This finding suggests an agenda-setting effect working at the subissue level of the main campaign issue.

Other studies of agenda setting at the subissue level include those by Atwater, Salwen, and Anderson (1985); Cohen (1975); Mikami, Takeshita, Nakada, and Kawabata (1995); and Salwen (1988). Each study demonstrated that the agenda-setting hypothesis was more or less supported, even at the subissue

---

[2]I admit the criticism by Kosicki (1993) is reasonable, arguing that agenda-setting research has used the term *public issue* as "a rather broad, abstract, content-free topic domain, devoid of controversy or contending forces" (p. 104). In the context of agenda-setting theory, a topic domain should imply an issue, but strictly speaking, it is not an issue itself. Literally an issue means what is in conflict in a certain topic domain. It seems to me that the study of attribute-agenda setting is an important step toward treating an issue not in the conventional sense but in the literal sense.

level. By designating what aspects of a certain issue to attend to, agenda setting at the subissue level can influence the perspective with which people see the issue as a whole.

Framing Research

Recent attention to attribute-agenda setting may be partly explained by the rise of the framing perspective in mass communication research. Framing research explores how the media frame an issue or a problem and how this affects people's understandings of that issue. Framing research includes studies with diverse assumptions and methods—too diverse, in fact, to lump together under the same label.

The concept of frame or framing itself has diverse theoretical origins. Scholars who are credited with the concept include Minsky (1975); Bateson (1972); Goffman (1974); Watzlawick, Weakland, and Fisch (1974); and Tversky and Kahneman (1981). Although they use the same word, the way it is conceptualized differs; however, most of them have something in common in that the word frame means the perspective a person applies to define an event or a problem (the word framing means the act of applying a frame). Among the scholars just listed, sociologist Goffman and cognitive psychologists Tversky and Kahneman might be the ones most referred to by framing researchers in mass communication.

Goffman's (1974) concept of frame—he owed this concept to Bateson (1955)—means the definition a person gives to the situation or context in which a human interaction occurs. This concept is applicable not only to face-to-face interaction but also to mass communication (Namba, 1993). In the latter situation, we use different frames according to types of media content. If we watch an advertisement on TV, we would apply the advertising frame to it, which is different from, say, the drama frame or the news frame. The advertising frame warns us, "The communicator has the intention of selling something to us." That is why we would not take the messenger's words of recommendation at face value. In terms of communication theory, the frame in Goffman's sense corresponds to a kind of metamessage.

On the other hand, Tversky and Kahneman (1981; Kahneman & Tversky, 1984) revealed in their experimental studies on decision problems that the way a decision problem is described or framed can affect people's preferences about the problem. For example, whether the choices are framed in terms of possible gains or possible losses is likely to give rise to shifts in preferences. Their theory could be applicable to the poll situations in which some differences in question wording influence the choices of the respondents.[3]

How have communication researchers made use of such concepts as frames or framing in their studies? At the risk of oversimplification, we could dichotomize the researchers into those who depend on the frame concept of sociological

---

[3]Communication researcher Lemert (1981) extended a similar argument independently, in which his concept of "attitude object changes" is similar to that of framing or reframing.

origin (that of Goffman) and those who follow the concept of psychological origin (that of Tversky & Kahneman). The former group includes Gamson (1989); Gitlin (1980); Neuman, Just, and Crigler (1992); and Tsuruki (1982); the latter group includes Iyengar (1991). Recently a few communication researchers have attempted to integrate the concepts of both origins (Entman, 1993; Pan & Kosicki, 1993).

The framing studies based on the concept of sociological origin are likely to analyze qualitatively the news content and infer its likely effects on the audience members or some interest groups. For example, Gitlin (1980) investigated how the media portrayed the anti-Vietnam movement by a new-left student organization in the late 1960s, and how the media representations contributed to marginalizing the organization. Gitlin saw news frames as a device with which the news organizations exert hegemony.

The main focus of the study based on the psychological concept, on the other hand, is the effects of message framing on the audience members. Iyengar (1991) classified the way TV news depicts such issues as poverty, crime, and so on into either the "thematic" framing or the "episodic" framing, and demonstrated in a series of experiments that differences in framing influenced people's perceptions of who was responsible for the problem (as a causal agent or as a treatment agent).

The emergence of framing research has stimulated agenda-setting research and helped correct the issue-centered bias of the latter. It seems that attribute-agenda setting is a natural extension of the agenda-setting concept, but as a result, agenda-setting research and framing research are exploring almost the same problem—that of the reality-definition function of the media.

It is not certain at the present time whether agenda setting and framing will converge or not. Gitlin (1978) criticized agenda setting as "too narrow and ahistorical: analytically it abstracts both media and audiences from their social and historical matrix" (p. 246). Other framing researchers with a critical perspective would agree with him. What Gitlin saw as faults with agenda setting must be the characteristics derived from the fact that it is a typical middle-range theory. A middle-range theory has merits of its own, however. The significance of agenda-setting research lies first in its presentation of an empirically testable hypothesis to explain social phenomena in a relatively restricted domain (i.e., mass communication effects), and second, in its presentation of methods enabling objective and systematic observations (excluding as much as possible arbitrary "readings" of data or texts). Third, as a middle-range theory, it has a theoretical flexibility to link with a variety of theoretical frameworks (see Barrat, 1986, for a reinterpretation of agenda setting effects in terms of the critical approach).

Agenda-setting research and framing research would benefit from each other, and both perspectives will contribute to exploring the reality-definition function of the media.

SOME RESEARCH AGENDAS

Some research agendas to elaborate attribute-agenda setting and promote the study of the media's reality-definition function are as follows.

Operationalization of Attribute Agenda

For a systematic study of attribute-agenda setting, some standard operationalization of attribute agenda is needed. Among the requirements of such an operationalization would be that it be applicable both to analysis of the media content and to measurement of cognitions of the audience members, so that we are able to compare the media data with the audience data.

Entman's (1993) discussion of the four functions of frames seems very useful in developing such an operationalization. Based on his theory, we can define and measure these four dimensions of an attribute agenda: (a) problem definition, (b) attributed causes, (c) moral judgments or evaluations, and (d) proposed remedies. These dimensions correspond to some structure of our understanding of issues. *Problem definition* means accounts of what a causal agent is doing with what effects, *attributed causes* means specifying the forces that create the problem, *moral judgments* denotes evaluations about causal agents and their effects, and *proposed remedies* means presentation of solutions to the problem.

As a research strategy, I would like to recommend that we should first focus on problem definition and causes—that is, we should first measure what the media (or the audience members) are saying about the problem situations and their causes. At the level of moral judgments, we probably can expect only a weak correlation between the media and the public, because media effects research has demonstrated that the media have little direct effect on the affective evaluations or attitudes held by the audience members. That is why moral judgment is given a lower priority. It is more important to explore the extent to which the media contribute to shaping people's cognitions on which, in turn, their evaluations or attitudes are based. The reason why proposed remedies is also given a lower priority is that there exist a number of issues around us that are serious and chronic in nature but difficult to find effective solutions for. Typical of that kind of issue may be environmental problems. Issues that were once a focus of public attention are often replaced by new issues without sufficient treatment, as the public gets tired of them (Downs, 1972).

A procedure of measurement might be as follows: Asking a small number of persons (with an open-ended questionnaire or in the context of a focus group interview) about their perceptions of the issue in question (i.e., in which perspective they see it); constructing the categories of problem definitions and attributed causes based on the collected information; applying the categories to content analysis; converting the categories into survey questions for a large sample; and so on. As to problem definitions, we could design a category of more general items, which is applicable across the issues. In that case, the model of problematic situations by Edelstein (1993) and the value-framing model by Ball-Rokeach, Power, Guthrie, and Waring (1990) must be useful guides.

Links to News Research

One of the important contributions agenda-setting research has made to mass communication research as a whole is providing the concept bridging between the tradition of effects research and that of news research. For example, issue-agenda setting research revitalized gatekeeping research (McCombs & Shaw, 1976; Whitney & Becker, 1982), and helped new studies emerge such as intermedia agenda setting (Reese & Danielian, 1989; Roberts & McCombs, 1994) and the study of the source–media relationship (Gandy, 1982; Turk, 1986). By dealing with the problem of how the media define a particular issue, attribute-agenda setting research will provide a stronger link between effects research and news research (for a recent review of news research, see Davis, 1990; Shoemaker & Reese, 1991).

Empirical examination of how the media's attribute-agenda is formed is indispensable to a full-fledged understanding of the media's role in defining reality. If the media adopt a certain perspective in defining an issue or an event, what are the intramedia/extramedia factors that influence the way the media define reality? For example, political communication researchers from a constructionist perspective argue that the media's definition of an issue is constructed as a product of complicated interactions and competitions among political elites, experts and scientists, interest groups, journalists, and so on (Gamson & Modigliani, 1989). On the other hand, Fishman (1980) hypothesized that news organizations are likely to depend on official sources for information and to reflect the view of officials in their news accounts.

The study of how the attribute agenda in the media is formed implies another frontier. It suggests the possibility of constructing a wider theoretical framework for exploring the reality-definition function of the media.

CONCLUDING REMARKS

In a recent review of agenda-setting research, McCombs and Shaw (1993) characterized the recent rise of attribute-agenda setting and framing research as follows:

> Bernard Cohen's classic summation of agenda setting —the media may not tell us what to think, but they are stunningly successful in telling us what to think about—has been turned inside out. New research ... suggests that the media not only tell us what to think about, but also how to think about it, and, consequently, what to think. (p. 65)

However, we must keep in mind that this is not a simple statement of "a return to the concept of powerful mass media." Mikami et al. (1995) examined agenda setting at the subissue level of the global environmental issue and found that people with a moderate interest in the environment were likely to show the strongest effect. They argued that people highly interested in the environment had a more fixed conception of what the important subissues were. Thus they were assumed to be less susceptible to media influence. This example suggests that considering contingent conditions is necessary for attribute-agenda setting as well as for traditional issue-agenda setting. Agenda setting is a very important but hardly a universal effect.

Attribute-agenda setting explores how media content is related not only to people's perceived salience of public issues, but also to their understanding of the substance of those issues. In this way, the development of agenda-setting research will shed new light on the role of news media in a contemporary mass democracy.

A final word is necessary about the roles of news media in the future. Recent years have seen the rapid and tremendous growth of Internet communication. More and more news sources such as political leaders, governmental agencies, political parties, business corporations, and so on, are establishing their own sites on the Web and seeking to directly reach publics. The Internet is giving would-be communicators new opportunities to make their voices heard without depending on the news media. Does this mean a declining importance in the roles of professional journalism in the realm of political communication? Not necessarily so, I expect.

Information on the Internet includes a mixture of wheat and chaff, that is, a jumble of true and false, useful and futile pieces of information. Even apparently reliable sources such as governmental agencies often provide some biased information in favor of their own interests. Altheide and Johnson (1980) called it bureaucratic propaganda. In such a situation, independent and reliable professional news media would be expected to serve as a reference point for ordinary citizens' understanding of what the world is like and for their evaluations of what the sources really mean. As long as the news media meet societal needs for surveillance and orientation, they will continue to play indispensable roles in the process of democracy, as will their agenda-setting functions.

3

The Press, Candidate Images, and Voter Perceptions

Pu-tsung King

In modern democratic societies, election campaigns have been portrayed as a three-player game involving the candidates, the media, and the voters (Covington, Kroeger, Richardson, & Woodward, 1993). Candidate images and campaign issues conveyed by the news media become important determinants of voting decisions (Choi & Becker, 1987). The media have emerged to fill the power vacuum created by the declining influence of political parties (Patterson, 1989) and have become a pivotal corner of the candidate–media–voter triangle, the so-called "golden electoral triangle" (Buchanan, 1991).

News media have been confirmed to have an agenda-setting function (McCombs & Shaw, 1972) that helps construct the pictures in our heads (Lippmann, 1922). Elements emphasized on the media agenda come to be perceived as important elements on the public agenda (McCombs, 1995).

Recently, McCombs (1995) proposed two levels of dimensions of agenda-setting effects. The first dimension is concerned with the transmission of object salience to the pictures in the heads of the public. The second dimension, which is viewed as new, refers to the transmission of attribute salience to the minds of the public. More specifically, each object has numerous attributes, or characteristics and properties,that fill out the picture of that particular object. As certain perspectives and frames are employed in news coverage, they can draw public attention to certain attributes and away from others. So far, compelling evidence of the second dimension of agenda-setting effect has been documented in some studies (Atwood, Sohn, & Sohn, 1978; Becker & McCombs, 1978; Benton & Frazier, 1976; Cohen, 1975; Iyengar & Kinder, 1987).

According to McCombs and Evatt (1995), the rediscovered domain of the second dimension of agenda-setting has opened new frontiers. Conceptualizing the candidate image in terms of a second dimension of agenda setting has offered communication scholars many research opportunities and challenges. In fact, previous studies have, either directly or indirectly, shown that media help set the agenda of attributes that define the pictures of candidates in voters' minds (Becker & McCombs, 1978; Robinson & Sheehan, 1983; Weaver, Graber, McCombs, & Eyal, 1981).

McCombs (1995) argued that media image agenda-setting effects work along two dimensions—the affective and the substantive. In the former dimension, the hypothesis is that candidate attributes described in positive, negative, or neutral terms in media coverage will influence voters' evaluations of those attributes. In the latter dimension, the attributes emphasized in news coverage are predicted to affect the kinds of characteristics the voters think about when they evaluate candidates. Moreover, candidates' attributes can be categorized into three themes: (a) ideology and issue positions, (b) qualifications and experience, and (c) personal characteristics and personality.

In the past, many researchers, especially those in political science, have been very interested in candidate image, which was described by Hellweg, Dionisopoulos, and Kugler (1989) as an illusive yet important phenomenon" (p. 44) of politics. However, the focus of most image studies has been on the relations between candidate images and voting behavior. Many studies have shown that candidate image is a significant, if not the best, predictor of voting decisions (Dennis, Chaffee, & Choe, 1979; Natchez & Bupp, 1968; Nimmo & Savage, 1976; Pike, 1985; Rarick, Duncan, Lee, & Porter, 1977; Zandpour; 1985). However, Kendall and Yum (1984) found that the perceived attitude homophily between candidates and voters, instead of image and issues, was the best predictor of vote decision.

Most political scholars generally consider candidate image a better predictor than campaign issues in deciding the outcome of elections. McGee's (1978) explanation was direct and simple: Asking people to vote on issues instead of images may be an impossible demand. With a thorough review of the issue–image literature, Hellweg et al. (1989) came to the conclusion that voters have a clear preference for image-oriented messages over issue-oriented messages.

Yet, although most studies seemed to treat issues and images as two separate entities, some scholars argue that issues and images are melded together as the electorate makes its voting decisions. Under the influence of the priming effect, issues may be used as criteria for evaluating a candidate's personal attributes and thus help a voter perceive differences between candidates (Davis, 1981; Husson, Stephen, Harrison, & Fehr, 1988; Jacobs & Shapiro, 1994).

DEFINITIONS OF IMAGES

There have been various definitions of the images of political candidates. McGrath and McGrath (1962) defined an image as different traits projected by candidates to influence voters, and Goffman (1959) saw such traits as expressions people give off as a way of managing the impression others have of them. Bowes and Strentz (1978) considered image the mental picture people have about a candidate, namely, the candidate's publicly perceived attributes. Kendall and Yum (1984) thought that the concept of image is very close to that of "ethos," or "source credibility," which originates with Aristotle's *Rhetoric*. Hahn and Gonchar (1972) maintained that "our image of a candidate is determined by the interaction of his personality and orientation to the world with ours" (p. 61). Nimmo and Savage (1976) gave a succinct working definition for candidate image: "a human construct imposed on an array of perceived attributes projected by an object, event, or person" (p. 8).

SOURCES OF IMAGES

It is noteworthy that the definition given by Nimmo and Savage provides a vital distinction between the "projected image" and the "perceived image," which alludes to the two major theses in relation to the sources of candidate image. They are the stimulus-determined thesis and the perceiver-determined thesis (Bowes & Strentz, 1978; Nimmo & Savage, 1976; Patterson, 1989; Sigel, 1964). The two theses are alternative conceptualizations of candidate image. The stimulus-determined thesis maintains that candidate image is a result of what a candidate projects. The perceiver-determined thesis asserts that candidate image is a result of what a voter projects onto the candidate (Garramone, 1983).

Nimmo and Savage (1976) argued that "there have been no sharp debates over the content of candidate image, but there have been clear, deep disagreement surrounding the sources of candidate image" (p. 81). The perceiver-determined thesis is based on the perceptual balance principle (Nimmo & Savage, 1976; Sigel, 1964). It argues that to avoid potential internal stress and conflicts, voters shape their perceptions of candidate image primarily according to subjective predilections, rather than the projected images cast by candidates. In other words, voters' partisan ideology, political values, prior commitment to a candidate, group identifications, or even demographic factors can be significant intervening variables in the formation of candidate images in voters' minds (Nimmo & Savage, 1976).

On the other hand, the stimulus-determined explanation stresses that the electorate is heavily under the influence of the created or projected images emanating from candidates. As a result, a successful projection of designed candidate images becomes extremely important in political campaigns. He or she who casts the most popular image wins the election (Graber, 1972; Sigel, 1964).

Evidence supporting either the perceiver-determined explanation or the stimulus-determined explanation has been documented, but both sides' explanations have been criticized for being too narrowly defined. It is believed that solely relying on only one thesis will not allow a complete explanation of voters' perceptions of candidate images (Nimmo & Savage, 1976). In contrast, Nimmo and Savage (1976) treated image as a transaction occurring between political stimuli and responding voters. Image is regarded not as a static product but as a process in evolution; various social and political restraints impact the transaction between the candidates and the electorate. Thus, in the image process, both the stimulus-determined thesis and the perceiver-determined thesis can, to a certain degree, explain the formation of candidate images. It is like a trade-off process, and the power of each side depends on the strength displayed by various intervening factors, including voters' political values, media exposure, and interpersonal communication.

From this perspective, news media undoubtedly are an integral part of the stimulus–perceiver transaction model. As Graber (1972) noted, "political stories in the mass media are significant in furnishing raw material for the formation of political images. Most people do not invent political images out of thin air. Rather they combine current political data supplied by the mass media with existing knowledge and attitudes and then weave these strands into a plausible and pleasing gestalt" (pp. 51–52). Covington et al. (1993) and Patterson (1989) also concluded that news media have an independent and significant role in the construction of candidate image in the minds of the public.

As for the influences of different news media on the audience, some studies found, contrary to many people's expectations, that newspapers were more powerful image-setters than television. Choi and Becker (1987) found that newspaper political article reading was particularly effective in helping voters discriminate images among candidates, whereas watching television news was not. The reason the newspaper is more powerful in helping the audience develop distinctive candidate images, according to Choi and Becker (1987), is because it has more space to cover candidate information and can be read repeatedly. Hofstetter, Zukin, and Buss (1978) found that voters' exposure to network news, specials, and political advertising only reinforced or intensified preexisting candidate images. Newspaper reading, however, had the strongest correlations with candidate imagery among voters. Graber (1972) stated that although television is the most widely used medium, when people need more complete or in-depth information, they turn to the newspaper.

RESEARCH IN TAIWAN

Image studies in Taiwan have primarily concentrated on investigating the relations between political party images, candidate images, and voting decisions (Chen, 1986, 1993, 1994; Wu, 1994). As the electorate in Taiwan tended to be candidate-oriented rather than issue-oriented or party-oriented in the past, political campaigns consequently have put a candidate's characteristics and personal attributes at the top of the priority list (Lai, 1992).[1]

In his study of Taiwan's voting behavior, Chen (1986) concluded that most voters were candidate-oriented in casting their votes, followed by issue-oriented voters, and then party-oriented voters. Chen (1993) also found that in the 1992 parliamentary elections, the two most influential factors for vote decisions were partisan identification and candidate image. Chen (1992) asserted that in the 1989 Taipei magistrate election, candidate image outweighed partisan identification in determining the election outcome. Therefore, although the ruling party Kuomingtang (KMT) outnumbered the opposition Democratic Progressive Party (DPP) in party members in the Taipei magistrate area, it lost the election.

COMPONENTS OF CANDIDATE IMAGE

Shabad and Andersen (1979) argued that in analyses of voters' perceptions of candidate images, the biggest methodological problem is the systematic categorization of personal attributes of the candidates. Sigel (1964) proposed that candidate image consists of two major components: job-crucial candidate attributes (such as intelligence and independence) and personal attributes (such as speaking ability and friendliness). By asking what voters liked or disliked about presidential candidates in the 1952 to 1972 campaigns, other researchers categorized respondents' answers into four items: experience, leadership ability, personal qualifications, and policy stands (Nimmo & Savage, 1976). When the American Institute for Political Communication (1970) studied the changes in the images of the candidates in the 1968 presidential election, it adopted a fivefold classification: leadership ability, political philosophy, speaking ability, intelligence, and honesty.

Nimmo and Savage (1976) used Q-sort methodology to examine image traits employed by voters in evaluating a candidate. They found that the content of images was multidimensional. When voters evaluated a candidate they looked for: (a) partisan style, or conformity to party standards; (b) political style as a working

---

[1] In Taiwan, electoral systems for electing representatives of local executive offices are different from those for electing parliamentarians. The former uses a plurality system under which each voter casts only one vote and the candidate who receives the most votes, not necessarily a simple majority of votes, is elected. However, for parliamentary elections, the electoral system is semiproportional—each voter has a single nontransferable vote in a multiseat district. Namely, there is more than one representative elected in one district, but each voter can have only one vote. As a result, candidates of the same political party have to compete with each other. Election campaigns thus become very candidate-oriented. Moreover, under such an electoral system, the larger the district, the easier a candidate from small parties can be elected. The ruling party Kuomintang (KMT) continually lost votes in the past parliamentary elections. It experienced a setback in the 1995 parliamentary election in which it received a record low 46.06% of the total vote. The government now is considering the possibility of adopting a system of single-membered constituency.

leader; (c) personal style in relation to individual characteristics; (d) political style of performance; and (e) both political style and personal style as a statesman.

In the 1989 Taipei Magistrate election study, Chen (1992) used five items to measure voters' evaluations of a candidate: integrity and virtues, working ability, enthusiasm, ability to make profits for the public, and representativeness of local voice. In a content analysis of media reporting about political figures, Hu (1987) used eight categories including experience and ability, leadership qualities, personal attributes, government management ability, philosophy of governance, policy stands, relations to others, and other. Yu (1982) found Taiwanese college students' perceptions of political figures tended to concentrate on personal attributes instead of political attributes.

So far, only a limited number of studies in Taiwan have been done to examine voters' perceptions of candidate images. Most were based on the perceiver-determined principle. No study has been done on the image agenda-setting effect of the mass media. By collecting data from the 1994 mayoral election of Taipei City,[2] the study reported here attempted: (a) to test the second dimension of media agenda-setting (candidate image-setting effect on the public), (b) to examine contingent conditions of the media image-setting effect, and (c) to investigate significant predictors of voters' affective evaluations of different candidates.

The 1994 Taipei mayoral election marked another milestone in Taiwan's political development. It was the first time a candidate from the opposition DPP seized this crucial executive office.[3] Moreover, the ruling party's incumbent candidate turned out to rank third in the election, which meant the ruling party was taken down two notches and became the Number 3 party in the capital.[4]

Research Design

The research design of this study primarily included two parts: (a) a content analysis of 4 months of coverage of candidates in the three leading newspapers,[5]

---

[2] This mayoral election was labeled as the warfare to defend the capital by the ruling party. The incumbent mayor, Huang Tar-Chou, was designated by the government. The two metropolitan cities, Taipei and KaosHuang, where the population is over 1 million, were formerly under the jurisdiction of the Executive Yuan. In the 1994 election, both cities' mayors were to be elected by popular vote.

[3] In addition to the fact that Taipei is the capital of the country, the annual budget of the city was estimated at about $140 billion NT (nearly $5.1 billion U.S.), a desirable administrative resource for any political party.

[4] The DPP mayoral candidate Chen Suei-bian obtained 43.67% of the total vote; the New Party's candidate, Chaw Shaw-kong, secured 30.17%; and the ruling KMT party got only 25.89%.

[5] According to the telephone survey conducted in this study, the most-often-read newspaper was the United Daily News (35.2%), trailed by the China Times (31.2%) and the Liberty Times (12.3%). These three newspapers combined accounted for nearly 80% of the readership market. Generally, the United Daily News is considered the pro nonmainstream faction in the ruling KMT, the China Times is considered the promainstream faction in the KMT, and the Liberty Times has a dual political stand—pro-opposition DPP and also the pro-mainstream faction in the KMT. The three newspapers pretty much reflect different stands in the political spectrum (King, 1994).

and (b) a cross-sectional telephone survey of Taipei voters that was conducted 1 week before the election of December 3, 1994. [6]

Content Analysis. A total of 486 news stories were selected from the three newspapers—the *United Daily*, the *China Times*, and the *Liberty Times*—from August 1, 1994, to December 2, 1994, 1 day before the election. The procedure of selecting a target story followed three steps: First, the news story had to be related to the 1994 mayoral election. Second, the story had to be related to at least one of the three leading candidates. Third, the story had to be related to personal attributes, issue or policy stands, or political identification of the candidates. Stories simply regarding candidates' campaign activities were excluded from the analysis.

Candidate images first were coded into 12 categories of attributes along three dimensions:

1. Personal attributes, which included four political attributes—ability, experience, leadership, and political style—and six nonpolitical attributes—integrity and virtues, personality, appearance, intelligence, education and family, and speaking ability.
2. Partisan affiliation.
3. Issue and policy stands.

Next, the statement of each attribute was coded as favorable (+1), unfavorable (-1), or neutral (0) to a candidate. For each news story, at most three attributes were coded, according to the level of emphasis on the attribute in the story.

The coders were two graduate journalism students from a national university in Taipei. Coder training sessions were administered by the author and another journalism teacher. Coder reliability tests were conducted by randomly selecting 50 sample stories from the population. The final intercoder reliability was 88.7%.

Telephone Survey. The survey was conducted by a Taipei commercial marketing research firm from November 28 to December 1, 1994. Based on systematic sampling from the most updated Taipei telephone directory, the survey completed 1,002 interviews. All respondents were over 20 years old. In comparing the demographics of the samples with those of the population, it was found that the low education subgroups (high school and below) were undersampled, and the high education group was slightly oversampled. [7] Therefore, weighting was used to address the problem of sampling inadequacies. [8]

---

[6] The official campaign period is supposed to begin 10 days before the election. However, almost every candidate jumped the gun under various excuses such as fund-raising dinners or parties.

[7] $Z = \dfrac{Ps - Pu}{\sqrt{PuQu / N}}$

[8] Except education level, the sample's other demographic variables were statistically representative of the population. In this study, the weight for the elementary group was 1.48; for the junior high group it was 1.37; for the high school group it was 1.17; for the college group it was .74; and for the graduate group it was .29.

The survey instrument was designed to measure voters' (a) political knowledge; (b) perception of and evaluation of three leading mayoral candidates; (c) media exposure; (d) political interest, political involvement, political leaning, and voting decision; and (e) socioeconomic status and demographic backgrounds. Respondents' perceptions of the three mayoral candidates' images and of an ideal mayor were measured by two open-ended questions: "When you think of _____, what do you think about (up to 5 items)?" and "What are the qualities, do you think, an ideal Taipei mayor should possess (up to 5 items)?"

For candidate evaluation, a Likert scale was used to measure voters' assessment of each candidate on six traits: integrity and virtues, friendliness, decisiveness, trustworthiness, speaking ability, and ability. Because each response was coded with a score from −2 to +2, each respondent had a total "evaluation score" ranging from −12 to +12 for each of the three candidates.

The scale for measuring voters' political knowledge had eight items, ranging from simple questions (such as candidates' names and party labels) to sophisticated questions (such as candidates' campaign slogans and policy stands). Because each respondent received 1 point by giving a correct answer to each question, the total "political knowledge score" a respondent had ranged from 0 to 8.

Findings

The Image Agenda of the Press.   According to the press coverage, the most emphasized attributes of Huang were his ability, followed by leadership/decisiveness, and personality. The most salient attributes of Chaw in the press were his partisan affiliation, followed by ability, personality, and issue and policy stands. As for Chen, the most often reported attributes were his personality, followed by partisan affiliation, issue and policy stands, ability, and integrity and virtues. [9]

Overall, the three candidates' image agendas were significantly different from each other in the press. When each candidate's image agenda in each individual newspaper was examined, it was found that the three newspapers showed a similar pattern of emphasis on the attributes of Huang and Chen. However, for Chaw, the *China Times*, compared with the other two newspapers, put significantly more emphasis on issue and policy stands and less emphasis on his partisan affiliation and personality.

The Image Agenda of the Voters.   The survey results showed that when Taipei voters thought of the three candidates, most of them often thought about their ability and party affiliation, and fewer thought about their issue and

---

[9] For Huang, of the 486 stories content analyzed, 26.1% mentioned the attribute of ability; 22.3% mentioned leadership or decisiveness; and 18.4% mentioned personality. For Chaw, 25.3% mentioned his partisan affiliation; 18.4% mentioned his ability; and 14% mentioned issue and policy stands. For Chen, 17.8% mentioned his personality; 17.4% mentioned partisan affiliation; 13.7% mentioned his issue and policy stands; 12.8% mentioned his ability; and 10% mentioned his integrity and virtues.

policy stands. Ability was considered the most salient attribute for the three candidates, and respondents had the most negative evaluation of Huang's ability and the most positive evaluation of Chen's ability. The evaluation of Chaw's ability was in the middle. As a whole, voters' evaluation scores of candidates turned out to be good predictors of the election outcome. The mayor-elect Chen had the highest mean score, and Huang, who obtained the least votes, had the lowest evaluation score.

The Image Agenda-Setting Effect of the Press. To examine the second dimension of image agenda setting, the rank order of candidate attributes stressed in the press was compared with the rank order of candidate attributes perceived by the voters. It was found that all three candidates' image agendas (the attributes emphasized) in the press were significantly correlated with their image agendas (the attributes perceived) in the minds of the voters. For Huang Dar-chou, the correlation coefficient (Spearman's Rho) between the two agendas was .64 ($p < .05$); for Chaw Shaw-kong it was .71 ($p < .01$); and for Chen Suei-bian, it was .54 ($p < .05$).

Briefly, the results of this study strongly supported the hypothesized image-setting effect of the press. That is, the attribute salience of the candidates in the press was correlated with the pictures in the heads of the public. From the perspective of the stimulus-determined thesis, it appears that the media, to a significant degree, determined which attributes the voters thought about when they thought of a particular candidate, although this study cannot control for time ordering.

To examine the media image agenda-setting effect more precisely, voters' candidate image agendas were compared with the image agendas projected in their most-often-read newspapers. It was found that the image agenda-setting effects were statistically significant for readers of the *China Times* (for Huang, Rho = .75, $p < .01$; for Chaw, Rho = .72 $p < .01$; and for Chen, Rho = .70, $p < .05$) and for readers of the *United Daily News* (for Huang, Rho = .66, $p < .05$; for Chaw, Rho = .59, $p < .05$; for Chen, Rho = .62, $p < .05$). However, this was not true for the readers of the *Liberty Times*. Nevertheless, after the amount of newspaper reading was controlled for, evidence of *Liberty Times* effects emerged. Among heavy readers of the *Liberty Times* (4 days or more per week), the perceived image agendas of Chen and Chaw, as expected, significantly matched the newspaper image agendas (Rho = .53, $p < .05$; Rho = .58, $p < .05$).

As for other contingent conditions of media image agenda setting, this study found different intervening variables for different candidates. In Huang's case, voters with blue-collar occupations and farmers were more likely to show a media effect. In Chaw's case, the effect was stronger for voters with a higher level of campaign interest. In Chen's case, the media effect was more pronounced for younger voters and those with lower education, a lower level of political knowledge, and a higher level of campaign interest. Gender, on the other hand, was not a significant factor in these correlations.

To sum up, the results of this study firmly supported the hypothesis of the second dimension of agenda setting. Salient candidate attributes in the press came to be salient elements in the perceived images of the voters. The results not only supported the media effect, but also, to a certain degree, bolstered the stimulus-determined explanation of image formation. In other words, according to the study, the voters appeared to be significantly stimulus-determined on the "substantive dimension" (McCombs, 1995) of image agenda-setting.

As a test of the "affective dimension" of the image agenda-setting effect, this study examined three personal attributes of candidates: ability, integrity and virtues, and speaking ability.[10] The findings showed that the affective image agenda-setting effect was nominally supported for Huang and Chen, but not for Chaw. The tone of the press coverage of Huang's ability and speaking ability was unfavorable, and voters' evaluations of him on these two attributes were also negative. On Huang's integrity and virtues, the coverage was favorable and so were voters evaluations. For Chen, the press coverage of all three attributes was very favorable and so were voters' evaluations. For Chaw, the press coverage of his integrity and virtues and ability were slightly negative and the coverage of his speaking ability was favorable, but voters' evaluations on all three attributes were favorable.[11]

When the three newspapers were examined individually, it was found that the coverage of Chaw's ability and integrity and virtues was either positive or neutral in both the *United Daily News* and the *China Times*, but the *Liberty Times* coverage was strongly negative and thus heavily influenced the mean tone of the aggregate coverage as a whole.[12] Moreover, it was found that voters who were more frequent newspaper readers (4 days or more per week) had a more negative evaluation of Huang than did voters who read less often.

In short, although the hypothesis of the affective image agenda-setting effect could not be statistically supported, the congruence in the tone of attributes between the press coverage and the public perceptions did suggest the possibility that the press was able to tell voters not only what attributes to think about, but also how to think about them.

Voters' Characteristics and Candidate Images.   Mindful of the importance of the perceiver-determined explanation of candidate images, this study included t-test analyses and one-way analyses of variance (ANOVAs) to examine the differences between voters with different characteristics (partisan identification, political interest, political knowledge, and demographics).

---

[10] The candidate evaluation scale included six items. However, only these three items were consistent with the categories used in the content analysis, which made the examination of the affective dimension of image agenda setting possible.

[11] The statement of candidates' attributes in a story was coded on a -1 to +1 scale, whereas voters' evaluation of candidates' was on a -2 to +2 5-point scale.

[12] As Chaw was a former KMT young turk and a nonmainstreamer, such a phenomenon probably is related to *Liberty Times'* aforementioned dual political stands. Chaw was one of the founders of the New Party, which was established in 1993.

It was found that voters with a high level of education (college and above) had more negative assessments of Huang than did voters with a low level of education. Voters with more political knowledge had a significantly lower evaluation of Huang than did voters with less political knowledge. The case was reversed for Chaw. Older voters (40 and older) tended to have a more positive evaluation of Huang than did younger voters, whereas younger voters had a more positive assessment of Chen.

In addition, partisan identification showed a strong influence on voters' perceptions of candidates. The results of the one-way ANOVAs suggested that beauty was in the eyes of the beholder. Huang received the highest evaluation from the KMT supporters, which was significantly different from the evaluation of the independents, DPP supporters, and New Party supporters. For Chaw, New Party supporters gave him the highest score, which also was significantly different from that of KMT supporters, DPP supporters, and the independents. Similarly, Chen received the highest score from DPP supporters, which was significantly different from that of KMT supporters, New Party supporters, and independents.[13]

And among the self-claimed independents, Chen enjoyed the highest evaluation mean score. That helps to explain the final victory of Chen in the election. Moreover, voters who claimed that they would vote for a particular candidate gave that candidate a significantly higher evaluation score than they gave to the other two opponents.

When stepwise regression was conducted to examine the relationships between a set of independent variables (media exposure, political interest, political knowledge, partisan identification, and demographics) and the dependent variable (candidate evaluation), it was found that the best predictor of voters' evaluation of Huang was their partisan identification, followed by education and age ($R^2 = .22, p < .001$). The best predictor for voters evaluation of Chaw also was partisan identification, followed by subethnicity ($R^2 = .26, p < .001$). For Chen, the best predictor of his evaluation was partisan identification, followed by subethnicity, age, and newspaper reading ($R^2 = .22, p < .001$).

In short, the results of the regression analysis, in large measure, supported the perceiver-determined explanation of candidate image at the affective level. Voters' partisan identification was the best predictor of evaluation for all three candidates. For Chaw and Chen, voters' subethnicity was also a strong predictor. For Chen and Huang, age was a good predictor. All in all, voters predispositions, especially partisan identification, proved to be the major determinant in explaining their affective perception of candidate images.

---

[13] The means of the evaluation scores for each candidate were as follows: For Huang, KMT supporters (.42), independents (-.07), DPP supporters (-.42), and New Party supporters (-.50). For Chaw, the means were: New Party supporters (1.2), KMT supporters (.31), independents (.32), and DPP supporters (-.07). For Chen, the means were: DPP supporters (1.3), independents (-.81), KMT supporters (.41), and New Party supporters (.11).

CONCLUSIONS

The transactional model of image sources stresses that it is not possible to explain candidate images by relying solely on either the stimulus-determined or the perceiver-determined approach. The findings of this study support this model. The findings show that the press significantly contributed to the construction of candidate images in the heads of the voters. Candidate attributes that were salient in the press become salient elements in the images perceived by the voters. Therefore, it is concluded that voters' images were likely to be more stimulus-determined or media-determined for the substantive dimension of image agenda setting. However, for the affective dimension of voter images, it was found that the perceiver-determined explanation seemed to gain the upper hand. Voters' predispositions, such as partisan identification, age, education and subethnicity turned out to be the significant predictors of their affective evaluations of candidates.

To sum up, according to this study, the stimulus-determined principle of image formation seems more applicable for the substantive dimension of image agenda setting, whereas the perceiver-determined principle is more useful for the affective dimension. Nevertheless, this study still identified some nominal evidence of media image agenda setting for the affective dimension. Certain candidate attributes that were negatively reported in the press were also negatively perceived by the voters. Future studies should adopt more vigorous methodology, including panel designs over time, to further test media image agenda-setting effects for this dimension.

This study also suggested that during the campaign, both the press and the voters were much more interested in candidates' personal attributes than in their issue and policy stands. In a political election, however, it is not possible for voters to make informed decisions without sufficiently knowing each candidate's issue and policy stands. It is understandable why voters are less interested in issue stands that may be boring and complicated, but because the media have assumed a pivotal role in the modern golden electoral triangle and have been shown to have agenda-setting effects on voters, it is inexcusable for the press to downplay the importance of candidate issue and policy stands. If the news media's role is to help create an informed democracy, as Buchanan (1991) argued, the Taiwanese press obviously did not fulfill this mission in the 1994 Taipei mayoral election. The press failed to emphasize each candidate's issue and policy stands in the election, and as a result, the voters did not perceive them as an important criterion for their evaluations of these candidates.

Future studies should try to further distinguish candidate image agendas projected in the press from the image agendas projected by the candidates. There certainly exist differences between the two. A well-designed study would allow researchers to separately isolate the image agenda-setting effects resulting from the two different image sources.

4

Television and the Construction of Social Reality:
An Israeli Case Study

Anat First

The idea of the second dimension of agenda setting is that "beyond the agenda of objects there is also another dimension to consider. Each of these objects has numerous attributes, those characteristics and properties that fill out the picture of each object. Just as objects vary in salience, so do the attributes of each object" (McCombs, 1995, p. 6). Thus McCombs argued, "How news frames impact the public agenda is the emerging second dimension of agenda setting" (p. 6). But through what process does transmission of attributes occur? We suggest that the second level of agenda setting can be understood best as a process of reality construction by individuals who combine elements of news with what they personally observe of life and events to make a sort of blended reality.

The media dependency hypothesis creates a link between construction of reality theory and media research (Adoni & Mane, 1984). According to that approach, mass media in modern societies are information systems involved in the processes of existence, change, and conflict on various levels of social activity—the individual, social group and social institutions, and society (Ball-Rokeach, 1985; Ball-Rokeach & DeFleur, 1976). DeFleur and Ball-Rokeach (1989) suggested that "An advantage of media system dependency theory is that we can use the same basic concepts that apply to the abstract macro relations between systems to examine the more concrete (and micro) relations between the individuals and the mass media" (p. 305). This media dependency mediates between social and individual constructions of reality. In addition, dependency theory claims that media contribution to the individual's construction of subjective reality is partly a function of one's direct experience with various social phenomena (Adoni & Mane, 1984), such as living in a certain religious neighborhood or in a city that is continually attacked by an enemy. Consequently, audiences develop a dependency on mass media content in order to shape their orientation and crystallize attitudes toward various events—even when they are living amid those events.

When television news is a major component of an individual's symbolic reality, we contend that it is also a dominant factor in his or her construction of subjective reality. Not only will individual priorities reflect those of the broadcasts (the first level of agenda setting), but to some extent understanding and attitudes will be shaped by the salience of attributes in the television coverage (the second level of agenda setting). Because reality construction is a dialectic process involving both media images and what one personally sees and hears, an individual's constructed, subjective reality—a combination of the two—provides the basis for his or her social actions. Television news is a major component of symbolic reality and is a dominant factor in constructing an individual's subjective reality.

In a brief test, this chapter shows the agenda-setting role (first and second levels) of television news in the social construction of views about the Israeli–Arab conflict by Israeli youth during the initial period of the Intifada—the 1987 uprising by Arabs in Israel for greater autonomy. We show how the conflict was presented on television news during a brief but important period and how that conflict was perceived by a young audience—Israeli Jewish school students, some perhaps not involved with the ongoing conflict. The Israeli–Arab conflict, which began more than 100 years ago, affects borders and political and social divisions within Israeli society. The Intifada reaches to the core of Israeli self-definition (Benziman & Manzur, 1992; Lissak, 1990; Reiter & Aharoni, 1992). Peacemakers and politicians have started negotiations and have proposed solutions to the conflict for years (Hareven, 1989). In 1996, that effort was still being made amid new conflicts in the streets.

The period examined here, December 1987 to March 1988, was the beginning of the Palestinian Intifada, when Israelis were forced for the first time since the establishment of the state of Israel to contend with an all-encompassing civil uprising. It was an intense time. The conflict, over time, has influenced the Israeli economy, the image and role of the Israeli Defense Forces, the relationship between political parties, and the ideological debate between a factionalized Israeli society and Israeli Arabs (Shalev, 1990). Television played a role in this and in creating a picture of the conflict that many Israeli students learned then, and perhaps still learn today.

MEDIA USE

In media research, the term *use* has a variety of meanings, ranging from simple exposure to a more or less well-motivated use of mass media content for fulfilling certain needs, as in most of the studies discussing uses and gratifications (Windahl, 1981). The focus of this chapter is not based on the uses and gratifications perspective, but we believe that in order to understand the construction of social reality based on television watching, more than one dimension of television use is needed. Our conceptualization is borrowed from Rosengren and Windahl (1989) and addresses three components:

1. There is the amount of consumption. We must study how much time is dedicated to watching television. During the last few years, other media (such as video games) have gained favor among children and adolescents. Yet, we maintain that watching television has become a way of life, of which "television is a major, perhaps the major, medium, occupying a large part of young people's free time" (Rosengren & Windahl, 1989, p. 18).

2. The type of content consumed is important. During adolescence, the amount of time spent watching entertainment programs declines, and the amount of time spent watching news broadcasts and programs on public and political issues increases (Chaffee & Yang, 1990). According to media dependency theory, an individual's dependence on television increases for political issues because these issues are usually somewhat remote from personal experience (Ball-Rokeach, 1985). Adoni, Cohen, and Mane (1984) found that the further a conflict is from the immediate experience of adolescents, the greater their dependence on television as a source of information and perception about the conflict. Even in small Israel, the Intifada did not touch directly on the lives of everyone, except via the news media or word of mouth.

3. The context of use can be influential. The context in which children and adolescents watch television—alone or in the company of others—is important. It is of special significance if youths watch the news with their parents (Liebes & Ribak, 1992). Rosengren and Windahl (1989) found, for example, that girls watch television with their parents more often than do boys and that this behavior is related to the learning of gender roles in Sweden, where parents control the television watching of girls more than that of boys. Other societies would also reflect unique patterns.

The amount and the context of adolescents' exposure to news broadcasts, their dependency on news broadcasts, and the extent to which they believe the broadcasts are the main source of political knowledge and understanding are central components in the process of the construction of reality, for which we propose a model here. Political attitudes, which are forming during the period of adolescence, also affect an individual's perception of the social reality.

SYMBOLIC REALITY

Lippmann planted the seeds of the modern theory of symbolic reality in the 1920s, but broader systematic work on the social construction of reality began in the 1960s with Schutz (1967) and others. Schutz, a sociologist, was fascinated by what he regarded as the mysteries of everyday existence. Just how do we make sense of the world around us so that we structure and coordinate our daily actions? How can we do this with such ease that we do not even realize that we are doing it?

Schutz argued that we can conduct our lives with little effort or thought because we have developed stocks of social knowledge to make quick sense of what goes on around us. Among the most important forms of knowledge we use are *typifications*, which enable us quickly to classify objects and actions that we have observed and then to which we respond (Baran & Davis, 1995). Schutz's ideas are elaborated in *The Social Construction of Reality* by sociologists Berger and Luckmann (1967). In explaining how reality is socially constructed by individuals, Berger and Luckmann argued that: "there is an ongoing correspondence between my meanings and their meanings in the world . . ." (p. 23).

Berger and Luckmann defined reality construction as a social process stemming from social interaction with an objective or symbolic character. It is a dialectical process in which the individual simultaneously creates, and is a product of, his or her social environment (Adoni & Mane, 1984; Baran & Davis, 1995). However, Berger and Luckmann (1967) recognized that individuals attach another kind of meaning to things in their nearest environments, a meaning that is subjective rather than objective. In fact, they identified three types of reality that interact:

1. The objective social reality that exists outside individuals. People experience this reality as the objective world, which confronts them as facts from their own eyes and ears. They apprehend this reality in a common-sense fashion, as a reality that does not need further verification. Human beings, of course, can doubt this reality, but they usually have to suspend any such doubt in performing the routine actions of daily life that ensure both their own existence and their interaction with others.
2. The symbolic reality, which arises from socially shared meaning based on any form of symbolic expression such as art, literature, or mass media content. News is symbolic (unless you are personally involved in the news event).
3. The subjective reality, in which both objective and symbolic realities merge inside of individuals. This is the reality to which we respond ultimately. In other words, if what we see and hear ourselves directly or from the media seems real, it is real.

We argue that symbolic reality—of which the media can be an important component—mediates the process of perception, affecting how individuals interpret both their objective and symbolic experiences. The model thus links phenomenological ideas about the construction of subjective reality to media dependency theory. As Adoni and Mane (1984) showed, the extent to which the media contribute to an individual's construction of subjective reality is a function of one's dependence on the media as a source of information. Depending on an individual's involvement with objective reality, the media serve as a direct input to the subjective construction of reality. However, I also contend that as part of symbolic reality, the media condition the individual's perception of objective experience. In other words, people use their thinking about symbolic reality to interpret objective reality.

Although Berger and Luckmann's book made no mention of mass communication, with the explosion of interest in the media that accompanied the dramatic social and cultural changes of the 1960s, mass communication theorists soon identified the book's value for developing media theory (Baran & Davis, 1995). I suggest that the second level of agenda setting can be best understood as the result of a process of reality construction.

A MODEL OF REALITY CONSTRUCTION

The model we offer (see Fig. 4.1) synthesizes these theoretical frameworks. Taking into account personal characteristics, television use, and attitudes about television, our model proposes that the individual's construction of subjective reality depends on perception of objective reality and perception of symbolic reality, including television presentations, and on the interaction between these two types of perception. The model describes the process through which an individual constructs his or her subjective reality. As part of symbolic reality,

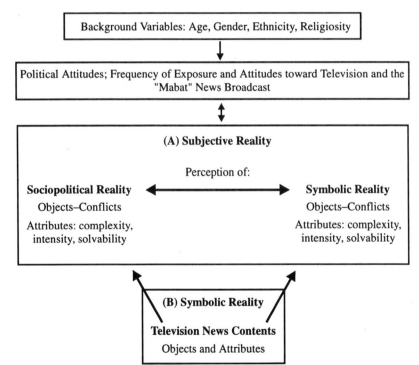

FIG. 4.1. The role of television news in the development of Israeli adolescents' attitudes toward the Israeli–Arab conflict.

television news influences both types of perceptions, and it may be the main—or even the sole—source informing perceptions of symbolic reality.

Our model is made up of two parts. The central component, Part A, represents the construction of subjective reality. It relates the subjective perceptions of the adolescents at two levels: the perception of (objective) sociopolitical reality and the perception of symbolic reality. The age, gender, and other socioeconomic characteristics of the adolescents influence perceptions of each level. In addition, a system of mutual relations between the perception of sociopolitical reality and of symbolic reality exists and it is also affected by adolescents' use of television and their attitudes about television.

Part B deals with the content of television broadcasts, which, for most individuals, is a critical aspect of their symbolic reality, especially with regard to public events. When we apply the model to television news, that medium—in terms of both the priority issues (agenda setting, first level) and the attributes ascribed to priority issues (agenda setting, second level)—wields considerable influence on perceptions of symbolic reality for many individuals.

THE ISRAELI–ARAB CONFLICT: A PARTIAL TEST

From the end of the 19th century to the present, the Israeli–Arab conflict has shaped the identity of Jewish society in Palestine and now Israel (Lissak, 1990). Although some participants in the conflict share language, culture, and religion, a complete understanding of the complexity of this situation requires identifying four distinct participants: (a) Arab states, (b) the Palestinians in the occupied territories, (c) the Israeli Arabs, and (d) the Jewish Israelis and the state of Israel. For the purposes of this study, we asked how the very first Israeli television news coverage of the Intifada simplified the conflict for viewers, Israeli school students who would be leaders for the Israeli "side" in the future.

To examine the relationship between television coverage of the Intifada and the adolescents' perceptions, we devised a quasi-experiment with two complementary methods of data gathering: survey and content analysis. The student survey and the codebook for the content analysis of the news broadcasts both define and operationalize the conflict in three dimensions (intensity, complexity, and solvability). We collected the data from the survey and for the content analysis at the same time.

In accordance with our model, we studied adolescents' subjective perceptions about the conflict at two levels: the sociopolitical reality and the symbolic reality. We wanted to compare their subjective construction of reality with television presentation of the national agenda (the objects), and of the intensity and complexity and the prospects of resolving the Israeli–Arab conflict (the attributes). We correlated the adolescents' perceptions of the conflict with the news content and then we asked them how importantly they ranked the three different aspects of news about one topic, the Israeli–Arab conflict. In other words, we took one issue and divided it into three parts, noting the relative emphasis given the parts by television and the relative emphasis learned by Israeli school youth.

News Intensity

This dimension deals with the attitudes and behavioral traits of the participants in the conflict. The intensity of the activity is a function of the efforts invested by both sides in achieving their objectives at the time of the struggle. For example, any conflict news—of which there was much—was judged intense (Kriesberg, 1973; Stagner, 1967). News of terrorist activities was also judged intense.

Complexity

This dimension deals with the general characteristics of a conflict and especially with the number of participants and the number of issues involved. Other characteristics related to the complexity dimension are the history of the conflict, its duration, and its possible effects on civic life. These were less mentioned in the opening news stories than was news of conflict or Israeli–Arab clashes.

Solvability

This dimension deals with news about the extent of possible conflict resolution. According to sociological analyses of conflicts, the difficulty of arriving at solutions arises from incongruity between or among the aims of the involved sides and from the estimated costs of possible solutions. Hence, conflicts over basic values and resources, such as territory, power, status, and religion, tend to be difficult to resolve (Cohen, Adoni, & Bantz, 1990; Kriesberg, 1973; Nordlinger, 1972).

Television news often creates the impression that conflicts are short-lived and relatively easy to solve (Cohen et al., 1990). We wanted to know if this generalization applied to Israeli news coverage of the Intifada. We sampled 54 news broadcasts of Mabat, the only nightly television news program in Israel at the time of the study, from December 1, 1987 through March 18, 1988. The Intifada erupted in 1987. From December through January, every other Mabat broadcast during the work week (Sunday through Thursday) was included—for example, Sunday, Tuesday, Thursday, the following Monday, Wednesday, and so on. From February through March, all weekly broadcasts were included. We included broadcasts during this period because these were the months when the survey data were being gathered. In our study, we concentrated on all stories that demonstrated themes of intensity, complexity, and solvability about the Israeli–Arab conflict, as well as all other topics, but here we analyze only the opening story, which operates like an introduction to the entire following broadcast. There were 54 of these lengthy stories, nearly all of which focused on the Israeli–Arab differences during the nearly 4 months in which the news was sampled. (There were 825 stories, including the introductory story, in the larger study.)

The Sample

The sample consisted of 466 urban adolescents, ages 12 to 18, including both junior high-school and high-school Jewish students. The schools were chosen from a sample of schools in the four major cities of Israel—greater Tel-Aviv, Jerusalem, Haifa, and Beer-Sheba. The respondents were pupils in classes chosen randomly from a representative sample of schools with varied social characteristics (secular and religious, academic and vocational).

The Questionnaire

The questionnaire included questions relating to patterns of media use, particularly the consumption of television news; questions about the way in which the adolescents perceived the conflict (the perception of objective social reality); questions concerning the adolescents' perceptions of the television presentation of the conflict (the perception of symbolic reality); and questions on background variables and attitudes of the respondents. Questions were closed-ended. Here we examine student media use with student judgments about what they regarded as important in their subjective assessments of differences with Arabs. The question was whether the students were most influenced by news that reflected the intensity of the conflict or by news that covered the complexity or solutions to Israeli–Arab differences.

RESULTS

The results show a partial working of the model. The content analysis of the news broadcasts showed that most opening news stories dealt with the Israeli–Arab conflict in some way, especially with the Intifada and terror (Fig. 4.2), or intensity. Nearly all of the 54 opening stories focused on some aspect of the Israeli–Arab conflict. Of these, 65% emphasized intensity, whereas the complexity (19%) and solvability (7%) of Israeli–Arab issues were less men-

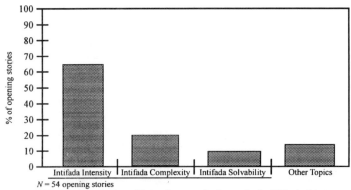

$N = 54$ opening stories

FIG. 4.2. Distribution of intensity, complexity, and solvability in 54 opening Mabat broadcasts.

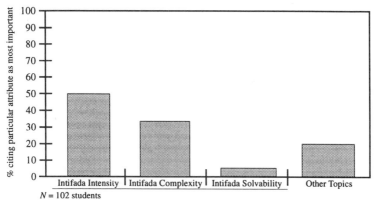

FIG. 4.3. Adolescent ranking of attributes of the Israeli–Arab conflict, by those who watched Mabat broadcasts six times a week.*

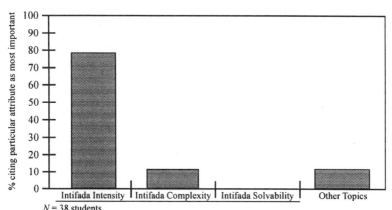

FIG. 4.4. Adolescent ranking of attributes of the Israeli–Arab conflict, by those who did not watch Mabat broadcasts at all.

tioned. Only 9% of these news openings mentioned other news topics (see Fig. 4.2). (If all 825 broadcast stories are considered—not just the 54 openings—the same general trend is demonstrated, although there are more stories on other topics later in the broadcast.)

Meanwhile, Israeli youth who were asked about their perceptions of the Israeli–Arab conflict—regardless of what television might have been saying—ranked the importance of the issues similar to the openings of the 54 newscasts. Those who watched all of the 6-day-a-week broadcasts especially reflected the same pattern of issues (see Fig. 4.3). (This was also true of those who said they watched even one broadcast a week.) Youth who said they never watched the newscasts were far more likely to mention as important only the most emphasized news approach of the Israeli–Arab conflict, intensity (see Fig. 4.4). For students who watched a lot, the order of issues closely matched the pattern of topic presentations, an example of a second-level media framing for that audience. For those who did not, only conflict (intensity) made much of a dent—perhaps a first-level agenda-setting effect— and they may have learned this issue from other people, not the news media.[1]

THE MEDIA AND SOCIAL COHESION

Because the unit of analysis in this study is the individual, our model takes into account a number of independent variables that influence the individual's perception of reality: age, gender, ethnic background, education, socioeconomic level, religiosity, and political attitudes. In this chapter we concentrate only on the contribution of television to the judgments of social-political reality of Israeli youth during a time of crisis, showing a second-level agenda-setting effect on those who watch a lot, and—perhaps—a first-level effect on those who said they never watched.

What does this mean? Kosicki (1993) argued that agenda-setting theory tries to provide a list of ranked issues where only one issue exists. In our case, there was one main issue—the Israeli–Arab conflict (the Intifada)—with many faces (attributes), of which we studied three—intensity, complexity, and solvability. We took a broad issue and divided it into three parts. Audiences seemed to learn the parts approximately the way television presented them. Stories are discrete and separable, but issues are integrated and complex. Agenda-setting research at present matches samples of public news with what is learned by individuals. This chapter suggests that one may not need media exposure to learn of the biggest issues, but one does need media exposure if one is to understand the ways in which the mass media frame, and the public, learns about issues. Democratic social systems can solve social problems only if citizens agree on the dimensions of the challenge.

---

[1]Not included here, the study showed that youths who watched television also remembered the TV issues close to the way that they actually were presented (when asked to cite what they had seen on television).

5

Agenda Setting and Priming:
Conceptual Links and Differences

Lars Willnat

Initially studied in the context of mass communication and voter behavior, media agenda setting (McCombs & Shaw, 1972) is based on the idea that the routine pattern of news coverage can structure and change audience cognition. Although the basic agenda-setting hypothesis has been widely supported, most communication researchers have failed to develop a comprehensive theory that would explain the underlying cognitive processes of exactly how development of issue priorities is influenced by the mass media. Instead, most research related to agenda setting has focused on associations between media content and response without much empirical or theoretical regard for the cognitive mechanisms involved (Kosicki, 1993).

Many of the earlier agenda-setting studies adopted a limited media effects model after finding only weak correlations between increased issue salience as a result of more media exposure and changes in political behavior (Rogers & Dearing, 1988). However, by limiting agenda-setting effects on audience cognition to changes in issue salience, researchers often ignored effects the media might have on links between political cognition and attitude formation. During election campaigns, such a link might exist if the media were to make salient certain issues or candidate attributes that enable the voter to assign a favorable or unfavorable value to a political candidate (Weaver, 1983).

Some recent agenda-setting studies have tried to include behavioral measures as dependent variables, but relatively little progress has been made in terms of theoretical explanations of this process (Rogers & Dearing, 1988). Weaver (1991), for example, showed that level of perceived issue salience can correlate with issue knowledge, strength and direction of opinion regarding the issue, and political behavior. Other agenda-setting studies focusing on the role of the news media in political election campaigns have successfully predicted voting patterns based on respondents perceived issue salience (Roberts, 1992) or found that television coverage of political issues can influence voters' party leaning (Brosius & Kepplinger, 1992). However, none of these studies was able to provide an explanation of how exactly issue salience might influence these observed behavioral consequences.

Another weakness of agenda-setting research has been its traditional bias toward aggregate-level analyses of public opinion. As Iyengar (1988) pointed out, individuals are not passive consumers of media messages, but they interpret, elaborate on, and evaluate information within an existing network of knowledge, attitudes, beliefs, and personal experiences. According to this perspective, individual differences in information processing are crucial factors for the perception of media messages because, "to the degree individuals take issue with the news or can call up information that challenges news items, agenda-setting is weakened" (Iyengar, 1988, p. 598). Although some theoretical concepts such as Weaver's (1977) "need for orientation" have been introduced to explain more clearly the cognitive processes that are involved in the agenda-setting process, little is known about how a person's political interest or knowledge might influence this media effect.

In response to calls for increased attention to the consequences of agenda-setting (Iyengar & Kinder, 1987; Weaver, 1984), a number of political communication researchers (Iyengar & Kinder, 1987; Krosnick & Kinder, 1990; Schleuder, McCombs, & Wanta, 1991) have linked the agenda-setting hypothesis and cognitive priming theory to analyze the effects of news coverage on people's evaluations and opinions of political leaders. Media priming studies have found strong empirical support for the priming hypothesis that television news coverage not only heightens viewer cognizance of certain issues, but also affects the criteria by which political leaders are judged (Iyengar & Kinder, 1987; Krosnick & Brannon, 1993; Krosnick & Kinder, 1990).

Although the priming hypothesis has been enthusiastically embraced by mass communication researchers, considerable disagreement exists about how the priming theory can be related to studies of agenda setting. Although media priming focuses on the cognitive and behavioral consequences of agenda setting, both approaches rely on issue salience or accessibility as a major dependent variable. Possibly because of this conceptual link, some researchers see media priming as an extension of agenda setting (McCombs, Einsiedel, & Weaver, 1991; McCombs & Shaw, 1993), whereas others describe agenda setting as "one particular variant of priming" (Price & Tewksbury, 1995, p. 8). Disagreeing with both of these viewpoints, Kosicki (1993) distinguished priming as "qualitatively different . . . separate both empirically and theoretically from agenda-setting" (p. 117).

Although the exact relationship of priming and agenda setting remains unclear in the present literature, the alliance of both approaches has unquestionably strengthened the theoretical base for media agenda-setting effects documented during the last 25 years. What is needed at this point is a better understanding of how and when priming can be applied to the traditional agenda-setting approach.

The intention of this chapter is to acknowledge the major opportunities and problems that have developed as a result of the combination of the traditional agenda-setting approach with cognitive priming theory. The chapter is organized in three parts. First, I briefly describe the theoretical conceptualization of media priming and how it has been linked in the literature to studies of agenda setting. The second part reassesses the applicability of cognitive priming theory to agenda setting based on conceptual definitions and findings of established media priming effects. I concentrate on the question of which conditions might facilitate the two related media effect processes to work together to produce significant changes in audience attitudes and behaviors. The final part of this chapter presents some suggestions for further research in the hope that a tighter integration of agenda setting and priming will allow a better understanding of how the mass media not only tell us "what to think about," but also "what to think" (Cohen, 1963).

COGNITIVE PRIMING THEORY

Cognitive priming, defined by Fiske and Taylor (1991) as the effects of prior context on the interpretation and retrieval of information, focuses on the effects of long-term memory on the processing of new information. In essence, priming is built on the assumption that the frequency, prominence, or feature of a stimulus activates previously learned cognitive structures and influences interpretations of an ambiguous stimulus. A simple illustration of the effect of priming on memory retrieval is found in the natural tendency to interpret a certain word in terms of the most recent encounter with it. If, for example, a person reads a newspaper article about a new computer virus that destroyed data stored on a government computer and an ambiguous conversational reference to "virus" occurs a few minutes later, the person is likely to think of "virus" as a destructive computer program rather than as a microscopic organism.

Two major information-processing models have been developed to explain the activation of prime-related concepts in long-term memory. The first model, proposed by Higgins and King (1981), suggests an *energy cell* process in which the energy or action potential of a mental category is increased whenever the cell involved is activated by recent or frequent exposure to related concepts or ideas. An alternative conceptualization by Wyer and Srull (1986, 1989) assumes that information is stored in memory in the form of a storage bin. According to this metaphorical model, primed categories will be retrieved from a storage bin and then, rather than being returned to their original location, they are placed on top of that bin. This means that more recently acquired and used information is nearer to the top of the bin and therefore more accessible in memory (Ottati & Wyer, 1991).

The underlying cognitive mechanism of both models can be explained by information accessibility, or the idea that recently and frequently activated or primed concepts come to mind more easily than concepts that have not been activated by prior stimuli (Higgins & King, 1981; Wyer & Srull, 1986, 1989). In other words, the frequency and intensity of media exposure to certain issues determines the likelihood that related concepts will be applied to new information in the minds of the individual audience members, as long as these concepts are applicable to the stimulus presented. The accessibility of a concept or idea in memory is determined by a variety of factors: the frequency (Higgins, Bargh, & Lombardi, 1985) and recency (Herr, Sherman, & Fazio, 1983; Higgins, Rholes, & Jones, 1977; Srull & Wyer, 1979, 1980) with which the concept has been used in the past, a person's goals at the time the information is received (Wyer & Srull, 1986, 1989), the level of prior knowledge about the person or object to which information pertains to (Wyer & Ottati, 1992), and the concept's applicability to the current stimulus (Price & Tewksbury, 1995).

A number of researchers have distinguished between the temporary accessibility of a construct and chronic (or baseline) accessibility based on the argument that more frequently activated concepts develop more and stronger associative links to other constructs in long-term memory (Bargh, Bond, Lombardi, & Tota, 1986; Bargh & Prato, 1986; Bargh & Thein, 1985; Higgins & King, 1981). Thus, chronic accessibility of a concept such as the president's foreign policy, for example, will be greater for individuals who have been exposed extensively to news stories about this issue in the past. Consequently, the temporary accessibility of a construct resulting from short-term media priming effects has to be measured against the baseline of chronic accessibility, which results from more long-term media exposure to an issue.

An instructive way to think about the effects of priming is in terms of a hierarchically organized network of concepts, schemata, or attributes (nodes) that are linked through associative pathways (Anderson & Bower, 1973; Collins & Loftus, 1975).

Based on earlier models of semantic memory and language comprehension, Collins and Loftus (1975) developed the spreading activation model, which represents memory as a collection of networks in which substantive elements of thought and feelings are linked associatively. According to this model, exposure to a certain stimulus with a particular meaning "primes" semantically related nodes and then expands or spreads along the associative pathways to other elements in the mental network. This mechanism first links all the nodes closely related to the original node, and then spreads to more remote nodes, thus providing a way to access indirectly associated thoughts or feelings. Thus, when people perceive an event via the mass media, concepts having a similar meaning are activated in their minds for a short time afterward, which, in turn, might trigger other semantically related thoughts or ideas.

Priming has been shown to influence a variety of perceptions, including word or letter recognition (Meyer & Schvaneveldt, 1976), retrieval of text in memory (Albrecht & O'Brien, 1990), formation of feelings (Berkowitz & Heimer, 1989), and judgments of life satisfaction (Strack, Martin, & Schwarz, 1988). Several other priming studies have shown that the mass media also can influence the worldview and subsequent behavior of people previously exposed to semantically related concepts such as helpfulness and cooperation (Holloway, Tucker, & Hornstein, 1977; Hornstein, LaKind, Frankel, & Manne, 1975). The majority of media priming research, however, has examined the potential connection between television viewing and aggressive behavior of children. A review of television programming effects on children's thoughts and actions by Berkowitz and Rogers (1986), for example, concludes that the mass media can activate thoughts and memories that "prompt people in the audience to act aggressively toward others or themselves, even when the portrayals of violence are fictional" (pp. 57–58).

COGNITIVE PRIMING AND AGENDA SETTING

The theory of cognitive priming has proven especially useful as an extension to the traditional agenda-setting hypothesis by addressing the importance of both the media agenda and media semantic content in influencing political communication. Iyengar and Kinder (1987) were the first to demonstrate that television news not only increases the perceived salience of those issues that are covered most, but also works to "prime" viewers to give these issues more weight in their overall evaluation of political candidates and parties. In a series of experiments designed to expose people to manipulated news programs, the authors found that the impact of increased media exposure to national problems such as energy, defense, and inflation substantially boosted the weight respondents assigned to these issues in their overall evaluation of President Carter.

Although the strongest empirical support for media priming comes from experimental studies, recent field studies of priming have provided some supporting evidence for the priming hypothesis under more natural conditions. Krosnick and Kinder (1990), for example, examined the priming effect of media coverage of the Iran–Contra scandal on perceptions of President Reagan in October 1986. The researchers took advantage of the fact that the disclosure of the Iran–Contra scandal took place in the midst of the National Election Study (NES) survey, and compared two groups of respondents—one interviewed before the disclosure and another afterward. The findings indicated that respondents in the postdisclosure group gave foreign policy more weight in their evaluation of President Reagan's overall performance than the predisclosure group did.

A later study by Iyengar and Simon (1993) used the NES surveys from 1988, 1990, and 1991 to analyze the impact of respondents' opinions and beliefs about foreign policy on assessments of Presidents George Bush and Ronald Reagan over time. The results showed that, in 1990 and 1991, the impact of foreign policy performance was more important than economic performance in respondents' assessments of President Bush. The reverse was true in 1988 for President Reagan. As in Krosnick and Kinder's (1990) earlier study, this change in the evaluation criteria was attributed to news coverage of U.S. foreign policy.

Iyengar and Kinder (1987) explained these findings by arguing that ordinary people, when facing complex political issues or events, do not conduct a thorough analysis based on all knowledge they may have learned because of limited information-processing capabilities. Instead, it is assumed that many people make judgments based on bits and pieces of information they could easily retrieve from the top of their mind. This would mean that individuals often base their decisions on a limited subset of the information available in memory so as to make satisfactory judgments without expending a great deal of effort (Krosnick & Brannon, 1993). Support for this claim is found in studies of information processing that show that many people only pay casual and intermittent attention to media presentations of political affairs and have a limited store of political knowledge to call upon (Kuklinski, Riggle, Ottati, & Wyer, 1991; Ottati, Riggle, Wyer, Schwarz, & Kuklinski, 1989).

Because most people rely on the mass media for information about political events and selectively attend to issues that seem important (Iyengar & Ottati, 1994), the accessibility of information in memory is determined to a great extent by which stories the media choose to cover (Iyengar & Kinder, 1987). Accordingly, issues that have been covered extensively by the mass media will make certain related considerations or ideas more accessible in people's minds (agenda setting) and, as a consequence, will have a greater impact on peoples' evaluations of political leaders than other nonprimed considerations (priming). Thus, according to the priming theory, the media not only affect the perceived salience of issues, but also influence the degree to which issues are used as criteria to evaluate political leaders.

It should be noted that the priming literature sometimes distinguishes between automatic and controlled information processing. Where controlled processing presumably requires conscious attention and depends on what a person's desires or intentions are at that moment, priming effects can operate automatically and without awareness (Bargh & Pietromonaco, 1982; Higgins et al., 1977; Schiffrin & Schneider, 1977). Sherman, Mackie, and Discoll (1990) found strong evidence for the influence of passive priming on evaluations of and preferences for political candidates. Individuals who were indirectly primed about a candidate's foreign policy experience with four associated prime words (diplomat, overseas, ambassador, consulate) were more likely to judge these candidates based on information relevant to the primed category than on another equally relevant but nonprimed category (economic matters).

Thus, even prime cues that are not directly related to the prime target can influence political judgments by passively priming people to consider semantically related aspects or issues when evaluating political leaders.

Modeling the Agenda-Setting and Priming Effects

During the past 10 years, cognitive priming has been primarily adopted by communication researchers to analyze the effects of television news on audiences' perception and evaluation of political leaders. One of the major accomplishments of applying the priming theory to agenda-setting research has been that it provided a plausible, theoretical model of how the media might influence people's perception of the importance of issues or events, and how these perceptions in turn might affect political attitudes, opinions, and behaviors.

Price and Tewksbury (1995), for example, argued that both agenda setting and priming rely on the same cognitive mechanism, which describes issue salience as the result of increased accessibility of mental constructs in long-term memory due to media exposure. They concluded that "agenda setting—commonly thought to be a kind of basic media effect upon which priming depends—is actually but one particular variant of priming, which is itself a far more general effect" (pp. 7–8).

Although there is considerable evidence supporting the use of heuristics in political decision making and the idea that people rely on what they already know when evaluating political candidates, the memory-based priming model reduces media effects to knowledge activation and leaves little room for alternative explanations of how people might form judgments based on information presented in the mass media. There are, for example, situations in which people might want to consider several different priming aspects of an issue before forming an opinion about it. In such a situation, people will actively seek out more information about that issue and then will base their judgments on the combined implications of the collected information. As Lau (1995) pointed out, during election campaigns, voters are undoubtedly "constrained by their own cognitive limits and by what information is available"; however, "within those constraints (or perhaps because of those constraints) people seek out highly diagnostic information (party identification) and other types of information they think is important" (p. 202). Moreover, it is also possible that memory search is affected by such matters as mood, social context, and other recent activities (Millar & Tesser, 1989; Zaller, 1992).

Memory-Based Versus Impression-Driven Model. The priming model has been especially criticized by a considerable research literature that argues that instead of making "memory-based" judgments from accessible ideas, people's judgments are normally made "online" as new issue-relevant information is acquired (Hastie & Park, 1986; Krosnick & Brannon, 1993; Lichtenstein & Srull, 1987; Lodge, McGraw, & Stroh, 1989; Lodge, Steenbergen, & Brau, 1995; McGraw & Pinney, 1990). Proponents of the online model believe that memory-based evaluations require too much cognitive effort because "they rely on the effortful retrieval of specific information from long-term memory, the weighting of evidence, and then the computation of a summary evaluation" (Lodge et al., 1989, p. 401). Lau (1995), for example,

showed that people often seek out far more information than they could possibly hold in working memory, which points to the importance of some other information-processing method, particularly for issues that are complex, ambiguous, or numerous and thus require an extensive information search. Other studies have found that the correlations between judgments of political candidates and memory are rather weak or nonexistent (Fishbein & Ajzen, 1975; Hastie & Park, 1986; Lodge et al., 1989; Lodge et al., 1995).

The online model of information processing tries to explain the weak relationship between judgments and memory by proposing that individuals who are exposed to new information can act as "cognitive misers" by simply retrieving issue-related evaluations from memory, updating their judgment, and then storing the new evaluation in long-term memory (Lodge et al., 1989). For example, when asked to express an evaluation of the president, people simply retrieve their current evaluation of the president from long-term memory, update this opinion with new information available, and then report it, rather than construct their evaluations on the basis of considerations most accessible (or salient) to them.

The advantage of the online model is that it allows people to take much more information into account when making their decisions, because they can update their judgments continuously and then forget the actual piece of information that contributed to the evaluation. According to Lodge et al. (1989), this might explain the observation that people are often able to tell whether they like or dislike something without being able to remember the reasons for their evaluation.

Although there is considerable evidence in support of the online information-processing model, its application to complex issues or events, such as a political debate among presidential candidates, is questionable.

Zaller (1992) pointed out that news stories are often too complex and refer to more issues than a person could possibly consider at the moment of encountering this information (as postulated by the online model). A televised debate between two presidential contenders, for example, might refer to a number of issues such as the budget deficit, foreign and domestic policy, or national defense. Obviously, people are unlikely to consider all these issues simultaneously (as proposed by the online model) and would have to rely on some form of memory-based evaluation. It is therefore reasonable to assume that, depending on the complexity of the issue, people either use the online or the memory-based information-processing approach.

Agenda Setting, Priming, and Political Involvement.
The information-processing approach underlying the media priming approach gives political knowledge a central place in how and when new information is stored and retrieved. Obviously, different people can be exposed to the same message and yet perceive it quite differently, depending on their prior knowledge about the issue under consideration. Theories of social cognition assume that an individual's understanding of political events and actions is determined by the interaction between existing cognitive structures and new information. Thus,

general political interest, knowledge about candidates or parties, or even a specific goal such as obtaining more information on a candidate's stand on certain issues, should strongly influence how mass-mediated information is processed by each individual.

Unfortunately, studies that have investigated the role of political involvement in agenda setting and priming have provided only inconclusive evidence. In their seminal study of agenda setting and priming, for example, Iyengar and Kinder (1987) found that the magnitude of the agenda-setting effect was negatively related with greater interest and participation in politics, whereas the priming effect was independent from political involvement. Findings from other priming studies indicated that individuals with lower levels of education, political interest, and political participation were generally more susceptible to media influences (Iyengar, Peters, & Kinder, 1982; Iyengar, Peters, Kinder, & Krosnick, 1984; Krosnick & Kinder, 1990).

Krosnick and Kinder (1990), for example, showed that among those who knew little about public affairs, extensive media coverage of the 1986 Iran–Contra scandal had a substantial priming effect on public support for President Reagan. Priming among political experts seemed confined to political aspects (economy, foreign policy) that were not directly implicated by media coverage of the Iran–Contra issue. A more recent priming study by Krosnick and Brannon (1993), however, showed that media priming was most pronounced for respondents with high levels of political knowledge, whereas higher levels of media exposure and interest reduced the priming effect.

These latter findings obviously challenge the conventional wisdom that political involvement facilitates the availability, organization, and recall of political information. Studies of agenda setting and priming have traditionally assumed that the more educated, interested, and involved segments of the audience can recall memorized information better than political "novices" when attending to the media because they possess more knowledge and informational support for their beliefs and thus should be less vulnerable to media influences. According to this perspective, political involvement might be associated with more intense cognitive activity because individuals actively respond to persuasive messages, counterarguing with those with which they disagree and elaborating favorably on those with which they agree (see, e.g., Iyengar & Kinder, 1985). Consequently, individuals with more political knowledge and higher levels of interest should be less affected by media priming.

Although the retrieval of political knowledge from memory might allow people to counterargue new information and thus protect them from media priming effects, political expertise might also influence the storage and organization of new information—possibly with opposite effects on the magnitude of media agenda setting and priming. Based on the assumption that people with substantial knowledge about politics are more easily able to interpret, encode, store, and organize new information in terms of concepts they have already formed, priming might especially affect those who can effectively assimilate and retain new information (Ottati & Wyer, 1991). This viewpoint was supported by Krosnick and Brannon (1993), who argued that "the more knowledge one has about politics, the more quickly and easily one can make sense of a news story and the more efficiently one can store it in, and retrieve it from, an elaborate and organized mental filing system" (p. 966).

The authors suggested, however, treating political knowledge and interest as distinct constructs, because they might have opposite effects on political information processing. Political interest, so the argument goes, limits the effects of priming because highly exposed and interested individuals are likely to consider a wide range of details so that the "priming impact of the principal message is likely to be diluted by the many other knowledge domains that are also primed" (Krosnick & Brannon, 1993, p. 965).

Similarly, Iyengar (1990b) hypothesized that, when evaluating a candidate, people tend to give greater weight to information pertaining to areas in which they hold more knowledge or have a particular expertise. In this way the information assumes a greater influence, which may cause a person with a particular background or knowledge in an area to selectively encode information relevant to his or her own area of expertise. As a result, one may be more likely to retain and be influenced by this subset of information, ignoring information relevant to other domains (Ottati & Wyer, 1991).

Salience and Issue Competition. The media priming theory explains the formation and consequences of issue salience in terms of temporary information accessibility, but little attention has been paid to the question of how people organize and relate the representation of multiple issues in memory (Iyengar & Ottati, 1994). One problem faced by agenda-setting and priming research is that our limited capacity for information processing might not only make us attend to one particular issue that is prominent in the media, but might also affect how many issues we can attend to at one time even when they are all equally prominent in the media. The limited processing abilities of the public on the one hand, and the competition of media issues for public attention on the other, leads to the important question of how issue competition influences people's considerations when they think about the most important issue facing the nation today.

As noted by Zhu (1992), many of the original agenda-setting studies relied on the implicit "zero-sum" principle that any new issue that appears on the public agenda might reduce or eliminate the perceived salience of older issues. This perspective has led many agenda-setting researchers to analyze multiple issues in terms of rank-order comparisons without considering the interaction that might exist between the perceived salience of these issues. Similarly, earlier media priming studies avoided the problem of salience interaction by assuming that media coverage of one issue primes only directly related concepts or ideas. The classic formulation of the priming hypothesis by Iyengar and Kinder (1987), for example, states that the "more attention television news pays to *a particular problem*—the more frequently a problem area is primed—the more viewers should incorporate what they know about *that problem* into their overall judgment of the president" (Iyengar & Kinder, 1987, p. 65, italics added).

Thus, if an individual is primed with media coverage of President Clinton's foreign policy, for example, only the weight of that issue should increase in people's overall evaluations of the president. It is also conceivable, however, that the news coverage of Clinton's foreign policy primes people to think of semantically related issues such as his domestic policy or national defense, therefore influencing the weight of ideas or concepts that are not directly implicated by the news story.

Whereas most previous studies found no "traces of spillover in agenda-setting whereby news coverage of some issues would also increase concerns for related issues" (Iyengar, 1988, p. 600), more recent analyses of media agenda setting and priming acknowledge and support the notion that media coverage of various issues can have some kind of interactive influence on issue salience. Comparing the agenda-setting effects of news stories about the recession, the federal budget deficit, and the Persian Gulf War between 1990 and 1991, Zhu (1992) found that although the emergence of the Gulf conflict decreased the salience of the budget deficit among the public, as assumed by the "zero-sum" principle, media coverage of the deficit and the war contributed to the perceived salience of the recession. A later study by Iyengar and Simon (1993) found similar evidence for such a "hydraulic pattern" in agenda setting, characterized by an increase in perceived salience for the Gulf War and the economy, and a corresponding decrease in salience for the problems of drug abuse and the budget deficit.

Because it is possible that the competition of news items for audience attention increases the perceived salience of conceptually related issues, Zhu's (1992) multi-issue analysis might be better modeled by priming and spreading activation rather than agenda setting. The observed relationships between the tested issues might be partly explained by the fact that news stories about the deficit and the war often explicitly speculated about the negative consequences of these two issues for the U.S. economy (Zhu, 1992). However, it is reasonable to assume that people, after being exposed to news about the budget deficit and the Gulf War, were more likely to base their overall evaluation of the U.S. recession on activated knowledge—or considerations related to the budget deficit and the Gulf War. This process would explain the additional increase in perceived salience for the recession issue attributed to the news stories about the budget deficit and the Gulf War.

Such a broader application of media priming would assume that news coverage not only increases the perceived salience (accessibility) of various issues, but that it also causes people to relate the issues to what they already know (knowledge activation) in order to calculate their relative importance. Unfortunately, we know little about the circumstances under which issue competition might take place and how people mentally calculate the relative weight of each issue. One factor that might determine whether issues can be mentally related or not is likely to be the specific characteristic of each issue under consideration. Most people should realize, for example, the relationship between the federal budget deficit and the recession, even if news stories do not explicitly make this point. The economic implications of the Persian Gulf War, however, are less obvious and thus might influence perceptions of the recession less than the budget deficit issue.

Naturally, explicit cues about the relationship of two issues should increase the magnitude of media priming effects. Iyengar and Kinder (1987), for example, showed that the weight accorded to economic performance in overall evaluations of President Reagan increased when individuals were given information about economic problems, and increased further when individuals watched news reports on economic problems suggesting that Reagan's economic policy was the principal cause of these problems.

Salience and Issue Content. In their review of agenda-setting research, Rogers and Dearing (1988) pointed out that priming theory has proven especially useful as an extension of the traditional agenda-setting approach by addressing the importance of both the mass media agenda and mass media semantic content in influencing political communication. Iyengar and his colleagues have shown that media coverage of political campaigns can prime individuals to consider particular personality or character traits, such as competence or integrity in their evaluations of political candidates (Iyengar et al., 1982; Iyengar & Kinder, 1987; Krosnick & Kinder, 1990; see also Conover & Feldman, 1986; Miller, Wattenberg, & Malanchuk, 1986; Rahn, Aldrich, Borgida, & Sullivan, 1990).

Based on the assumption that people tend to interpret ambiguous stimuli in terms of the trait category that is most accessible, media priming theory contends that those traits made more accessible by extensive media coverage tend to bias the way people evaluate the overall performance of a political candidate. Iyengar and Kinder (1987), for example, analyzed the influence of media content on priming by comparing news stories that either did or did not emphasize the president's responsibility for a national problem. As expected, the authors found that the priming effect was more pronounced for those news stories that contained explicit references to the president's responsibility for a problem.

Whereas these initial findings support the idea that the semantic content of news stories influences the priming effect, recent media priming studies have neglected the potential differences that might result from news content. Most analyses have relied on simple counts of how often an issue is mentioned in the media without paying much attention to the way the issue was covered.

Especially missing from the current literature are analyses of how positive and negative news coverage of political issues influences the cognitive priming effect. Because the media priming theory is based on the assumption that both the issue salience and the semantic content of a news story lead to the activation of prime-related knowledge, we might expect that the tone of a news story (positive, negative, or neutral) can influence what kind of prime-related ideas come to mind as the result of media exposure to certain issues.

Moreover, if priming can activate related ideas in memory via associative pathways as proposed by the spreading activation model, negative news stories about a political issue also might prime related negative feelings or emotions toward a political candidate. Various experimental studies have shown, for example, that individuals, after constructing sentences using words with aggressive connotations, tended to evaluate a target person unfavorably (Wyer & Hartwick, 1980), or were more likely to deliver the most intense electric shocks to a fellow student whenever that individual made a mistake. Obviously, the exposure to aggression-related cues can activate or prime other aggression-related thoughts that color an individual's judgment of a person and might even lead to aggressive behavior. During an election campaign, this could mean that negative news coverage or advertising not only primes people to consider certain issues as more important when evaluating a political candidate, but also prompts them to feel more negatively about the candidate as a result of negative emotions activated by negative issue coverage.

Television Versus Print Media Effects. Another underdeveloped area that might provide room for a more general application of the priming model is the analysis of print media priming effects. Ironically, although the majority of agenda-setting research has focused on print media as the major force of influence on audiences, almost all media priming studies have analyzed the effects of television news. Iyengar and his colleagues justified the focus on television in analyses of agenda setting and priming with the argument that television news is regarded by many Americans as an authoritative and accurate source of public affairs information (Iyengar, 1988) and because its "vivid pictures and dramatic stories" (Iyengar & Kinder, 1985, pp. 118–119) can evoke strong emotions in the audience—both factors that should bolster the effect of media exposure on issue salience.

However, such arguments do not consider that media channel characteristics are crucial determinants of cognition, because the processing of visual and verbal messages from television differs significantly from information processed through reading text. Memory research has demonstrated, for example, that brain activity is greater for reading than for watching television (Weinstein, Appel, & Weinstein, 1980). Thus, information derived from the print media might be encoded, stored, and retrieved more efficiently than visual information coming from television. Moreover, print media generally provide more information for each issue or event than television news and provide more complex coverage of news stories (Graber, 1993).

At this point, evidence for different priming effects depending on the type of media exposure is limited to studies that do not directly relate to agenda setting and have analyzed the priming effect mainly for different types of television exposure. Schleuder, McCombs, and Wanta (1991), for example, compared the priming effects of political advertisements and news stories on television. Their results suggest that the ability of a viewer to activate semantically related issues and candidate knowledge stored in long-term memory is not affected by message form. However, respondents' attention and visual memory were better when the information was presented in advertisement form than when it was presented in a news story.

In a similar study, Schleuder, White, and Cameron (1993) found that priming effects of news teasers resulted in improved attention to news stories that followed and better recall of verbal information in the primed news stories. The recall of visual information, however, was not improved by priming. The only study that directly compared the priming effects of television and print found little difference between television and newspaper users (Mendelsohn, 1994).

THE FUTURE OF AGENDA SETTING AND PRIMING

As we have seen, media priming theory challenges the old and often cited maxim of agenda setting that "the media may not be very successful in telling us what to think, but they are very successful in telling us what to think about" (Cohen, 1963, p. 13). Although priming has provided agenda setting with a psychologically plausible theory of how media influence political perceptions and behaviors, the cognitive expansion of agenda setting has also resulted in many conceptual problems that remain unexplored.

Overall, media priming has opened up many potentially exciting venues for further research. However, we need to expand the application to a wider range of issues and test the theory against other models of media effects. It seems that the most important obstacle for the future of media priming in mass communication research is the question of whether this theory can be applied to a wider range of public affairs issues, or whether this particular media effect is confined to its traditional application in appraisals of presidents and political leaders. Many communication researchers agree with the view that the influence of the mass media "is due in large part to the activation of concepts and propositions semantically related to the event depicted" (Berkowitz & Rogers, 1986, p. 61), but limited evidence exists for the application of priming to the broad range of issues that have been tested successfully in agenda-setting research.

Although priming has been shown to influence a variety of factors (evaluations of political candidates, formation of feelings, judgments of life satisfaction, aggressions, etc.), most priming studies that have analyzed media effects on the perception of public affairs have used evaluations of political leaders as the ultimate dependent variable. Compared to the well-researched structure of candidate representations in memory, however, we know virtually nothing about how ordinary issues such as the economy or foreign policy are represented in the minds of the public.

In view of the findings by Zhu (1992), which showed that the coverage of some issues can boost the perceived salience of conceptually related issues, it seems important for studies of agenda setting and priming to consider how issues might be represented in memory and how they might be mentally related. Only then should we consider applying Iyengar and Kinder's (1987) original conceptualization of media priming theory to other issues by substituting judgments of political leaders with judgments of other public affairs issues.

I have also tried to show that the concepts of knowledge activation and issue accessibility have to be considered carefully in the context of agenda setting because their applicability might depend on the type of issue under consideration and the personal background (i.e., political knowledge or interest) of each media user.

According to the priming theory, media exposure presumably causes the activation of related knowledge, which is then more likely to be retrieved and used in later judgments because it is more accessible in memory and comes to mind spontaneously and effortlessly. Critics of this memory-based model of political judgments have pointed out that many issues are too complex to be processed in such a heuristic way. They have suggested that the complexity of the issue(s) under consideration will determine to a large extent whether individuals will retrieve related thoughts or ideas when exposed to some stimulus from the mass media (priming), or whether they will evaluate issues based on impressions that have little connection to information stored in long-term memory (online information processing).

It is thus questionable to categorize agenda setting exclusively as the result of knowledge activation, as suggested by Price and Tewksbury (1995). Rather, priming should be seen as one possible explanation of how agenda setting might work under certain conditions (e.g., with issues and individual differences that support knowledge activation).

Also needed are studies that close the methodological and conceptual gaps that previous studies of media priming have left. As mentioned already, priming should be tested for the print media and television. Although there are good arguments for the persuasiveness of television in agenda setting and priming, potential print media effects cannot be ignored. Another point that has to be cleared up is the presumed duration of the priming effect. Iyengar and his colleagues have provided little information about how long priming is assumed to work after exposure. At this point, most studies seem to indicate that the priming effect might be observed about a week after exposure (Iyengar & Kinder, 1987; Willnat & Zhu, 1996). Moreover, as already pointed out, the priming effect is not only dependent on the recency of media exposure, but also on the frequency of exposure. Thus, future studies should investigate in more detail how the potentially different effects of repeated versus most recent media exposure influence media priming.

Because political persuasion is difficult to achieve and political news probably has only small direct effects on the electorate, it seems of great importance to search for other, more indirect ways the media might influence our political views and decisions. In view of the cognitive shortcomings of the traditional agenda-setting approach, priming provides an improved explanation of the ways people think rather than what they think about. Priming may offer the best foundation for a new understanding of political media effects within the agenda-setting framework, because it combines the importance of mental links between cognition and political attitudes with agenda-setting ideas, resulting in a more general information-processing model.

II

THE AGENDA-SETTING PROCESS

6

Susceptibility to Agenda Setting:
A Cross-Sectional
and Longitudinal Analysis
of Individual Differences

Jian-Hua Zhu with William Boroson

Who is most susceptible to media agenda-setting influence? The question has important implications for both scholarly research and the democratic process. From a theoretical point of view, the answer provides insights on the power of the media and the nature of the audience, two central issues of long concern to media scholars. If some members of the audience prove to be less vulnerable to media agenda-setting effects than others, then there is reason to believe that the media have a limited power on the sophisticated segments of the audience. Methodologically, the study of individual differences in the agenda-setting process provides a testing ground for a number of long-debated issues such as individual-level versus aggregate-level analysis, cross-sectional versus longitudinal comparison, and statistical versus substantive significance. Finally, policymakers may use the findings from this line of research to identify the "victims" of agenda setting (Iyengar & Kinder, 1987) and equalize the gap in issue salience among different segments of the public.

Agenda-setting research has attended to individual differences from the outset. In their seminal study, McCombs and Shaw (1972) compared the different agenda-setting effects across voter groups (i.e., Democrats, Republicans, and Independents), and explicitly noted that the purpose of the between-group analysis was to examine the "individual differences" that might be lost in the overall design of "lumping all the voters together in an analysis" (p. 181). Unexpectedly, they found an across-the-board function of agenda setting because the variations among different voters across various issues and media channels were quite minimal. The search for individual differences has since continued, spanning a variety of individual characteristics such as political partisanship (Iyengar & Kinder, 1987; McCombs & Shaw, 1972; McLeod, Becker, & Byrnes, 1974), campaign interest (McLeod et al., 1974), age (Weaver, Graber, McCombs, & Eyal, 1981), and media preference (Benton & Frazier, 1976). Despite the impressive quantity of studies, the accumulated evidence is conflicting and confusing. Some studies have found no significant differences among individuals, whereas others have reported significant differences in opposite directions from one study to another. Moreover, the selection of these individual characteristics has been criticized as "ad hoc" because they "have no explicit theoretical grounding" (Swanson, 1988, p. 605). However, there do exist theoretical models of audience susceptibility, with the following three concepts most worthy of further exploring in the current chapter.

COGNITIVE SOPHISTICATION

MacKuen (1981) offered two competing theories (attentiveness vs. cognitive framework) of why some members of the audience are more susceptible to agenda setting than others. The attentiveness model holds that the audience's susceptibility to the media agenda is a function of the individual's attentiveness toward incoming information and his or her cognitive ability to process the information. Operationally, attentiveness is measured by interest in politics, and cognitive ability by years of education. Specifically, the theory predicts that the higher the political interest and/or educational level a person has, the more susceptible the person is to media agenda setting. On the other hand, the cognitive framework theory contends that those with higher education and political interest have developed a more effective self-defense mechanism against external influence and thus are less subject to agenda setting.

MacKuen's empirical test of the two rival models produced evidence in favor of the attentiveness theory. However, a later study by Iyengar and Kinder (1987) found that better education and higher political interest made the audience less susceptible to media agenda setting. Therefore, they concluded that "The power of television news to set the public agenda depends partly on which public we have in mind. Television coverage is particularly effective in shaping the judgment of citizens with limited political resources and skills" (p. 60).

The first objective of this study is to examine whether agenda-setting effects are contingent on the audience's cognitive sophistication; specifically, whether the sophisticated or the naive audience is more easily moved by media coverage of an issue. Following MacKuen (1981) and Iyengar and Kinder (1987), we use education to measure cognitive sophistication. Converse (1972) succinctly justified the use of education alone as a sufficient surrogate for cognitive sophistication:

There is probably no single variable in the survey repertoire that generates as substantial correlations in such a variety of directions in political behavior material as level of formal education. Whether one is dealing with cognitive matters such as level of factual information about politics or conceptual sophistication in its assessment; or such motivational matters as degree of attention paid to politics and emotional involvement in political affairs; or questions of actual behavior, such as engagement in any of a variety of political activities from party work to vote turnout itself; *education is everywhere the universal solvent,* and the relationship is always in the same direction. The educated citizen is attentive, knowledgeable, and participatory, and the uneducated citizen is not. (p. 324, italics added)

Because the better educated members of the audience are more attentive to public affairs, it is reasonable to expect them to be more responsive to media agenda-setting effects than the less educated.

ISSUE SENSITIVITY

Independent of cognitive ability, the audience's predisposition may be another contingent factor for media agenda-setting effects. Erbring, Goldenberg, and Miller (1980) called this predisposition an "issue-specific sensitivity" and argued, "As individuals obviously differ in their issue sensitivities and preoccupations, we do not expect the impact of issue coverage by the media to occur in a blanket sweep across the entire population" (p. 28). In their view, media coverage of an issue serves as "a trigger stimulus" (p. 45) to the audience's preexisting perception of issue salience. This formulation of issue sensitivity resembles "issue relevance," one of the two key components for the concept of need for orientation (Weaver, 1977).

The audience's issue sensitivity has been operationalized in several ways depending on the nature of the issue under examination. In Erbring et al.'s study, the presence of a union member or an unemployed person in the family was taken as a measure for sensitivity to unemployment, personal income for sensitivity to inflation, age and gender for sensitivity to crime, and political interest and party membership for sensitivity to trust in the government. Those with a union member or unemployed person in the family were more responsive to media agenda-setting effects about unemployment than those without any of these family connections; women and senior citizens were more affected by media agenda setting about crime than men and the younger generations. However, contrary to their hypothesis, those with a lower level of political interest were more prone to agenda setting about government trust. The impact of income on agenda setting was also unexpected because those at the middle range of income were more subject to media coverage of inflation than those at either end of the income scale. The observed impact of issue sensitivity was further impaired by the lack of control for education (i.e., the differences between the sensitized and insensitized audiences might be due to different levels of cognitive skills) and by the cross-sectional design of the study.

Our second objective in this study is to investigate the role of issue sensitivity in agenda setting while holding the audience's cognitive sophistication constant. Family income is used as the only measure of sensitivity to all four issues under study: inflation, unemployment, international problems, and government spending (there is detailed discussion of the issues later). It is hypothesized that those with higher levels of income are less sensitive to inflation and unemployment because they are proportionally less affected by these issues than those with lower levels of income. On the other hand, the wealthier are expected to be more sensitive to international problems (which may affect their domestic and overseas investments) and government spending (which has direct relevance to their taxes).

OBTRUSIVENESS ISSUE

Although our interest centers on the contingent effects of individual characteristics, it is necessary to control for issue characteristics because there may be some interaction between the two. For example, the sophisticated audience may be more susceptible to agenda setting for unobtrusive issues whereas the naive audience may be more vulnerable for obtrusive issues. According to Zucker (1978), an issue is obtrusive if the public has direct experience with it, or unobtrusive if the public has no direct contact with it. Domestic economic issues such as inflation and unemployment are often cited as examples of obtrusive issues, whereas foreign affairs is considered a typical unobtrusive issue. The distinction between obtrusive and unobtrusive issues has been empirically tested. For example, based on a factor analysis of 11 issues, Eyal (1979) identified two distinctive sets of issues: an obtrusive set including inflation, unemployment, and the economy and an unobtrusive set involving welfare, the environment, and foreign affairs. Blood (1981) reported that the respondents in his survey rated inflation as the most obtrusive and the Iran hostage issue the least obtrusive, with economic recession falling in between.

Zucker argued that the media agenda-setting effects are stronger for unobtrusive issues because the audience has to rely on the media for information about these issues. On the other hand, the audience is less susceptible to agenda setting about obtrusive issues because these issues can be learned from one's own experience or personal networks. A number of studies have found strong media agenda-setting effects for unobtrusive issues (Eyal, 1979; Zucker, 1978), and weak or even null agenda-setting effects for obtrusive issues (Iyengar, 1979; Palmgreen & Clarke, 1977; Winter, 1980). However, a more recent study by Yagade and Dozier (1990) has raised doubts about the obtrusiveness hypothesis. Using a different terminology, "concreteness versus abstractness," the authors observed that the media agenda-setting power was enhanced for concrete issues, but diminished for abstract issues. Although Yagade and Dozier drew a distinction between concreteness and obtrusiveness, the examples they used clearly indicate that obtrusiveness and concreteness are equitable. For example, they defined the nuclear arms race as an abstract issue and found no agenda-setting effects for it; when the issue was treated as an unobtrusive issue in earlier studies by Zucker and others, stronger agenda-setting effects were observed.

To control for the interaction between audience characteristics and issue obtrusiveness, we have included four issues in the current study: inflation, unemployment, federal government spending, and international problems. There are both conceptual and pragmatic reasons to choose these issues. Conceptually, based on previous studies (Blood, 1981; Eyal, 1979), we have an objective measure of obtrusiveness for these issues, with inflation and unemployment being the most obtrusive, international problems the most unobtrusive, and government spending in between. Practically, these four issues have been prominent in the public's issue agenda (e.g., accounting for up to 80% of the answers to the question of what the most important problem facing the nation is in Gallup polls), whereas other issues such as the environment, drug abuse, crime, or abortion tend to be present sporadically and sparsely.

GROUP-LEVEL ANALYSIS

Data

The data on the public's issue salience are extracted from 35 Gallup surveys that contain a question on "what is the most important problem facing the nation" (MIP hereafter) between 1977 and 1986, archived at the Roper Center for Public Opinion Research at the University of Connecticut. The unavailability of many Gallup MIP surveys after that period prevents us from extending the series up to the present. Nevertheless, the current data pool, with a total of 39,914 individuals interviewed at 35 points in time, provides a sufficient basis to test the hypothesized differential effects of media agenda setting. As did many earlier studies of agenda setting, we use the open-ended question on MIP as a measure of perceived issue salience. As discussed earlier, we chose two individual characteristics, education and income, to divide the surveys for cross-sectional comparison. To keep a balance between enough groups for comparison and enough individuals in each group, we classify both education and income into three levels.[1] The procedure results in nine audience groups (three levels of education x three levels of income).

---

[1]For education, those with 8 years of schooling or less are labeled low, those with 9 to 12 years of schooling are middle, and those with any college education or more are high. For income, no fixed threshold value is used because family income in dollar amount increases all the time. Thus, all 35 samples are divided as evenly as possible into three income levels.

The data on media issue coverage are based on a content analysis specifically carried out for this chapter. The content analysis involves counting the number of news stories on inflation, unemployment, international problems, and government spending aired by *ABC World News* during the same 10-year period. The definitions of inflation, unemployment, and government spending are self-explanatory, and international problems refers to all kinds of "bad news" abroad such as wars, riots, coups, scandals, economic crises, and natural disasters. ABC was selected to represent national television newscasts because previous studies have shown a high degree of homogeneity in news content among the three networks (e.g., Zhu, 1992). Using *The Vanderbilt Television News Index and Abstract* as our source, we examined every news item on the *ABC World News* for the 10 years. If *ABC World News* was off the air for a given day (e.g., a Saturday or Sunday) we substituted first with *CBS Evening News* for that day, followed by *NBC Nightly News* if *CBS Evening News* was also off the air on that day.

VISUAL INSPECTION

Before performing any formal test, we plot the public's issue salience of the four issues, along with media coverage of these issues, in Figs. 6.1 to 6.4, to help identify visible patterns for (a) media agenda-setting effects over time, and (b) differentials in agenda-setting effects across groups. For an easy reading of the figures, only five out of the nine audience groups are shown, with four intermediate groups omitted. Before the omission, however, we checked all nine series to ensure that all the excluded series fell into the middle of the displayed areas.

Figures 6.1 to 6.4 reveal a certain degree of correspondence between the public's issue salience and the media's coverage of the issues. For example, both the public and the media had a fairly high level of concern about inflation at the beginning of the 10-year period (Fig. 6.1). After a dip, both rose to a new height in January 1978 and stayed there for about 2 years. The 1980s, however,

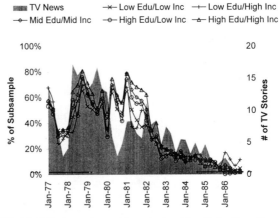

FIG. 6.1. Inflation as the most important problem facing the nation.

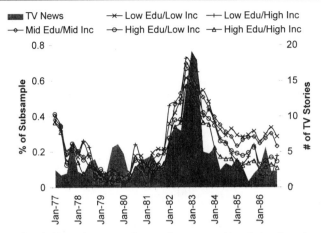

FIG. 6.2. Unemployment as the most important problem facing the nation.

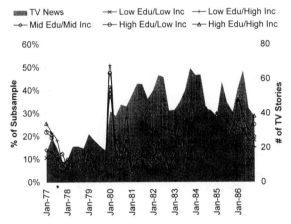

FIG. 6.3. International problems as the most important problem facing the nation.

witnessed a gradual decline in the prominence of inflation in both the public's mind and the media's spotlight, although the latter lost interest in the issue much quicker. Unemployment went through a different course, but the parallel trends between the public and the media are quite visible (Fig. 6.2). For example, after paying little attention to the issue, both the public's concern and the media's coverage of unemployment rose suddenly in January 1982 and peaked in 1983, then both displayed a downward trend. The parallel between the public's salience and the media's coverage of international problems is more complex because there were several ups and downs throughout the entire period (Fig. 6.3). However, a careful check of these cycles reveals a close match between the two agendas. For example, January 1980 saw an abrupt rise of international problems in both the public and the media agenda (mostly regarding U.S. hostages in Iran). Parallel trends can also be found in several other peaks and valleys of international problems between 1983 and 1986. Government spending seems to be a weak case for media agenda setting because the public did not become concerned about the issue until January 1984, whereas the most intensive coverage of the issue occurred between 1981 and 1983 (Fig. 6.4).

Figures 6.1 to 6.4 also show some differences among the five audience groups. However, both the magnitude and the direction of between-group differences vary over time and across issues. For example, the differences were much larger in the first 5 years (1977–1981) than in the last 5 years (1982–1986) for inflation (Fig. 6.1), but smaller in the first half of the period than the second half for unemployment (Fig. 6.2). A larger between-group discrepancy was also observed during the second half of the period for both international problems (Fig. 6.3) and government spending (Fig. 6.4). In general, the high-education/high-income group had the highest level of issue salience and the low-education/low-income group had the lowest level of concerns. This pattern shows up even for inflation, which seems to be contradictory to the issue sensitivity hypothesis. However, the reverse holds for unemployment, in which the high-education/high-income group was the least concerned whereas the low-education/low-income group was the most concerned (Fig. 6.2), which is consistent with the sensitivity hypothesis. When the level of media coverage is taken into account, it becomes clear that the high-education/high-income group shows the closest match with the media.

The most striking observation in Figs. 6.1 to 6.4 is, however, that the cross-sectional variations appear to be much less dominant than the longitudinal variations within each group. That means, despite the different levels of concerns, various groups of the public behave quite consistently with each other over time. Even when there was a large difference in the magnitude of issue salience across the groups (e.g., 1981–1982 in Fig. 6.1, 1983–1986 in Fig. 6.2, 1980 in Fig. 6.3, and 1983–1986 in Fig. 6.4), it is important to note that all the groups followed a similar trajectory along with the changes in the number of television news stories. The displayed series represent the

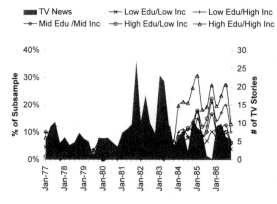

FIG. 6.4. Government spending as the most important problem facing the nation.

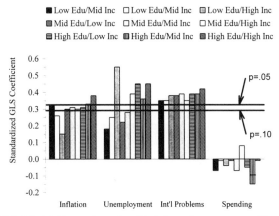

FIG. 6.5. Media agenda-setting effects by audience groups and issues.

maximum contrast among the nine groups. The between-group differences across the entire sample would appear even less visible had the four intermediate groups been included.

TIME SERIES ANALYSIS

However informative they might be, visual impressions are not always reliable, especially because we are dealing with such complex scenarios that involve multidimensional comparisons. To formally test the differential effects of media agenda setting, we have applied generalized least squares (GLS) regression to the data. The GLS estimation controls for the autocorrelation present in the time series data (Hibbs, 1974). The dependent variable for the regressions is issue salience (i.e., the percentage naming an issue as the MIP by an audience group), whereas news salience (the number of ABC news stories on the issue) serves as the independent variable.[2] A quarterly interval is used for the series, which amounts to 40 time points for the 10-year period. There were five quarters in which Gallup did not conduct an MIP survey. The missing points have been linearly interpolated. Because there are 36 series of issue salience (nine audience groups x four issues), we performed the same GLS regression 36 times. The results are summarized in Fig. 6.5.

The vertical axis displays the estimated standardized GLS regression coefficients, which represent the agenda-setting effects of television news coverage about the four issues on each of the audience groups.[3] Not shown

---

[2]More precisely, a cumulated number of stories is used (= $News_t$ + .5$News_{t-1}$ + .25$News_{t-2}$ + .125$News_{t-3}$, where t is the current month, t-1 is the previous month, etc.). See Zhu, Watt, Snyder, Yan, & Jiang (1993) for details.

[3]Strictly speaking, a comparison across regressions should be based on the unstandardized coefficients. However, plotting the unstandardized coefficients may make the interpretation unnecessarily complicated. Thus, the standardized coefficients are used here.

in the figure, however, is the significance test for each of the coefficients. Given the degrees of freedom for the regressions, ($\pm$ .28 is the minimal value for a coefficient to be marginally significant at the .10 level (which may be acceptable given the small N, 40, for all the regressions), and ($\pm$ .32 is minimally required for significance at the .05 level. Judged by these two yardsticks, media coverage of the first three issues seems to have a significant impact on the audience (on seven groups for inflation, six for unemployment, and all nine for international problems). On the other hand, television news about government spending appears to have no effect on any of the nine groups. It should be noted that, although eight of the nine coefficients for government spending are negative, all of them are far from being significant. Thus, the data do not lend support to the so-called reverse agenda-setting hypothesis (i.e., the audience sets the agenda for the media).

Because we are more interested in whether the agenda-setting effects are differentiated across various segments of the audience, it is necessary to take a closer look at the between-group differences in Fig. 6.5. Three patterns seem to emerge: First, all of the nine groups are responsive to media agenda setting for international problems (i.e., all coefficients are significant beyond the .05 level). Second, none of the groups is affected by agenda setting for government spending. Finally, the groups show a varying degree of susceptibility to agenda setting for inflation and unemployment, with the agenda-setting effects being significant on some groups (three for inflation and five for unemployment), marginally significant on other groups (four and one, respectively), and not significant on still other groups (two and three, respectively).

However, it is premature to accept the differential effects of media agenda setting for the last two issues simply based on the significance level of the GLS coefficients. The significance level generated from the regressions does not directly test the null hypothesis that there is no difference among the regression coefficients; instead, it tests the null hypothesis that each of the regression coefficients is zero in the population. Thus, if we ran two GLS regressions and found one yielded a significant coefficient (say, $p = .049$) but the other yielded a nonsignificant coefficient ($p = .051$), the significance test does not imply that the two estimated coefficients are significantly different (as one can expect from this hypothesized case, the two coefficients are most likely to be equal in the population). A formal test of the heterogeneity across the estimated coefficients is therefore called for.

HETEROGENEITY TEST

We have chosen Rosenthal's (1991) heterogeneity test to assess whether there are indeed differential effects of agenda setting across the nine groups.[4] To

---

[4]The test is based on $\Sigma(n_i - 3)(z_i - z)^2$, where z_i is Fisher's transformation of the standardized regression coefficient for Group i (= 1 to 9), z is the weighted mean for the nine zs for an issue, and n_i is the number of cases for Group i (= 40 for each of the nine groups). The resulting statistic is distributed as χ^2 with k -1 degrees of freedom (k is the number of coefficients in the test).

control for the issue characteristics, the test is performed separately for each issue. The procedure results in four scores for the heterogeneity statistic: 1.365 for inflation, 6.159 for unemployment, .230 for international problems, and 1.159 for government spending. The statistic has a χ^2 distribution with $k - 1$ degrees of freedom (k is the number of coefficients tested). If the statistic is 15.51 (the critical value of χ^2 with $df = 8$ for $p = .05$) or greater, then we can conclude that the nine coefficients under examination are significantly different at the level of .05 or beyond. Obviously, none of the four heterogeneity statistics survives this test. In fact, the significance level is above the .50 level for the most heterogeneous issue (unemployment). In addition to the test of the overall difference among the nine groups as a whole, we have also checked the pairwise difference between any two groups for each issue. Among the 144 possible pairwise comparisons, there is no single pair of coefficients different from each other at the .05 level.[5]

Because the heterogeneity test shows no significant difference among the nine groups for each issue, we can legitimately combine the GLS coefficients into a weighted mean to summarize the agenda-setting effects on the entire sample. Following Rosenthal's (1991) procedure, we have obtained four weighted mean GLS coefficients and their corresponding significance levels ($\beta = .300$ and $p < .01$ for inflation; $\beta = < .345$ and $p < .01$ for unemployment; $\beta = .375$ and $p < .01$ for international problems; and $\beta = -.035$ and $p > .50$ for government spending). As the results show, the agenda-setting effects on the entire sample are significant for the first three issues, but not significant for government spending.

INDIVIDUAL-LEVEL ANALYSIS

Unlike most other time series studies of agenda setting in which the aggregated issue salience is regressed on media content, our study disaggregates the public into nine groups in terms of cognitive sophistication and issue sensitivity. This group-level approach reduces, if not completely eliminates, the ecological fallacy that is often associated with aggregate-level analysis. However, our approach still suffers from a loss of power of analysis when we transform the original individual-level data, which include nearly 40,000 respondents, to 36 group-issue series. In other words, there might be a high degree of Type II error in our findings of no differential effects of agenda setting based on a comparison of 36 cases. Thus, before drawing any firm conclusion, we need to cross-validate the findings with individual-level data.

---

[5]Only two pairwise comparisons are marginally significant at the .10 level (the low-education/high-income group vs. the low-education/low-income group, and the former group vs. the middle-education/low-income group, both for unemployment).

The validation is carried out by fitting a series of log-linear models to the 35 original individual-level Gallup MIP data sets. To assess the between-group difference over time, the 35 surveys are stacked into one data set, which contains 39,914 cases and five variables: issue, education, income, year, and news. All of the variables except news are treated as categorical variables. Issue has four categories, representing the four issues under study. Both education and income are coded into three levels, ranging from low through middle to high, the same as in the group-level analysis. Year has 10 categories, ranging from 1977 to 1986, each for a particular year in which the surveys were conducted. This variable is used to account for the changes in the distribution of issue over time. We treat year as a categorical variable rather than a continuous variable in order to examine (a) the unique contribution of year, and (b) its interaction with education and income, both of which are possible only when year is included as a categorical variable in the log-linear models. On the other hand, news (the number of stories aired by *ABC World News* on each of the four issues in a given year) remains as a continuous variable because it does not have cross-sectional variation (i.e., news is a constant for all nine groups at a given time).

Issue is the dependent variable in all of the log-linear models we have tested and news is always entered as a covariate. The models differ only in the specification of three independent variables: education, income, and year. First, we fitted a null model that assumes the distribution of issue is not affected by any of the independent variables. As one can expect, this null model fits the data poorly, as reflected by a large and significant L^2 relative to its degrees of freedom ($L^2 = 15,075.28$, $df = 264$, $p = .000$).[6] Although this null model does not offer any theoretically interesting information, the resulting L^2 represents the total variance in issue, a baseline from which improvements made by subsequent models can be calculated.

Next, we searched for a best fitted model that explains the most variance in issue with the fewest predictors. The resulting model, including all three independent variables and their two-way interactions, provides a very good fit to the data, given the huge size of the sample ($L^2 = 110.80$, $df = 108$, $p = .41$). Absent from the model is the three-way interaction among education, income, and year. Had the three-way interaction been included, we would have had a saturated model, which by definition fits the observed data perfectly (i.e., $L^2 = 0$, $df = 0$, $p = 1$). However, the difference between the best-fitted model and the saturated model is not statistically significant ($\Delta L^2 = 110.80$, $df = 108$, $p = .41$), suggesting that the more parsimonious model (i.e., the best-fitted model) is superior. On the other hand, a comparison between the best-fitted model and the null model shows a significant difference ($\Delta L^2 = 14,984.57$, $df = 159$, $p =$

---

[6] L^2 stands for log-likelihood function, a measure of the discrepancy between the observed frequencies (e.g., the mentions of various issues as the most important problem) and the expected frequencies (e.g., given the joint distribution of education, income, and year). Thus, a large, significant L^2 indicates a poor fit of the theoretical model to the data, wheras a small, nonsignificant L^2 suggests a good fit between the model and the data.

.000), which justifies the inclusion of these predictors. Furthermore, the best-fitted model explains 99.3% ($=\Delta L^2 / L^2_{\text{null model}}$) of the variance in the null model. The remaining 0.7% of unexplained variance is due to the three-way interaction omitted from the best fitted model.

Our primary interest is not in the best fitted model per se, but in the relative contribution made by each of the independent variables. Thus, we have examined three partial models that contain all the predictors of the best fitted model except one: education, income, and year, alternatively. Because these partial models use one fewer predictor than the best fitted model, they necessarily fit the data less well. As it turns out, all three partial models do not fit the data adequately ($L^2 = 282.05, df = 114, p = .000$ for the education-excluded model; $L^2 = 246.40, df = 114, p = .000$ for the income-excluded model; and $L^2 = 5,690.89, df = 131, p = .000$ for the year-excluded model). Thus, each of the three independent variables has an indispensable influence on issue salience. In other words, unlike the time series analysis at the group level, log-linear analysis of individual-level data shows significant differences both cross-sectionally and longitudinally.

As in any other causal study, we should be concerned with both the *significance* and the *size* of the effects. The best indicator of the size of effect for a variable is the unique contribution made by the variable over and above all other variables present in a model. Thus, we have calculated the difference between a partial model and the best fitted model divided by the null model, which gives the proportion of variance solely attributable to the variable excluded from the partial model. For example, the unique contribution of education is given by ($L^2_{\text{Education}} - L^2_{\text{best-fitted}}) / L^2_{\text{null}} = (282.045 - 110.80) / 15.094.37 = 1.1\%$. By the same token, the estimated unique contribution is .9% for income and 37.0% for year.[7] As explained before, year captures the changes in the distribution of issue for a given group over time. Therefore, to borrow the analysis of variance language, education and income together represent the between-subjects variance, whereas year indicates the within-subjects variance. In other words, the log-linear modeling shows that the within-subjects factor (i.e., comparison of the individuals within the same group over time) accounts for almost 20 times more variance in issue than do the between-subjects factors (i.e., comparison of individuals across groups at a given time). This finding is consistent with the time series analysis of group-level data that shows significant agenda-setting effects over time but few differences across groups.

CONCLUDING REMARKS

Who is most susceptible to media agenda-setting effects? The answer seems to be everyone, or no one, depending on the issue context. In this study, we have found that various audience groups are equally subject to media agenda-setting

---

[7]The remaining explained variance in the best fitted model is attributable to the joint force of the three independent variables.

influence for inflation, unemployment, and international problems, but the same groups are equally unresponsive to agenda setting for government spending. In other words, the audience is homogeneously susceptible to the media agenda for some issues and invariantly insensitive to the media agenda for other issues. This uniform process of agenda setting seems to be quite robust given the fact that our evidence is derived from 35 nationwide samples spanning 10 years and analyzed at both group and individual levels.

One may argue that the homogeneous agenda-setting effects are not warranted because the individual-level analysis did show significant differences across levels of education and income. This brings up the traditional debate between statistical significance and substantive significance. Yes, the between-group differences detected in the individual-level analysis reach a high significance level ($p < .001$). However, in terms of the size of the effects, the between-group factors (i.e., education and income) together account for only 2% of the variance in issue salience, which pales compared with the 37% of the variance explained by the within-group factor (year). In other words, the media agenda-setting effects are not manifested in creating different levels of salience among individuals, but are evident at driving the salience of *all* individuals up and down over time.

One may challenge our findings of homogeneous agenda-setting effects based on the particular way the public is classified. There are certainly a variety of alternatives for grouping the public, such as by exposure to media (which seems to be more appropriate to testing media agenda-setting effects), interest in public affairs (e.g., Iyengar & Kinder, 1987; MacKuen, 1981), personality (e.g., measured by the Strength of Personality; Weimann & Brosius, 1994), and occupation or union membership (Erbring et al., 1980). However, we suspect that the results would not be any different if any of these classifications was employed, because these variables are highly correlated with education or income, the variables used in this study. For example, in Weimann and Brosius (1994), the rank-order correlations between opinion leaders (i.e., the highest 10% on the Strength of Personality scale) and opinion followers in Germany are mostly above .80 and .90 across issues and over time, which suggests a highly homogeneous agenda-setting process in that country.

The multilevel approach used in this study appears to be both crucial and fruitful to testing the differential effects of agenda setting. The most important outcome from this exercise is, of course, that uniform effects of agenda setting consistently emerged at both the group and individual levels. Each level of analysis offers additional insights. For example, the time series analysis of the group-level data provides a justification for the conventional time series analysis of the correspondence between the aggregate public issue salience and the media agenda. On the other hand, the log-linear modeling of individual-level data helps consolidate the mixed results from previous studies regarding individual differences in agenda setting. Other factors aside, the size of sample employed seems to be closely related to whether a study finds significant differences across individuals. As clearly demonstrated in this study, a large sample makes the significance test very sensitive to any small difference across individuals. Although this is certainly a desirable strength of a large sample, we should also be concerned with the substantive meaning of the significance by examining the size of the difference.

Do the characteristics of an issue make a difference in agenda-setting? This study does not offer any conclusive evidence. Agenda-setting effects are observed in an unobtrusive issue (international problems), as well as two obtrusive issues (inflation and unemployment). On the other hand, agenda setting is absent from government spending (which presumably is an unobtrusive issue). However, a strong case of agenda setting for government spending was found elsewhere (Zhu, 1992) based on a subsequent time span (1990–1991). Conversely, an earlier study (Behr & Iyengar, 1985) reported no agenda-setting effects for unemployment during an earlier period (1974–1980). Thus, it appears that media agenda setting can take place for both obtrusive and unobtrusive issues, depending on the specific time period under study. This is, of course, not a satisfactory answer. A particular difficulty in testing the contingent impact of issue characteristics is the limited number of issues that are salient to the public at any given time. A fruitful approach in future research will be meta-analysis that provides a quantitative and systematic means to integrate a diverse body of studies on issue characteristics.

ACKNOWLEDGMENTS

This research was supported in part by a grant to the first author from the University of Connecticut Research Foundation (No. 440632). The authors would like to thank the Roper Center for Public Opinion Research at the University of Connecticut for providing the survey data.

7

Political Advertising's Influence on News, the Public, and Their Behavior

Marilyn Roberts

In Protess and McCombs' (1991) edited collection of seminal agenda setting research, the initial introduction to the public agenda discussion begins with the following statement:

> Each generation writes its own history of the world. This is not because of any pernicious desire to cast aside the worldview of their fathers and mothers or even to rewrite history more to their liking! Although these motives may not be totally absent, each generation creates a history differing in significant details from previous versions principally because they came of age under a new set of circumstances. (p. 1)

As each generation of communication researchers has written about the world as they see it, few concepts have endured the repeated empirical testing that agenda setting has undergone. The process of agenda setting has exhibited a unique durability despite the rapid proliferation of mass communication message delivery channels. This notion of how media are influential has endured due to its most simple premise, the transfer of salience. The agenda-setting process is about the transfer of salience in varying degrees of time among specified segments of information consumers.

The process of agenda setting can no longer and must not in the future be thought of as an exclusive activity of print and broadcast journalists, which solely occurs as an unintended consequence through the normal flow of news.

The failure to extend the process of agenda setting would surely ignore political advertising as a pervasive force in today's electoral process. To fail to do so would ignore the application of the enduring process to the rise of corporate, governmental, and nongovernmental organizations' paid advertisements, whose competing messages attempt to shape public opinion, media coverage, and public policy in a democratic society. How political and information campaigns use the agenda-setting power of advertising to impact the electorate, news coverage, and public policy in an age of integrated, market-driven information and new media technologies is the focus of this chapter.

LAYING THE GROUNDWORK

Specific studies focusing on agenda setting and political advertising appeared in the early 1970s including one by Bowers (1973) that indicated a high correlation between the issues appearing in candidate advertising and voter emphasis. Shaw and McCombs' (1977) Charlotte study speculated on the integrated processing of information by voters. They stated, "In our minds, news flows into commercials into feature stories. Most likely our minds synthesize diverse information into a coherent picture of the campaign so that we can vote as the campaign comes to an end. The montage becomes a picture" (p. 24). On examining the news, public, and candidates' agendas in the Charlotte study, Bowers (1977) concluded that candidates have the ability to influence voters directly through paid advertising and indirectly through their campaigns' attempts to manipulate news coverage. Results of the study also suggested a triad relationship such that a high level of television exposure leads to a high level of advertising exposure, which in turn leads to high affect toward the candidate and high salience of issues stressed in the candidates' advertisements.

Additional works such as Atkin, Bowen, Nayman, and Sheinkopf (1973) demonstrated that political advertising was a contributing factor to candidate choice in the decision-making process. Atkin et al. also suggested that a particular advertisement may have a variety of effects based on voters' needs, motivations, predispositions, and the actual qualitative production qualities contained in the ads themselves. The work of Atkin and Heald (1976) showed that voters' knowledge of the candidates' issue positions was correlated with political advertising exposure. Atkin and Heald suggested that there was a functional relationship between the voters' agenda and the candidates' agenda.

Finally, Kaid's (1976) study intended to demonstrate the direct influence of political advertising on the voting decision. Kaid's findings showed that exposure to advertising accounted for only a small percentage of the unique variance in explaining vote choice. She concluded that knowledge of a person's mere exposure to candidate advertising alone was a poor predictor of candidate choice. To more fully capture advertising's influence on the news and public agendas, as well as on voter behavior, more complex measures of the levels of exposure to both mediated and nonmediated sources of information are necessary.

REPLICATION IN A HOTLY CONTESTED RACE

Perhaps in the 1990s one might say that you know what to think about and then ask what you are going to do about it. This statement more closely reflects the two-step process in a more hostile and competitively market-driven media environment. Roberts (1991) attempted to replicate as closely as possible the Charlotte study of the agenda-setting hypothesis including the examination of contingent conditions and the two-step process of agenda setting that Ghorpade's (1986) research implied. Roberts examined the agenda-setting power of televised political advertising during the 1990 Texas gubernatorial campaign between Democrat Ann Richards and her opponent, Republican Clayton Williams. Three research questions formed the parameters of the study. First, the research sought to determine if televised political advertising had specific agenda-setting functions that were distinctively different from general media (editorial) content. It seemed critical to demonstrate political advertising's ability to uniquely affect the public agenda. Second, if distinctive agenda-setting functions did exist, what characteristics such as specific demographics or sociocultural or media usage patterns differentiate televised political advertising's ability to transfer salience to the public's issue agenda? The question explores which contingent conditions currently enhance or constrain the agenda-setting function of political advertising. The final question asked if specific groups of voters can be identified and impacted by these characteristics in predictable behavioral patterns. In other words, is it possible to correctly identify and predict voters' candidate choices based on the saliencies of issues?

A voter panel contained 238 respondents who participated in all three waves of the study. The respondents were registered voters of Travis County, Texas, which contained the city of Austin. All were randomly selected from 189 precincts and had voted in either the spring 1990 Republican or Democratic primary elections. (In Texas, voters cannot register to vote in the state as Independents.) The panel was comprised of 52.5% males and 47.5% female respondents, with 37% reporting at least a bachelor's degree. Partisanship was balanced, with 49.6% registered Republicans and 50.4% registered Democrats. Approximately 90% reported an annual household income of at least $20,000, and 29% reported income levels of $60,000 or more. The average respondent read the newspaper daily, watched the local news broadcast 5 or 6 days per week, and 70% reported relying on television and newspapers at least somewhat to very often for political information.

The Wave 1 interview period was conducted approximately 1 month before the election. Wave 2 was 3 weeks later and fell during the final week of the campaign and Wave 3 immediately followed the election. Using Stempel and Westley's (1989) constructed week form of content analysis, three local television newscasts and the major local newspaper's stories about the campaign were monitored and coded for the two 3-week periods prior to Wave 1 and Wave 2. Riffe, Aust, and Lacy (1993) supported the superiority of constructed week sampling over simple random and consecutive day samples of newspaper content. Because news coverage about the governor's campaign included daily television coverage, the constructed week format appeared appropriate. The unit of analysis for the media was the individual news story about the gubernatorial campaign.

All political advertisements that aired for the candidates during these same time periods were coded. The unit of analysis was the individual commercial. The coding instrument was developed and adapted from instruments used in previous agenda-setting and political advertising studies (Bryan, 1987; Faber, Tims, & Schmitt, 1990; Ghorpade, 1986, Kern, 1989; Shaw & McCombs, 1977). The code sheets for content analyzing both television newscasts and political advertisements were the same. The newspaper coding instrument was adapted as closely as possible to the electronic one.

The monitoring period prior to Wave 1 became known as the "early campaign" period, and the monitoring period prior to Wave 2 was referred to as the "late campaign" period. Twelve issues were selected for study: crime, the state's economy, drug abuse, state taxes, public education, the state budget, abortion, insurance, women's issues in general (other than abortion), the gubernatorial candidates' personal backgrounds, the rise in negative political advertisements, and the environment.

ADVERTISING'S INFLUENCE ON THE PUBLIC AGENDA

The results of Roberts (1991) show that issue concerns over the rise in negative campaigning and the abortion issue in Wave 1 and the concern for women's issues in general in Wave 2 suggest specific agenda-setting functions for the recall of political advertising that were distinctively and significantly different from general media (editorial) content. Thus, the findings support the first research question that political advertising can play an independent role in the agenda-setting process.

An array of control variables were examined to determine their association with the issues tracked. The study suggests that the characteristics that appear to temper the salience of voters' recall of political advertising are the following: the degree of certainty in voting for a particular candidate; the level of media reliance on either newspaper or television for political information; the number of days per week spent either reading or viewing local news or newscasts; age, gender, education, and household income levels of the respondents; the level of concern over who won the election; and the level of interest in following the campaign. Absent, at least in this study, is the appearance of partisanship as a significantly associated control variable for the recall of political advertising about the governor's race. One explanation for this is that the high level of exposure to commercials for both candidates overwhelms the effect of partisanship in heavily advertised campaigns. An indirect reflection of partisanship can be found in the variables of candidate choice or voter intention, which are highly correlated with partisanship.

THE PUBLIC'S BLURRING OF NEWS AND ADS

The major finding of Weaver, Graber, McCombs, and Eyal (1981) was that the media appear to have the greatest and most immediate effects in the realm of candidate images, even more so than in issues. Graber (1972) argued that "the mass media are significant in furnishing raw material for the formation of political images . . . they [the public] combine current political data supplied by the mass media with existing knowledge and attitudes and then weave these into a plausible and pleasing Gestalt" (pp. 50–51). Early agenda-setting studies acknowledged the strength of another intermediary system of influence—interpersonal communication. The overall agenda-setting function of the various systems of intermediaries solidified the various bits of information to form voters' mental picture of candidates in their heads. Biocca (1991) stated that "the struggle over the candidate's image is the struggle over the semantic processing of political commercials by voters" (p. 27). Jamieson (1992) coined the term *pack rat* to describe the schematic storage of various bits and pieces of information. Shaw and McCombs (1977) addressed the idea of blurring by noting that "news flows into commercials into feature stories" (p. 24).

Jamieson (1992) argued that blurring does not occur by chance. Political consultants intentionally use pseudo-events to manipulate the campaign visuals that appear on the news. Recently, news stories about the accuracy and fairness of negative campaign ads have had more media coverage. There has also been an increase in the use of news coverage quoted and used as source validation for claims made in ads. The 1992 presidential campaign saw the rise of the campaign "infomercials," a form of paid advertising that has the illusion of being legitimate news coverage.

Rosenberg and McCafferty (1987) examined the question of whether political consultants could manipulate voter impressions of political candidates and affect candidate preference. Rosenberg, Kahn, and Tran's (1991) work indicated that candidate image has a potent impact on electoral outcomes. The results of Rosenberg and McCafferty (1987) and Rosenberg et al. (1991) were both limited to only photographic manipulations of appearance conducted in experimental settings using fictitious candidates' images in artificial elections. Left unanswered was whether political consultants could shape candidates' images in actual campaigns and affect voters' real candidate preferences.

The purpose of Roberts, Anderson, and McCombs (1994) was to determine whether voter decisions in the 1990 Texas gubernatorial campaign were shaped by a composite of image and issue information obtained from a variety of intermediary sources. The study tested the "pack rat" hypothesis which asserted that voters would recall a gestalt image of the candidates rather than specific categories of information. The independent variables for the study were candidate image, media use, and interpersonal communication; the dependent variable was candidate choice. To measure the respondents' perceptions of candidates Richards and Williams, 16 image and attribute items were developed to measure candidates' images at Times 1 and 2. These measures were adapted from Faber, Tims, and Schmitt. (1990), a study that had measured candidate perceptions in a U.S. Senate campaign in Minnesota. Respondents were asked the 16 image questions and indicated on 3-point scales whether they believed that a specific attribute better described Williams, Richards, or if there was no difference between the two (see Roberts et al., 1994, for a detailed description of these image items). The 16 items were summed and averaged to create Time 1 and Time 2 candidate-image indices, which exhibited strong coefficient alpha reliabilities (.92 and .90, respectively).

Media usage was measured at Times 1 and 2 by asking respondents to rate on a 4-point scale how often they remembered hearing or seeing television news stories, reading newspaper stories, and hearing or seeing paid political advertising for the gubernatorial candidates. Interpersonal communication was only measured at Time 2 when state politics was salient enough to generate variance in the interpersonal measures. Respondents were asked how often they discussed politics, with whom they most often discussed politics, and what role they played when they discussed politics.

A principal components analysis of the 16 image items yielded two distinct factors; one defined the entire set of items measured in Time 1 and the second factor defined the entire set of items from Time 2. A hierarchical logistic regression identified the composite candidate image from Time 2 as the only significant predictor of the respondents' actual reported vote. Prediction of the vote from this variable alone correctly forecasted more than 90% of the actual votes. The findings of Roberts et al. (1994) suggest the overall interplay between the various systems of intermediary influence (news, ads, and interpersonal communication) solidify information to form a unified schematic mental image of the candidates. These findings empiricize the notion Shaw and McCombs (1977) only speculated that "Most likely our minds synthesize diverse information into a coherent picture of the campaign so that we can vote as the campaign comes to an end" (p. 24). The Time 2 effect supports the conceptual model that Roberts et al. set forth: Various mass and interpersonal communication sources create candidate images and these, in turn, influence voters on election day—demonstrating evidence of a two-step agenda setting process from salience to behavior outcome. The study supports the results of Weaver et al. (1981) in that it is in the realm of candidate images, even more than the realm of issues, that the media appear to have the greatest and most immediate effects on election outcomes.

INFLUENCE OF POLITICAL ADVERTISING ON NEWS

Currently an evolving phase of agenda-setting research looks inward and focuses on who sets the media's agenda. (Gandy, 1982; Turk, 1985, 1986). The number of potential sources of influence in shaping the media's agenda is large. Those extending influence can range from external sources in government and the private sector to the idiosyncrasies of individual journalists, as noted by McCombs, Einsiedel, and Weaver (1991). Intermedia agenda setting has been defined in terms of the influence that the news agendas of different news organizations have on each other.

Earlier studies of intermedia influence focused on the standardization of news stories among newspapers due to their use of wire services (Hirsch, 1977; McCombs & Shaw, 1976; White, 1949). More recently, Reese and Danielian's (1989) work on coverage of the drug issue suggests that elite newspapers influence each other, and sometimes they influence the national network television news agendas as well. Danielian and Reese (1989) wrote, "These questions [about influence] are becoming more important given the central role of media in political life. Consequently, we need to be fully aware of all the factors that set the agenda of the media, causing them to converge on certain issues, sources, and themes" (p. 65).

Gans (1979) commented that "although it takes two to tango, either sources or journalist can lead, but more often than not, sources do the leading" (p. 116). The warlike strategies and tactics used by candidates and their political consultants aim to dominate both the advertising agenda and the news agenda. The agenda represented by the candidates' political advertisements is the most visible indicator available of the agenda that the candidates wish to advance. The advertising agenda established by candidates through their television advertising must be added to the model of the agenda-setting process.

Roberts and McCombs (1994) used the 1990 Texas panel study's content analyses of the candidates' issue agenda, the television issue agenda, and the newspaper issue agenda to more fully examine who sets the media's agenda. To ensure the accuracy of the construction of the candidates' issue agenda, it was weighted by the actual frequency of airing per issue. Going beyond the content analysis of 21 different ads, the weighting reflected the level of actual airing during the two monitoring periods. No newspaper political advertisements or major radio advertisements were placed in the market during the two monitoring time periods. All three agendas indicated considerable diversity in the emphasis on the 12 tracked issues in total time covered.

The rank-ordered candidates' agenda for Time 1 indicates that the most frequent issues to appear were drug abuse, insurance, concern for the candidates' personal backgrounds, and public education. The issues of crime, taxes, and negative advertising appeared somewhat less often; the issues of the economy, abortion, women's issues in general, the environment, and the budget appeared least frequently. Three issues dramatically shifted position during Time 2. The topic most emphasized at Time 2 was negative advertising, a rise from sixth position at Time 1. Also rising was the issue of the economy, moving from tenth at Time 1 to tie for third position at Time 2. In contrast, the top issue at Time 1, drugs, fell to seventh position in the later period.

The television news agenda was constructed from a sample of 68 newscasts drawn from Austin stations KTBC, KVUE, and KXAN during the two constructed time periods. The Time 1 television news agenda indicates that the issue of negative political advertising was covered most often in news stories about the gubernatorial campaign. The issues of abortion, crime, insurance, and concern for women's issues in general rounded out the top five issues. Other issues covered less often were public education, the environment, drug abuse, and concern for the gubernatorial candidates' personal backgrounds. The issues of the state's economy, taxes, and the state budget appeared least in television news stories during Time 1.

The Time 2 monitoring period indicated a different rank order of issues than had been seen during Time 1. Public education, taxes, and concern about the gubernatorial candidates' personal backgrounds were the most frequently covered issues across all local newscasts in Time 2. These issues all rose from much lower rank orders at Time 1. Insurance remained as the fourth-ranked issue in both time periods. The tax issue rose most dramatically from the bottom of the rank at Time 1 to second position in total time of coverage in Time 2. Coverage of women's issues in general decreased from the early period to the late period. The issues of drug abuse, the economy, the environment, and the state budget continued to have little or no time devoted to them in television in Time 2.

The newspaper agenda of issues covered by the *Austin American-Statesman* was constructed by using the ISYS content analysis software plus a coder manually examining the program's results for accuracy and context. The highest ranked issues during Time 1 were public education and insurance. State taxes, the candidates' personal backgrounds, and the state budget rounded out the top five issues covered by the newspaper in Time 1. The issues of negative political advertising, abortion, women's issues in general (other than abortion), and the state's economy received secondary levels of coverage in Time 1. Three issues—crime, drug abuse, and the state's environment—received the least newspaper coverage at Time 1.

Coverage of drug abuse dramatically rose to rank first at Time 2. Stories about the candidates' personal backgrounds rose from the fourth position at Time 1 to the second position at Time 2. The state budget, insurance, and public education rounded out the top five issues. Education had previously ranked first and slipped to fifth. Abortion remained fairly stable, rising slightly from the seventh to the sixth position. Women's issues in general, crime, and negative advertising received low levels of coverage at Time 2 and the issues of taxes, the state's economy, and the environment received little or no newspaper coverage.

To sort out the flow of intermedia influence in the three issue agendas of newspaper stories, television news, and the candidates' advertising, three cross-lagged correlation analyses were performed. In doing so, two opposing hypotheses about the time order of influence were juxtaposed. The principal findings of the cross-lagged correlation analyses were the impact of televised political advertising on both the newspaper and the television news agendas.

The findings show a strong correlation (+.734) between the newspaper agenda at Time 1 and the television agenda at Time 2. A second influence on the television news agenda was identified: televised political advertising (+.524). Results also show a strong correlation of the political advertising agenda at Time 1 with the newspaper agenda at Time 2 (+.638). Additional correlation analyses resulted in all cross-lagged correlations—zero-order, first-order partials, and second-order partials—exceeding the Rozelle–Campbell baseline levels for significance. Thus, strengthening the claim that political consultants make political campaigns, the agenda set and paid for by the candidates can set the news agenda.

QUESTIONS OF A TWO-STEP PROCESS

Two studies from the 1980s focused on the notion that the agenda-setting function of political advertising goes beyond simple awareness. Sutherland and Galloway (1981) raised the question of whether advertising's role is persuader or agenda setter. They suggested that "through media emphasis, individuals learn how much importance particular issues, persons, or attributes are 'supposed' to have, and they internalize a similar set of weights" (p. 26). Applying agenda setting's implication to advertising strategy, the authors speculated that "the major goal of advertising may be to focus consumers' attention on what values, products, brands, or attributes to think about rather than to try to persuade consumers what to think of these" (p. 26).

Grounded in marketing research literature, the study of Sutherland and Galloway (1981) expanded the notion of agenda setting, stating that "salience in the public mind is correlated with behavioral outcomes such as purchase and market share" (p. 27), thus implying a two-step agenda-setting process from concern (transfer of salience) to candidate choice (behavioral outcome). The authors also equated advertising frequency with media coverage emphasis. They concluded that "ad frequency or media weight is analogous to the media emphasis that is given to a news item over a period of time" (p. 27).

Ghorpade (1986) empiricized the two-step model by examining the 1984 senatorial race in North Carolina between Republican incumbent Jesse Helms and Democratic challenger Jim Hunt. Television news and television commercials were recorded off the air from two television stations. Both newscasts and commercials were coded for candidate images, positive and negative. Telephone survey data were collected from 796 respondents using a random survey of registered voters to construct the voter agenda. Ghorpade's findings suggest that the reasons that respondents gave for selecting a specific candidate were positively associated with both the television news and the candidate advertising agendas. His work also suggests that voters learned from both sources. An alternative explanation could be that voters could not differentiate between television news and candidates' advertising agendas. Ghorpade's work provides support for agenda-setting effects of advertising in a more current political environment. Future research in this area should be encouraged.

TESTING THE PREDICTABILITY
OF ISSUE SALIENCE

The final research question that Roberts (1991) examined was whether it was possible to correctly identify and predict voters' candidate choices based on the saliency of issues. Wave 3 contained the panel sample's reported actual gubernatorial vote. In order to test the predictability of voter behavior by the levels of issue concern, a computer program was written that randomly selected 80 respondents from the 137 who had reported voting for Richards. Because 80 respondents had reported voting for Williams in Wave 3, each group now had an equal sample size. Next, 50 respondents from each group were randomly selected by the computer program in order to form the analysis sample. The remaining two groups of 30 respondents formed the holdout sample (n = 60). If a case had at least one missing discriminating variable (level of issue concern) it was eliminated from the analysis.

The model correctly classified 70% of the respondents' actual reported votes for governor by the level of issue concern over time, regardless of controlling for other selected variables. The discriminant analysis results show that the model correctly grouped 84% of the male respondents, predicting 26 of 35 (74.3%) of the males who voted for Richards and 43 of 47 (91.5%) of those who voted for Williams (Wilks' lambda=.45, $p < .01$). The model correctly classified 91% of the female respondents with 39 of 41 (95.1%) who voted for Richards and 20 of 24 (83.3%) who voted for Williams (Wilks' lambda=.39, $p < .01$). When using other control variables such as the respondents' partisanship, the degree of media reliance on either television or newspaper for political information, concern over who won the campaign, and the closeness of attention paid to the campaign, the correct classification exceeded 80% and produced significant Wilks' lambda statistics (see Roberts, 1992, for detailed results).

These results suggest that the process of agenda setting does occur in a two-step process, from one of merely awareness followed by a behavioral outcome. These findings suggest that the mass media may not only tell the public what to think about specific issues, but may actually influence the public's voting decisions based on those issue saliencies.

NEW FRONTIERS FOR AGENDA-SETTING RESEARCH

As each generation creates a history, those coming after must also create a future. The proliferation of competitors who desire salient voices of influence in a democratic society requires that future research no longer be limited to traditional news and thought of solely in terms of unintended consequences of media influence. Because we have come of age under a different set of circumstances, the arrival of political consultants, corporate issue managers, powerful professional associations, market-driven celebrity pundits and journalists, and globalized meganews and entertainment organizations are dramatically impacting the democratic process.

The challenge before us in this new era is to systematically push open new frontiers of communication research. We must sort out the direct and indirect influences of these fiercely competitive entities at the individual level, the aggregate or public level, the intermedia and intramedia levels, and the various levels of public policy formation to better assess, whether individually or collectively, their mediated efforts are beneficial, harmful, or harmless to democratic societies. Some argue that these competing entities that rival for influence are destabilizing the very institutions required to manage the governance of a strong democratic society. Others assert that these nontraditional voices of influence beyond the media are adding to the marketplace of ideas and increasing public dialogue and participation. The world today is but a pale remnant of the world of 1972 when the first empirical test of the agenda-setting hypothesis was published. The growing complexity and proliferation of not only the number of information sources, but the sheer amount of news and information available on an individual, national, and global basis in increasingly compressed time frames will forge new streams of agenda-setting research. These new streams will differ in significant details from previous versions with one exception. Each will have at its core the examination of the transfer of salience in varying degrees of time and specified amounts and forms of information consumption. It is highly doubtful given the growing complexities of contemporary political communication environments that any single medium or entity can solely serve as the agenda setter. Instead, the individual influence of any particular entity must participate as an agenda builder. The convergence of issue and image saliencies from multiple influencers share in the agenda setting process. What the works in this chapter have attempted to demonstrate is that the process of agenda setting does not pertain exclusively to the news media. The chapter has also attempted to more fully examine the currently evolving phase of research that asks who sets the media's agenda. Evidence suggests that the process of agenda setting can be expanded to a two-step process from salience to behavior outcome. The new frontiers of agenda-setting research are imbued with opportunities to apply the agenda-setting process' central concept, the transfer of salience, to all forms of corporate, governmental, and nongovernmental organizations' paid advertising efforts that attempt to shape public opinion, media coverage, and public policies in democratic societies.

8

Economic Headline News on the Agenda: *New Approaches to Understanding Causes and Effects*

Deborah J. Blood
Peter C. B. Phillips

More than two decades of agenda-setting research have established our belief in the capacity of mass media news coverage to set the public agenda. Arguably, there is no other news topic where this effect has such potentially far-reaching consequences as economic news. Many have charged the media with portraying economic issues unfairly and excessively negatively in the newsroom pursuit of the vivid and the newsworthy, and foretold economic and political fallout as a result. From undermining consumer sentiment and delaying an anticipated economic upturn to losing a president his reelection, the potential consequences of agenda setting are now seen by many to extend well beyond issue salience, the original dependent variable of early agenda-setting research.

Criticism of economic news writers and fear of the impact that their stories and reports may have on the real world are based on three assumptions: (a) the media's portrayal of the economy is negatively biased, (b) economic news coverage is capable of shaping the public's perception of the nation's economic well-being, and (c) adverse economic news may itself ultimately influence the economic and political landscape.

Yet, when these assumptions are put to empirical test, findings are mixed concerning the direction and the degree of influence of economic news. In studies of this kind there are four key variables involved and interest centers on the causes and effects among them: economic news coverage, the public's perception of the economic health of the economy (commonly measured as consumer sentiment or confidence), the actual state of the economy, and presidential popularity. In short, these variables encompass four very large and different empirical arenas—the economy, politics, people's perceptions, and the media. Given their disparity and the multitude of ways in which these variables may be measured, it is hardly surprising that investigations regarding the relationships between them have yielded mixed results. Many researchers have found media effects in general, and economic news effects in particular, on the other three variables, but the influence has also been found to work in the reverse direction—that is, some investigators have found the content of economic news stories to be determined by real-world economic conditions, prevailing consumer sentiment, and presidential approval.

Further, because of the difficulties of dealing simultaneously with four very different variables, most research efforts have been directed at determining the nature of bivariate relationships between some of these variables. Mixed findings may be due, in part, to their failure to take the effects of the other variables into account. Some studies have explored three variables in their analysis, for example, the relationship between economic news and consumer sentiment controlling for real-world conditions (e.g., Behr & Iyengar, 1985; MacKuen, 1981; Stevenson, Gonzenbach, & Prabu, 1991). And MacKuen, Erikson, and Stimson (1992) examined the relationships among all four variables (consumer sentiment, economic conditions, presidential popularity, and economic news) employing some of the time series techniques described in this chapter, but they used consumer perceptions of economic news rather than actual economic news reported in the press as their media variable.

Empirical investigations of these variables involve time series data and all of the series have distinct characteristics. For instance, macroeconomic time series tend to move in a secular way over time representing the growth and cyclical behavior of the actual economy. Presidential approval ratings have a tendency to wander around as if they had no fixed mean, their level depending on the prevailing climate of public opinion (*inter alia*). In a similar way, consumer sentiment series wander over large periods of time in a manner that shows no tendency to return to one constant level. Such time series are said to be nonstationary.

Many agenda-setting studies involving some of these variables have employed statistical analyses that do not take into account this dominant nonstationary characteristic of the data. Conventional statistical procedures call for detrending (and, hence, prefiltering) of the data before analysis can be performed, at the cost of losing valuable information and at the risk of wrongly determining the existence or absence of agenda-setting effects between series comprised of filtered or manipulated data.

A specific aim in this chapter is to draw attention to the usefulness of some recently developed time series methods for analyzing nonstationary data and their application to the empirical problem of detecting agenda-setting effects.

Given the dynamic nature of the agenda-setting process and the characteristics of the series representing the variables of interest, these techniques offer the ability to analyze the data in its original form. We illustrate this new approach by examining the evidence of long-term cause-and-effect relationships between economic headlines, consumer sentiment, real-world economic conditions, and presidential popularity in order to establish whether the assumptions about the effects of economic news that were discussed earlier have any empirical basis.

ECONOMIC HEADLINE NEWS:
CAUSES AND EFFECTS

We begin with a very brief review of theories, empirical findings, and speculations that shed light on the potential interrelationships among these variables. First, there has been much research interest in the cause-and-effect relationship between economic news coverage and the economy. Addressing the question of who sets the media agenda, some investigators have tried to determine if there is any correspondence between actual economic conditions and the news items representing them to media audiences. The tendency for the media agenda to be influenced by, or to mirror reality, is an "event-centered theory" of media content (Gans, 1979). In looking for evidence of event-driven content in economic news coverage, some researchers have reported a failure of economic reporting to reflect actual economic conditions. For instance, the Institute for Applied Economics (1984) reported that, from July 1983 to December 1983, 95% of the economic statistics were positive, whereas 85% of the in-depth stories on network television were primarily negative. The Media Institute found that during the nonrecessionary period between 1982 and 1987, 4,500 out of 5,300 television stories on the economy had a negative tone (see Glassman, 1993). The absence of correspondence between economic reporting and real-world conditions has led some to charge that economic news content bears little association with the facts. Such evidence is often proffered to support the charge of media bias. Other researchers have focused their attention on the alternative direction of influence between these two variables; that is, the adverse effect of unfavorable news on subsequent economic performance. During the 1987 financial market fall, for instance, the use of alarming language and comparisons with the stock market crash of 1929 were seen as fanning the growing alarm and further weakening the markets (see Graber, 1993). More generally, the phrase *media malady* was coined to describe the role that negative news may play in delaying an otherwise anticipated economic upturn (Kurtz, 1990; see Stevenson et al., 1991). This alternative perspective invests considerable power in the media to impact the very economic environment it purports merely to describe.

The second assumption of economic news critics concerns the power of economic news to influence consumer sentiment, or more generally, the ability of the media to sway public opinion, a process immediately recognized by readers as the original subject of agenda-setting research (McCombs & Shaw, 1972). Agenda-setting investigations were first conducted in the context of national and local political elections and focused on the ability of the news media to lead the public in assigning relative importance to various public issues. It was not long before this notion was extended to other contexts. One context that has gained in importance is the impact of economic news on consumer confidence. Given the fact that individual consumer spending accounts for two thirds of the U.S. national expenditure, it is not surprising that the relationship between consumer confidence or sentiment and economic news reporting has been of interest. In particular, scholars have been concerned with establishing the direction of influence between them.

As would be predicted by agenda-setting theory, some studies have found economic news to be the determining influence on subsequent public opinion (Behr & Iyengar, 1985; Neuman, 1990). Yet others have reported the effect to be, at least initially, in the other direction. For example, Stevenson et al. (1991) found in their study that it was the media agenda that was influenced by public opinion, but the media "in turn picked up public concern and influenced public perception at a later date" (p. 13). This supports the counternotion (to agenda setting) that news reporting is itself consumer driven, whereby media personnel are merely providing news perceived as of interest to their audiences. Shoemaker and Reese (1991) described this influence as a market approach: Media content is driven by the editor's desire to give news consumers what they want in order to ensure large audiences for the products of their sponsors.

There have been attempts to resolve this rather confused picture and determine once and for all the direction of influence between economic reporting and consumer confidence. Testing causal effects in both directions for the period 1990 to 1993, Fan (1993) found that media effects dominated consumer sentiment effects. However, there was no control for real-world economic conditions in Fan's bivariate analysis. Real-world indicators need to be considered in order to test the sensitivity of economic news coverage to economic conditions and to distinguish between the effects of news coverage and real-world conditions on public opinion (Neuman, 1990).

Studies such as those by Behr and Iyengar (1985) and Stevenson et al. (1991) did treat economic indicators as a control variable, but with contradictory results. In the former study, the authors found media agenda setting effects on public concern for the topics of energy and inflation, but they found no agenda-setting effects for unemployment. For Stevenson et al., the issue was recession, and their results showed a predominant effect of public opinion on the media agenda, as already discussed.

When economic indicators are included in the analysis, but treated only as a control variable, one loses the opportunity to assess any role that economic news may play in influencing the state of the economy. Blood (1996), testing for all possible directions in a 13-year data set that included a determining role for the economy itself, found that headlines concerning the general state of the economy had strong agenda-setting effects—but for the specific topics of recession and unemployment, which were more sporadically occurring events, headline numbers were driven by consumer sentiment over the long term. A recursive analysis in that study revealed that there were agenda-setting effects by recession headlines on consumer sentiment only during the periods when recession was occurring. This led the author to speculate that the detection of economic news agenda-setting effects is a function of the specific time periods examined, the nature and severity of prevailing economic events, and whether consumers feel themselves to be directly affected by such events or not.

Zucker (1978) was the first to argue that the obtrusiveness of an issue may be an important determining factor in whether or not agenda setting takes place. Although economic matters may be considered to be obtrusive compared to, say, many foreign policy issues, some economic events are likely to be more obtrusive than others. Economic issues that audiences experience directly and dramatically, such as unemployment or recession, may leave less room for media effects—except when editors respond with a plethora of bad news headlines, in which case consumer sentiment effects on media content are outpaced and media agenda-setting effects predominate. On the other hand, the general state of the nation's economic health may be a less obtrusive issue, leaving editors with the opportunity (and in some cases, perhaps, mission) to raise concern when the public does not anticipate or feel directly the effects of economic downturn.

The ability of economic news coverage to affect presidential popularity invests agenda setting with political consequences. For example, former President George Bush's failure to secure a second term of office was attributed in part to adverse economic news (see Graber, 1993). In their seminal work on this general topic, Iyengar and Kinder (1984) discovered that in paying attention to some problems and ignoring others, network television news programs alter the criteria by which viewers evaluate presidential performance, which they called the *priming effect.* Elsewhere, it has been noted that changes in presidential approval ratings are often highly correlated with the favorability of news stories (Graber, 1993).

As for the inverse direction, there is evidence that presidential popularity can have an effect on the economic news agenda. Stevenson et al. (1991) noted that the negative coverage of the economy revealed in their study appeared to grow as a result of Bush's approval ratings over his handling of the Gulf. They suggested the press may have turned adversarial eyes toward the economy at a time when Bush was strongly supported on foreign policy. Blood and Phillips (1995) found evidence that presidential popularity during the Gulf War period did indeed appear to spawn increasing numbers of negative economic headlines out of proportion with the actual economic conditions at that time, seemingly supporting the notion of an "adversarial press" suggested by the Stevenson et al. study.

When considering potential causes and effects between variables, it has been noted that the past values of a variable are often its own best predictor. For instance, in the early Charlotte study of media agenda setting, Shaw and McCombs (1977) performed a cross-lagged correlation on media content and public opinion at Times 1 and 2. Although they found evidence of newspaper influence on subsequent opinion, the largest correlation of all was the autocorrelation between the public agenda at Times 1 and 2, suggesting that the public was more affected by the stability of public opinion than by the media. Moreover, this correlation was close to unity. From a time series perspective, this suggests the presence of a unit root in the statistical mechanism behind a series. Unit root effects allow for the possibility that a series' own past history, dominated by the level of the immediately preceding value, will produce the best predictor of its future. In this respect, a unit root is more specific than an autocorrelation effect wherein a series is indeed influenced by its past history but not necessarily the level of its immediately preceding value.

A NEW STATISTICAL APPROACH

As indicated earlier, many agenda-setting studies have employed statistical analyses that do not take into account the dominant time series properties of the data, notably their inherent nonstationarity or tendency to drift over time. Techniques that have been developed in the field of econometrics over the last decade (see Hamilton, 1994, for an overview and references to the literature) allow for the analysis of nonstationary data in their original form to test for potential links or comovement between the series, as well as causal effects between them.

Recently, Blood and Phillips (1995) used some of these nonstationary time series techniques to examine the interrelationships of all four variables, controlling for the effect of each in a recession headline study that examined a 5-year time period straddling the Persian Gulf War. In this chapter, we use the Blood–Phillips methodology and extend the investigation of the interrelationships among these four variables to a much longer time frame, from June 1980 to December 1993, a period of history that saw the full and partial tenures of four presidencies (i.e., Carter, Reagan, Bush, and Clinton), times of economic expansion, and the occurrence of two economic recessions. The time series tools described in this chapter take into account the inherent time series properties of the data that have been mentioned already, such as their tendency to drift stochastically over time (which is manifest in the presence of unit roots), cointegrating links among them (Engle & Granger, 1987), differing degrees and directions of causal influence (as evidenced by Granger causal effects), and switching causal patterns that may be present over the whole time frame but may not apply to certain subperiods (as revealed by a recursive analysis).

The software package COINT 2.0 (see Ouliaris & Phillips, 1994) of time series procedures for unit root analysis and cointegrating regressions was used for the data analysis. Interested readers may refer to Blood (1996) for a detailed analysis of the results of this investigation, which are presented only in general terms here. The technical terms unit root, cointegration, Granger causality, and recursive analysis will be clarified for readers in our discussion of the statistical methodology used here and by references to the relevant statistical literature.

The Data

Time series data representing each of the variables were compiled from a variety of sources. Each series comprised 163 observations, covering the time period from June 1980 to December 1993 and the time unit of analysis was 1 month.

As a measure of present and prospective real-world economic conditions, the Leading Economic Indicator Index (issued by the U. S. Department of Commerce) was used. This is a composite measure comprising the following 11 leading indicators: average weekly hours for manufacturing, average weekly initial claims for unemployment, new orders of consumer goods and materials, vendor performance, contracts and orders for plant and equipment, building permits, changes in unfilled orders for durable goods, changes in sensitive materials prices, stock prices, money supply, and the index of consumer sentiment.

The monthly Index of Consumer Sentiment (ICS), compiled by the Survey Research Center at the University of Michigan, was selected for the consumer sentiment series used here. Our presidential popularity series was derived from the monthly aggregate percentage of approval ratings of the incumbent president's performance (e.g. "Do you approve or disapprove of the way Ronald Reagan is handling his job as President?") obtained from national opinion polls and archived at the Roper Center for Public Opinion Research at the University of Connecticut. Four different presidencies occurred within this time frame: the complete tenures of Ronald Reagan and George Bush, and the partial tenures of Jimmy Carter and Bill Clinton.

Representing economic news were headlines concerning the U.S. economy that were retrieved from the *New York Times* Library of the NEXIS database. The *New York Times* was chosen because of its position as an elite newspaper and model for other newspapers (Crouse, 1973; Kinder & Sears, 1985; Neuman, 1990; Stevenson et al., 1991; Winter & Eyal, 1981), as well as its influence on television network news coverage (Brown, 1971). Headlines rather than stories were selected to represent economic news because many researchers believe that headlines are powerful texts capable of wielding considerable influence on readers (Allport & Lepkin, 1943; Bleske, 1995a, 1995b; Blood, 1996; Blood & Phillips, 1995; Emig, 1928; Hilliard, 1991; Pasternack, 1987; Tannenbaum, 1953; Winship & Allport, 1943). When one also takes into account the possibility that headlines may not be representative of the stories they precede, but may present a biased perspective of the story (Pasternack, 1987), the case for using headlines as a measure of economic news in agenda-setting studies rather than the content of the stories themselves becomes stronger still.

The series comprised only headlines describing the U.S. economy. This general topic was chosen in order to observe an ongoing generic pattern of economic news data over the time frame studied compared to more sporadically occurring economic news issues such as energy, inflation, recession, or unemployment. Headlines were coded according to whether the economy was portrayed in positive terms, negative terms, or mixed or neutral terms. Newspaper headlines are often difficult to comprehend because they can be "syntactically impoverished" and ambiguous as a result: for example, "Pentagon Plans Swell Deficit," and "Union Demands Increased Unemployment" (Perfetti, Beverly, Bell, Rodgers, & Faux, 1987). In such cases, ambiguous headlines were rated as neutral. The economic headline series was then transformed in order to orient it toward negativity; that is, unfavorable economic news. Only positive and negative headlines were included in the series (neutral and mixed headlines were excluded) and extra weight was given to front-page headlines.

Compilation of the series revealed the presence of emotive headlines that might well be perceived as capable of undermining consumer sentiment: for example, "The Week in Business, the Economy: God Help the American People" (6/1/80); "Economic Scene: Dancing On the Titanic" (6/13/80); "Around the Nation: Watch Out, It's The Economic Flu" (3/29/81); "Economic Scene: Is Depression Lurking?" (3/3/82); "Economic Scene: Is a Recession Coming in '85?" (11/2/84); "People Found Anxious on Economy and Goals" (6/8/88); "Currency Markets: Dollar Has Sharp Decline on Fears About Economy" (11/6/90): "School Districts Reeling in Weakened Economy" (6/5/91); "Weather and the Economy Fill Homeless Shelters" (1/5/92); and "Economic Scare Stories" (10/16/92). The series comprised 2,280 headlines in all, with 308 coded as positive, 596 as negative, 127 as mixed, and 1,249 as neutral.

There were considerably more negative than positive headlines, but this study did not reveal the very high levels of negativism reported elsewhere, such as the Media Institute's finding of 85% negativism in television news stories (see Glassman, 1993). On the other hand, these results may lend some support to Glassman's contention that newspapers' coverage of the economy typically is more balanced and less dramatic than television network news treatment.

STATISTICAL ANALYSIS AND RESULTS

Time series analyses were performed on the data series to test the nature and the direction of influence among the variables of interest. Each series was analyzed to isolate its principal characteristics (particularly the presence or absence of an autoregressive unit root), and tests for comovement (formally, cointegration; see Engle & Granger, 1987) between the series were conducted.

Vector autoregression was used to model the joint determination of the series, and tests for Granger causality were conducted to determine the nature and direction of causal influence among the series. Finally, recursive analysis was employed to assess whether the causal patterns observed over the whole data set were sustained over subperiods. The procedures followed in this analysis are described briefly along with the results obtained at each stage (see Blood, 1996, for a full description of procedures and findings).

First, each series was analyzed to identify its main features, particularly to determine whether the series were stationary or nonstationary. The leading example of a stochastically nonstationary series is a random walk. Unit root models allow for more general dependence over time than random walks but they have the same wandering characteristics. Many time series of economic data have been found to have unit root nonstationarity—some display secular growth characteristics (like Gross National Product), whereas others randomly wander like exchange rates. We sought to determine whether these features were evident in our four variables of interest: economic headline news, consumer sentiment, leading economic indicators, and presidential popularity. The tests used here come from the econometric literature and are the same as those used in Blood and Phillips (1995) for the shorter period 1989 to 1993.

The empirical results of the unit root tests revealed that the leading economic indicator, consumer sentiment, and presidential approval series are all nonstationary. These series are depicted with the economic headline series in Fig. 8.1. The nonstationarity of the consumer sentiment and presidential popularity series is clearly evident in this figure. The nonstationarity of the leading indicator series is less visually obvious due to the scale of this figure, but was

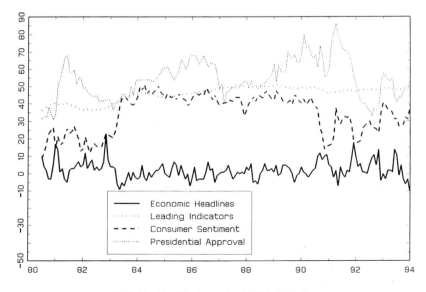

FIG. 8.1. Monthly time series 1980:6–1993:12.

strongly supported by the statistical test. Each of these three series shows a tendency to drift over time, in addition to having periods of decline during the 1982 and 1991 recessions.

There is no empirical evidence from the tests in support of a unit root for the economic headline series. The graph of this series (shown in Fig. 8.1) appears to be stationary throughout the entire time period, fluctuating around the same mean level, with some limited peaks of negative reporting around the recessions and periodic episodes of favorable economic headlines.

Of central concern are the potential linkages among the time series. For example, we are interested in whether movement in consumer sentiment is associated with changes in economic headlines over time. One way of exploring such linkages (without explicitly addressing causal effects) is to consider whether the series themselves move together in a meaningful way over time. When the time series are individually nonstationary, as three of our series are, such comovement is known in the econometric literature as *cointegration*. The concept of cointegration was introduced by Engle and Granger (1987) and statistical tests for the presence of cointegration have been developed by Phillips and Ouliaris (1990), Johansen (1988) and others. Empirical tests for comovement or cointegration in the series were conducted using the residual-based test procedure of Phillips and Ouliaris (1990).

To estimate the linkages among the series and allow for nonstationarities, a modified least-squares regression technique called fully modified (FM) regression (see Phillips & Hansen, 1990) was used. The results of this regression are analyzed in the same way as a conventional least-squares regression.

- Tests indicated a strong degree of comovement between economic headlines and leading indicators. The regression beta coefficients revealed a significant, negative relationship between the two series.
- Tests also indicated a strong degree of comovement between the headline series and consumer sentiment. Regression analysis revealed a significant, negative relationship between the series.
- Tests showed evidence for cointegration between presidential popularity and the headline series. Test results from the bivariate regression did not confirm a significant relationship at this stage.

Next, we used vector autoregressions (VARs) to explore linkages between the series over time and potential causal effects. VARs are helpful in our context because they allow for quite general temporal dependence as well as potential unit roots and comovement over time. The analysis of causal effects was conducted with four variable VARs to explore the direction of causality between leading indicators and headlines for each headline series.

VAR causality tests assess whether a series can be predicted better by using the history of other series as well as its own than it can be by using only its own past history. If such an improvement in prediction capability is found, one deduces that there is explanatory power in the history of other series that is useful in predicting the future course of the given series. Such predictive capability is described as a causal effect, or Granger causality following the original work by Granger (1969). A recent exposition of the approach in the context of VARs was given by Lutkepohl (1993).

Wald tests were constructed to test the hypothesis of noncausality in the VARs, allowing for lag lengths in the autoregression from 1 to 6 lags (each lag represents 1 month).

- Strong evidence was manifested for media agenda-setting effects on consumer sentiment over the period of the study and at all lags. The sign of the influence was also in the expected direction and uniformly so, that is, the rising numbers of "ailing economy" headlines appeared to dampen subsequent consumer sentiment, and positive economic headlines boosted consumer sentiment.

- Further evidence of a strong media influence was manifested in the relationship between leading indicators and economic headlines, this time in the form of the so-called "media malady effect." Headlines had considerable long-term effects on the economy: With up to 5 lags (and marginally so with 6 lags) rising numbers of unfavorable economic headlines had an adverse effect on subsequent leading indicators and did so uniformly and persistently. As for the reverse effect, only with 3 lags (a 3-month period) was there any evidence that the leading indicators themselves had any influence on subsequent economic headlines. These results suggest that the amount and tone of economic news exerted a powerful influence on the economic environment and further, that the economic news agenda was generally not being set by prevailing economic conditions.

- An analysis of the causal relationship between presidential popularity and economic headlines revealed that, after the first lag (where the effect was insignificant), presidential popularity had a direct influence on subsequent numbers of "bad news" headlines; that is, an increasingly popular president appeared to inhibit unfavorable economic news over and above the prevailing economic conditions at the time. This finding supports Entman's (1989) argument that media content can display an evaluative bias in that journalists, sensitive to the prevailing popularity of the president in residence, are likely to be critical of presidents when they are unpopular but uncritical when their level of public support is high. Note that our investigation here focuses on headlines describing the general economy only. When examining recession headlines over the same time frame, Blood (1996) found brief displays of adversarial press behavior (Blood & Phillips, 1995; Stevenson et al., 1991) whereby journalists produced increasingly scathing reports (over and above prevailing economic conditions) about the recession at a time when Bush's popularity was highest during the Gulf War. This appears to have been an aberration to the general pattern seen over the long time frame examined here and we comment on this later.

• As for any influence of economic headlines on presidential popularity, there was no evidence of a priming effect here. The Blood (1996) study on a variety of different economic-related headlines revealed that headlines concerning unemployment did exhibit a priming effect on presidential approval. Clearly, not all issues on the economic agenda and their effects on the economic and political scene are the same: Presidential popularity may be particularly vulnerable to increasing waves of headlines announcing more layoffs.

As discussed earlier, the 13 years of data (1980–1993) covered in this study includes two periods of economic recession, a sustained economic expansion, and the full and partial tenures of four presidencies. With these subperiods that have very different economic and political characteristics, it is of interest to assess whether the causal patterns observed over the whole data set are sustained over the various subperiods. Recursive analysis allows the data to be informative about the presence of any regimes over subperiods of the sample by computing the test statistic of interest in a recursive way as one moves progressively through the time series. Recursive calculations allow the data to highlight points (or periods) in time where the test statistics undergo major changes. For example, the tests may indicate "acceptance" of the null hypothesis of no causality over the first part of the sample $t = m, \ldots ,M$, but rejection of the null over the full latter period $t = M + 1, \ldots N$ or a subperiod such as $t = M + 1, \ldots , P$ where $P < N$. In such cases, the data point to M and P as potential break points in the sample; that is, points where there is a potential shift in regime.

The major interest here centers on the causal patterns and the extent to which these are sustained over subperiods of the full sample. Thus, the Wald statistics that test for causal effects were calculated recursively in the manner previously described for $m \leq n \leq N$. Here $N = 163$ and the starting value was set at $m = 26$, so that there were enough data (n) to initiate the recursion for a four-variable VAR with 4 lags.

• The recursive causality tests indicate that in the relationship between consumer sentiment and economic headlines, the predominating effect throughout the 13-year time period was that of economic headlines on consumer sentiment, lending support to the agenda-setting theory of media influence. Figure 8.2 graphs the results of the recursive analysis (shown here at 4 lags). Noteworthy is that long-term media effects that are shown here (i.e., media effects after a 4-month period) do not become significant until mid-1990, during the Bush presidency, and then remain so for the rest of the period. This suggests that during Bush's presidential tenure there was a change in the dynamics of the press–consumer sentiment relationship that was then sustained throughout the rest of the time frame under study

• In the relationship between leading indicators and economic headlines, the recursive analysis confirmed the dominance of "media malady" effects (i.e.,

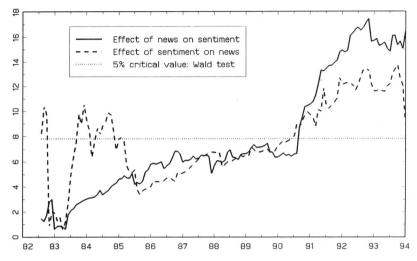

FIG. 8.2. Recursive causality analysis (news data = economic headlines).

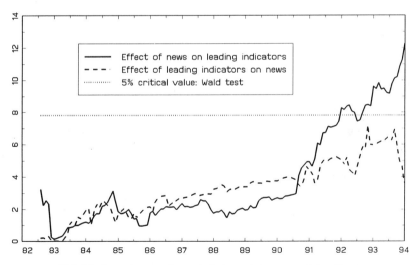

FIG. 8.3. Recursive causality analysis (news data = economic headlines).

media effects on leading economic indicators). However, it was revealed that the longer term influence (the impact of headlines on leading indicators 4 months later) only took effect at the close of 1991 and continued thereafter for the rest of the period (Fig. 8.3, shown at 4 lags). These results give some further evidence regarding the special nature of the 1991 subperiod when the dynamics between the press and real world economic conditions also appeared to change.

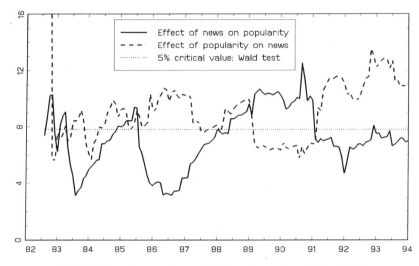

FIG. 8.3. Recursive causality analysis (news data = economic headlines).

• Prior causality tests between presidential popularity and headlines showed that the dominant influence overall was that of presidential popularity on subsequent numbers of economic headlines. However, recursive analysis uncovered brief periods of priming effects when headlines significantly influenced presidential popularity, notably during the 1989 to 1991 period, with the most dramatic peak occurring after mid-1990 (shown in Fig. 8.4 at 3 lags). Again, these results are consistent with the notion that there was an important shift in the causes and effects of the economic news agenda during this period of the Bush tenure, a time of war overseas and economic upheaval at home. They demonstrate the helpfulness of recursive analysis in detecting subperiods of change in empirical relationships under investigation that might otherwise go undetected.

DISCUSSION

The findings just outlined are part of a larger dissertation study by Blood (1996) that set out to explore the relationships between the press, the public, the presidency, and the economy over a time frame of extended economic and political changes. Using headlines to represent economic reporting and new statistical procedures from the field of econometrics to analyze the data, insights were gained on the relationships between the variables of interest that consolidate some earlier findings and speculations and challenge others. What follows is a summary of the main findings to emerge from this investigation, which cast light on the causes and effects of economic headline news.

• Although unfavorable economic headlines did dominate favorable head-lines in this study, the proportion of negative headlines found was modest compared to the extraordinary levels of negativism reported by the Media Institute (Glassman, 1993). However, the less than two-to-one ratio of negative to positive headlines reported here may lend some support to Glassman's contention that newspapers' coverage of the economy typically is more bal-anced and less dramatic than television network news treatment.

• The statistical procedures used here allow for economic headline news, leading economic indicators, consumer sentiment, and presidential popularity to be analyzed simultaneously and in their original form. There is no need to alter the data before analysis by trend elimination or filtering, as the techniques are designed specifically for analyzing data that may be nonstationary. The procedures also allow for the effects of other variables in the system to be controlled for when the relationship and causal effects between two of the variables are being studied. The empirical results confirm the importance of controlling for real-world variables, as argued by MacKuen (1981) and Neuman (1990), but they also illustrate the important role that is played by the past history of the variables themselves, especially when there is evidence of unit root nonstationarity, as there is with the data analyzed here.

• A number of causal effects were uncovered by the VAR analyses. The findings provide clear empirical evidence in support of the agenda-setting effects of media influence, where the media are believed capable of having an important influence on people's attitudes and behavior. Here, negative eco-nomic headlines were found to have a significant and negative impact on subsequent consumer sentiment at all lag lengths. However, media influence was found to be more far reaching, extending to the economic environment. Economic headlines had an adverse effect on subsequent leading economic indicators up to a 5-month time lag, a finding that lends empirical support to accusations made by some in the early 1990s that excessive negative economic news had a depressing effect on the economy.

• As for relations between the press and the presidency, there was a persistent influence of presidential popularity on economic headlines, whereby rising approval ratings for the president discouraged negative headlines on the general topic of the economy, and falling approval ratings spawned increasing numbers of them, more than were warranted by the economic conditions prevailing at the time. However, recursive analysis revealed subperiods of a priming effect, where presidential popularity was affected by unfavorable economic headlines. This finding demonstrates the usefulness of a recursive analysis that can help to reveal subperiods of causal effects that would not otherwise be detected.

Evidence here and elsewhere (Blood, 1996; Blood & Phillips, 1995) also points to a disruption in long-established patterns of relationship among the press, the public, and the presidency over the 1990–1991 period, a time of foreign and economic upheaval for the Bush administration, when a president enjoying high approval ratings over his handling of the Gulf Crisis faced increasing criticism from the press over his handling of the economy. Although this was undoubtedly a recessionary period at home, Blood and Phillips (1995) showed that the economic coverage of the recession was not related to the actual state of the economy at the time, as measured by the leading indicators. This raises the possibility of a pack journalism mentality (Graber, 1993) whereby news leaders set a norm for interpreting and reporting on the recession that was widely adopted and resulted in a deluge of negative headlines, with dampening effects on consumer sentiment and the economy as a result.

• Findings of powerful media effects here lend encouragement to agenda-setting researchers, as well as researchers in other fields of communication research, who seek media effects beyond the cognitive level. They should also be of some interest to economists with interests in the behavior of leading economic indicators and consumer sentiment. Our results offer a clear refutation of Linden's (1982) dismissal of economic news as an important influence on consumer confidence when he opined, "the average individual . . . does not, evidently, follow the economic news with any degree of sophistication but is quite responsive to personal day-to-day experiences" (p. 355). In short, media variables should not be overlooked when trying to understand the movements in these series.

• At the same time, the findings of powerful media effects on the economic and political landscape should raise some concerns for media scholars. Clearly, news organizations hold the power to effect change, or to maintain the status quo, in our social and economic systems. Although outside factors such as consumer sentiment, leading indicators, and even the popularity of the president may be seen to determine the media agenda at times, the ultimate driving force behind such effects may be the economic interests of the media organization owners themselves. Although it is critical that media content remains independent and devoted to the public welfare, it has been noted elsewhere that organizational interests, dictated by media ownership, may be the ultimate determinant of media content (Shoemaker & Reese, 1991). It is essential that media scholars closely monitor the influences on the production of economic news, cognizant of its potential to sway the public's assessment of the state of the economy and the presidency, and the very economy itself, to ensure that economic reporting is, in the end, determined by virtue of its service to the public good rather than by virtue of an economic impact designed to serve media ownership interests.

• Finally, media scholars must also be concerned with the capacity of media headlines to sway consumer sentiment and presidential popularity, and ultimately threaten the integrity of our democratic process of leader selection. Seymour Martin Lipset (cited in Patterson, 1993b) argued that George Bush lost his presidential reelection bid in 1992 not on the basis of the actual state of the economy, but on people's perceptions of the state of the economy. The findings here and elsewhere (Blood, 1996; Blood & Phillips, 1995) suggest that it was media representations of the state of the economy rather than actual economic conditions that influenced people's evaluations of their president and the economic health of their nation. If so, then, the media may facilitate the selection of a political leader in our democracy, not on the basis of a rational choice, but on the basis of an irrational one.

9

A Brief History of Time:
A Methodological Analysis of Agenda Setting

William J. Gonzenbach
Lee McGavin

Research examining the relationships among agenda setting's primary variables presents a rather confusing picture. The inconsistency of the results may be due in part to the agenda-setting effects of specific issue types; however, Iyengar and Kinder (1987; cited in Rogers & Dearing, 1988) offered much more serious and biting reasons for the inconsistency of results:

> Although research on agenda-setting has proliferated over the past decade, so far, the results add up to rather little. With a few important exceptions, agenda-setting research has been theoretically naive, methodologically primitive, both confused and confusing. . . . Agenda-setting may be an apt metaphor, but it is no theory. (p. 557)

Iyengar and Kinder's conclusion about agenda-setting methodologies may have merit, but this analysis takes issue with the spirit of the statement. Agenda-setting research presents many methodological problems concerning the measurement of agendas and agenda relationships over time; however, the body of research indicates that the methodological approaches have grown with the emerging time series databases and methodological techniques and have built on the efforts and visions of the field's fledgling analyses.

Agenda setting is by definition a time-related process. Many of the early agenda-setting studies were based on cross-sectional data, which by definition cannot directly capture the relationships of the agendas over time (Rogers &

Dearing, 1988; Weaver, 1987). A social process may go through various phases, rising and falling with the influence of various agendas and their operatives' efforts to frame and energize the issue for the public, who may in turn affect the life of an issue via their public outcries. The effects that one measures will certainly depend on where in time and space one happens to examine the process of a specific issue. A cross-sectional study's static design cannot account fully for the dynamic nature of the agenda-setting process (Behr & Iyengar, 1985), nor can it account at all for time lags of possible effects (Brosius & Kepplinger, 1990a).

Early agenda-setting research focused too narrowly on short time frames because the researchers came from an effects tradition, but the methodological progression in agenda-setting research has moved from "one-shot, cross-sectional studies to more sophisticated research designs that allow more precise exploration of agenda-setting as a process" (Rogers & Dearing, 1988, p. 572). This methodological progression can be categorized into five relevant methodological arenas: cross-sectional studies, trend studies, panel designs, time series designs, and nonlinear approaches (see Kessler & Greenberg, 1981).

CROSS-SECTIONAL STUDIES

Change effects in cross-sectional studies are inferred from variations between units at a single point in time. Although valuable insights can often be gleaned from this method, the approach is seriously flawed because it only measures synchronous relationships (relationships at the same point in time) and therefore cannot directly address time-based causality (Kessler & Greenberg, 1981). This approach should be avoided if possible whenever cohort or historical effects are presumed, at least when the focus of the research centers on change. In agenda-setting research, this approach is exemplified by the seminal research on agenda setting, in which media salience and public salience were correlated at one point in time (see McCombs & Shaw, 1972). Other studies used cross-sectional analyses to investigate the intervening role of individual-difference variables (e.g., Weaver, 1980) and other studies lagged media measures prior to a one-shot survey to examine the intervening roles of social category and social relationship variables (e.g., McLeod, Becker, & Byrnes, 1974) and to document time lags (Stone & McCombs, 1981).

TREND STUDIES

When a researcher is content with simply determining how much a single variable has changed in a population, he or she can gather measures from successive samples from the same population at different points in time and examine the change in the variable over time (Kessler & Greenberg, 1981). This type of study is referred to as a *trend study*. In agenda-setting research, the key weakness of trend analysis is that researchers have generally "eyeballed" the trend over time with rather simple graphic representations or applied analytic methods that do not adequately address the often complex mathematical nature of the time series processes (Brosius & Kepplinger, 1990a; McCleary & Hay, 1980). However, these early studies made an important contribution to agenda-setting research in that they sought to examine the agenda-setting process over long periods of time and to disentangle the complexities of relationships of issue agendas over time.

The seminal trend analysis in agenda setting explored the dynamics of public opinion for eight issues from 1964 to 1970 (Funkhouser, 1973). The study examined, in chronological order, annual measures of the country's "most important problem" (MIP) question from national surveys and then expanded on the basic trend approach by eyeballing the trend in opinion for these eight issues in relation to the annual number of articles that appeared in three national news magazines about each issue and to rather vague measures of real-world cues. As an example, media coverage of the drug issue roughly paralleled the rise in the real-world cue of actual drug use. However, the only evidence offered for the real-world cue was that "LSD was first noted in 1963, and from that point the use of that and other hallucinogenics (especially marijuana) accelerated through 1970" (p. 71). In general, Funkhouser's analysis of several issues over the 1960s suggested a limited role for real-world indicators. When the mass media coverage of the issue and the real-world indicators varied, the public agenda mirrored the media agenda more than the real-world cues. Funkhouser's study generally found strong associations between the media agenda and the public agenda and weaker associations between real-world indicators and either the media agenda or the public agenda

In a similar vein, another analysis eyeballed the trend in opinion regarding the abortion issue with annual data from 1972 to 1976 (Tedrow & Mahoney, 1979). Unlike Funkhouser's (1973) study, it did not examine the data in relation to the media and real-world cue agendas; rather, it examined change in opinion in regard to gender, education, occupation, religion, and church attendance.

Beniger's (1978) study argued that media emphasis could be used as a surrogate measure for public salience and included a measure based on the Greenfield Index computed from the number of stories about an issue indexed in the *Reader's Guide to Periodical Literature*. The study examined annual measures of media coverage from 1945 to 1975 for numerous issues including drugs and eyeballed this media coverage in relation to real-world cues about accidental drug deaths (only from 1966–1972), measures of self-reports of drug use (only from 1966), and the percentage of responses giving drugs as the country's MIP (only from 1969–1975). It concluded that media coverage may be more closely associated with public attitudes and opinion than are more objective measures.

Finally, a study by Smith (1980) examined the trend in opinion for numerous social issues from 1946 to 1976 based on the percentage of responses to MIP questions from national surveys. The analysis eyeballed the trends in opinion over time and then, like Tedrow and Mahoney (1979), it examined these trends in opinion in relation to several demographic variables. However, d-systems, which are linear-flow graphs, were used to determine the differences for each of the demographic subgroups over time.

PANEL AND TIME SERIES DESIGNS

Researchers use panel and time series designs to examine the differences between units in patterns of change, or to determine the effects of a change in one variable on another variable. The investigation of such questions is aided by the collection of data at more than one point in time on the same units of analysis. The most commonly used design of this type is the time series, for which observations are collected on one person or other unit of analysis for a large number of time intervals (Kessler & Greenberg, 1981). The second method is the panel study, in which observations are collected for a number of individuals (or other units of analysis) instead of only one, at two or more points in time. In agenda-setting research, the major difference between the two is that in a panel study the unit of analysis is the individual, who is typically surveyed at only a few points in time; in a time series analysis, the unit of analysis is typically an aggregate measure, such as the frequency of news stories, the percentage of the population believing an issue is the country's MIP, or a real-world cue measure such as the unemployment rate. The typical time series study usually includes numerous time points and an explanation of second-order relationships. In this analysis, two types of time series analyses are examined separately: The first type uses correlation and regression methods to examine the time series process; the second type uses Autoregressive, Integrated, Moving Average (ARIMA) models to mathematically model the various time series components (McCleary & Hay, 1980).

Panel Designs

Panel designs are powerful methods to provide information about cross-sectional and longitudinal variation (Kessler & Greenberg, 1981). In agenda-setting research, cross-lagged correlations are typically used to examine the relationship between two agendas. For example, a 1972 study of the national presidential election conducted in Charlotte, North Carolina, compared the rank-order correlations of the media agenda of issues (both newspaper and television) and the public's agenda of issues (voter's agenda) from June 1972 to October 1972 (Shaw & McCombs, 1977). The study hypothesized that if Media ($X1$) was a stronger cause of Public Opinion ($Y2$) than Media ($X2$) was of Public Opinion ($Y1$), the correlation $rX1Y2$ should be larger in magnitude than the correlation $rY1X2$ (see Fig. 9.1). The study indicated a strong agenda-setting effect for newspapers on public salience based on this cross-lagged correlation analysis; however similar support was not found for television.

This simple comparison presents several problems (Kessler & Greenberg, 1981; Markus, 1979; see Fig. 9.2). One type of problem involves temporal misspecification, or temporal erosion. If X and Y are measured at slightly different times, the misspecified causal lags can create significant observed cross-lagged correlation differences even when they do not exist in the true causal processes. Another class of problems concerns the consistency of effects across time, also called *stationarity*. If the reliability of one of the variables changes over time, or if the relationship between the measured variable and the underlying construct to which one is making some inference changes through time, the cross-lagged correlations will attenuate in ways unrelated to the relative causal influences. Finally, the cross-lagged correlation is inappropriate as a test of relative causal influence because lagged cross-correlations are determined not only by the differential stabilities of X to Y and from Y to X, but also by the differential stabilities of X to X and Y to Y.

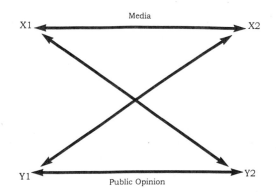

FIG. 9.1. Shaw and McCombs' agenda-setting panel study model.

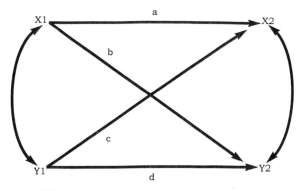

FIG. 9.2. Kessler and Greenberg's panel study model.

The cross-lagged correlations can be expressed as follows from the fundamental theorem of path analysis:

$$rX1Y2 = b + drX1Y1$$
$$rY1X2 = c + arX1Y1. \tag{1}$$

The cross-lagged correlations receive contributions from the true causal coefficients b and c, but they also receive contributions proportional to the stabilities of a and d. Only when the stabilities of a and d are equal does equality of the causal coefficients b and c follow from equality of the cross-correlations. If a and d are not equal, no inference about the relative strength, or even sign, of the true causal inferences can be determined. If the purpose of one's analysis is to estimate causal parameters, then a multiple regression approach should be used in which the cross-lagged partial regression coefficients can be compared in a number of ways, or preferably, the correlation $rX2Y2$ can be decomposed into its component causal parts so that the relative influences of the cross-coefficients can be examined (Kessler & Greenberg, 1981).

Time-Series Designs

Like panel designs, time series approaches are concerned with differences between units in a pattern of change, or in the effects of a change in one variable on another over time; however, unlike panel designs, the variables (at least in agenda-setting research) are typically aggregate measures collected over numerous points in time. Time series designs in agenda-setting research build on the agenda-setting trend studies by charting agenda-setting measures over relatively long periods of time, but then use correlation and regression to empirically quantify the relationships of the measures over time.

The first such study examined the relationship between media coverage of an airport noise problem and public complaints to the Federal Aviation Administration's noise complaint telephone service over 253 consecutive days (Watt & van den Berg, 1978). The time series cross-correlation analysis indicated the minimal conditions for support were present only for direct and indirect effects, agenda-setting, and reverse agenda-setting theories. The authors concluded that the interpretation of the time lag information between presumed cause and effect limited the plausible theoretical explanation to direct effects. The study is important because it addressed the issue of autocorrelation, which was defined as the "correlation of a variable with itself at different time intervals" (p. 219; see also Ostrom, 1990). Unfortunately, the study did not integrate the autocorrelation modeling into the cross-lagged correlation analysis (nor did it address the issue of stationarity) and thus the significance tests of the cross-lagged correlations may not be reliable (McCleary & Hay, 1980).

A study of civil rights used correlation methods to examine the relationship between public opinion and media coverage of the issue from 1954 to 1976

(Winter & Eyal, 1981). The public opinion measure comprised 27 measures of civil rights as the country's MIP from national polls, gathered at unequal intervals, which were compared to a media measure comprising the *New York Times* front-page coverage of the issue that was collected for the 6 months preceding each poll. The study examined the correlation of the media agenda at monthly lags of 1 to 5 months to the public agenda. Although not presented under the guise of autocorrelation, the analysis partialed out prior monthly effects, which may have controlled for autocorrelation in the media series, whereas the study did not address autocorrelation in their "dependent" public opinion series, nor did it address the issue of stationarity. The findings of the study suggested that for the first month prior there was a "recency effect" that was not highly related to previous months, whereas for the other months there was a cumulative effect that was related to the media agenda in previous months.

A study by Behr and Iyengar (1985) provided an important contribution to time series agenda-setting research by examining contrasting regression models that controlled for autocorrelation in the series to examine the relationships of television news coverage and public opinion, controlling for real-world cue measures. In the study, which examined the obtrusive issues of energy, unemployment, and inflation, public opinion was measured by responses to MIP questions for 42 consecutive bimonthly periods from 1974 to 1980. The analysis contrasted two regression equations for each issue:

$$\text{TV News} = c + \text{Real World} + \text{Issue Importance} + e$$
$$\text{Issue Importance} = C + \text{TV News} + \text{Real World} + E,$$
$$\text{where } c \text{ and } C \text{ are constants and } e \text{ and } E \text{ are error terms.} \qquad (2)$$

The study moved beyond cross-lagged correlation approaches and addressed the issue of autocorrelation, although it did not address the issue of stationarity. The study's experimental evidence indicates that the agenda-setting effect is unidirectional: News coverage boosted public concern for the issues of energy and unemployment, but public concern did not alter the level of coverage—although there was some indication that concern for inflation did increase coverage of that issue.

Another important study by Smith (1987) examined the relationships among the media agenda, public concerns, and public evaluations about local governmental services in Louisville, Kentucky, with eight annual surveys conducted from 1974 to 1981. The findings of the study suggested that the amount of newspaper coverage was related to higher evaluations of concern about community issues and poorer evaluations of government services. The study examined the relationships with a regression method based on the idea of Granger (1980) causality, a popular technique developed by an economist for estimating causality among variables measured from repeated cross-sectional surveys:

A variable is said to Granger cause Y, if Y can better be predicted from the past history (i.e., the lagged values) of X and Y together than the past history of Y alone. Sims (1972) has demonstrated that a necessary condition for a variable X to be considered exogenous (i.e., a causal predictor) to variable Y is that Y fails to Granger cause X. When X is found to Granger cause Y and Y Granger cause X, a two-way effect is indicated. (K. A. Smith, 1987, p. 386)

Shoemaker, Wanta, and Leggett (1989) examined the media agenda and public opinion of the drug issue in the United States from 1972 to 1986 with a hierarchical regression approach that did not address the problems of autocorrelation or stationarity. The findings suggested that the more the media emphasized drugs, the more people thought drugs were the MIP and that there was no evidence of similarity in coverage among the media; the *New York Times* and the *Los Angeles Times* accounted for almost all of the total effect of the nine media on public concern with drugs. The study also found evidence for media agenda-setting effects in two time periods—one during the weeks immediately preceding the poll and one about 3 months prior to the poll.

Kepplinger, Donsbach, Brosius, and Staab (1989) investigated the relationship between media coverage of German Chancellor Helmut Kohl in seven leading German print media outlets and the opinions of the German public about the politician between 1975 and 1984. Cross-lagged correlations were used, which did not address autocorrelation or stationarity, to examine the relationship between media coverage and approval. They correctly qualified the analysis by saying that ARIMA modeling or Granger causality was not used because of missing values and the less-than-optimal quality of the data. The study concluded the evaluation shifts in the media preceded similar evaluation shifts in public opinion with a time lag of about 3 to 6 months for the whole period of investigation, and a somewhat shorter time lag for the period of Kohl's chancellorship.

HIGHER ORDER RELATIONSHIPS

The early agenda-setting studies using cross-sectional methods assumed that social science research did not find many second- or third-order relationships. In 1990 several researchers made important contributions to time series analysis in agenda setting by creating process models of agendas with longitudinal data. Neuman's (1990) strategy was to define real-world variation as an important but unmeasured variable and proceed to model the relative response functions of the media and the public. The S-shaped logistic curve, defined as

$$Y = e^x/(1 + e^x) \tag{3}$$

was determined to be "an attractive candidate" for the agenda-setting response function and the analysis specifically used Downs' (1972) notion of the issue–attention cycle. Neuman argued that the public perception of most crises does not reflect changes in real conditions as much as the operation of a systematic cycle of heightening public interest followed by a saturation or boredom effect and general public decline of attention.

Downs (1972) identified five stages of the issue–attention cycle:

1. The preproblem stage—the problem exists but has not captured public attention.
2. The discovery stage—here there is a sudden steep ascent of attention and transition from nonproblem to problem, which Neuman (1990) termed the threshold.
3. The plateau—there is a gradual realization that the problem is not easy to solve and that it is quite complex.
4. The decline—the public becomes inattentive and possibly frustrated with the problem.
5. The postproblem period—the problem enters a period of inattention, although its objective conditions have not changed significantly as the public awaits a new issue and new hope.

In the analysis of 10 issues, Neuman first eyeballed the relationship of the "raw metrics" between the media and public opinion, much like Funkhouser (1973), from which he developed four issue types.

The *crisis* category is exemplified by an issue like Vietnam, which had a clear beginning, middle, and end. The drug issue exemplified the *symbolic crisis* as did pollution and poverty, in which a combination of events and the responses of the government, the public, and the media led to a public definition of the problem of crisis proportions for a limited period of time. The *problem* category is exemplified by an issue like inflation, which is an issue without a story line. Finally, the *nonproblem* category is exemplified by the crime issue, in which there are weak public-opinion effects, moderate media coverage, and a weak relationship between the two (Neuman, 1990). Next, linear regression equations were used to model the slopes of the response functions, with public opinion as the dependent measure and media coverage as the independent measure, although the analysis did not appear to account for stationarity and autocorrelation in the series. There appeared "to be ample evidence indeed that the media and the public have unique dynamics in their response to real-world cues" (p. 172); however, Neuman never examined real-world cues in the model, nor did he account for stationarity and autocorrelation in the models.

Brosius and Kepplinger (1990b) questioned the linearity assumption underlying most of the longitudinal agenda-setting research and derived four alternative nonlinear models of the relationship between media coverage and public opinion. The *threshold* model indicates that a certain threshold of media attention must be met to affect public salience. The *acceleration* model suggests that problem awareness increases or decreases to a larger degree than corresponding media reporting; the same changes in media reporting have different effects on the problem awareness depending on the level of previous reporting and the public reacts more sensitively to issues that are already on the media agenda. The *inertia* model is the reverse of the acceleration model and proposes that problem awareness decreases or increases to a smaller degree than media reporting. Finally, the *echo* model proposes that extraordinary peaks in media reporting have long-term effects on public awareness.

Finally, Brosius and Kepplinger (1990a) investigated static (cross-sectional) and dynamic (longitudinal) approaches to agenda research. In this study, the focus moved from nonlinear modeling to an examination of cause and effect. As in the previous study, regression methods with Granger causality tests were used, in which two competing models for the dynamic analysis were tested: media salience leads to public salience versus public salience leads to media salience. The study also attempted to address the issue of nonstationarity. Significant time lags between 1 and 3 weeks were found for both directions of causality. These higher order research findings tend to suggest the need for more research to determine the linear and nonlinear relationships of the primary variables in the agenda-setting process.

ARIMA TIME SERIES MODELS

In this section, the issues of stationarity and autocorrelation, as well as other components of a time series, are addressed and a method, ARIMA modeling, is presented to model these components in a time series analysis. Then, several studies that incorporate ARIMA modeling in time series analyses of agenda setting are examined.

Autocorrelation and ARIMA Modeling

In ordinary least-squares regression, the following three assumptions are made: (a) the error term has a mean of zero, (b) the error term has a constant variance over all the observations, and (c) the error terms corresponding to different points in time are not correlated. Of the three, the third assumption is often the most important (Ostrom, 1990). When the observations of one variable from different points in time are correlated, the error process is said to be autocorrelated and the third assumption is violated. Autocorrelation in the error term has three primary causes: a misspecified model; omission of important variables, the result of which shows up in the error term; and errors in measurement, which are repeated over time and show up in the error term (McCleary & Hay, 1980). When the third assumption is violated, the estimated regression line fits the data very well, leaving small estimated residuals. Therefore, the estimated variances seriously underestimate the true variances.

The estimated variances are extremely important in the construction of confidence intervals, testing hypotheses, and computing *t* ratios. Therefore, when a time series has autocorrelated error terms, the coefficients are unbiased, but the variance and standard deviation are underestimated and tests of significance are inaccurate. In regression analysis, one common method to test for first-order autocorrelation (correlation between successive error terms) is the Durbin–Watson d-statistic (Ostrom, 1990). Some of the agenda-setting studies using time series regression analysis (e.g., Behr & Iyengar, 1985) use this test for first-order autoregressive processes, and Granger causality tests, in effect, model this first-order autoregressive process into the regression equation. Most time series in the social sciences are first-order autoregressive processes. However, this is a critical assumption because the time series may be a second-order autoregressive process (correlation between the current error term and the two preceding error terms; McCleary & Hay, 1980; Ostrom, 1990). In addition, a time series contains several other components, such as stationarity, that must be modeled to accurately determine coefficients and test for statistical significance. ARIMA analysis provides a means to model these components.

Although elements of ARIMA modeling can be traced back some 50 years, Box and Jenkins (1976) have been credited with integrating the elements into a comprehensive method, extending it greatly, and popularizing it. ARIMA models posit a random shock, a_t, as the driving force of a time series process. The most important tenet is that the present input, a_t, will have a greater impact on the present output, Y_t, than any earlier input; that is, the influence of a past event (or input, a_t) diminishes as time passes. ARIMA models, which are based on maximum likelihood estimation, require approximately 40 to 50 time-ordered observations, the interval of which should be constant. Also, the discrete time series data set should provide an adequate representation of the continuous, underlying process of the variable over time (McCleary & Hay, 1980).

A time series has two basic components: (a) a deterministic component that measures the systematic behavior of a time series process and is represented by all the parameters of the time series that are not dependent on the error structure; and (b) a stochastic (or "noise") component that describes the underlying process of the unobserved errors, which makes the observed time series somewhat unpredictable. The stochastic component follows certain laws of probability and has two parts: (a) the systematic part—that which is unobserved and is responsible for the autocorrelation in a time series; a major objective of ARIMA analysis is to determine and model the structure of the systematic part of the stochastic component in the corresponding equation so that unbiased estimates of standard deviations can be calculated and correct inferences for the significance tests can be drawn; and (b) the unsystematic part—that which is the unexplained variance left after the systematic part is modeled (McCain & McCleary, 1979).

ARIMA Parameters

ARIMA analysis models three parameters of the systematic part of the stochastic component through the process of identification. These three parameters are the trend component (d), which addresses the issue of stationarity; the autoregressive component (p), which addresses the issue of autocorrelation as discussed in the sections on panel studies and correlation and regression in time series; and the moving average component (q), which is another form of autocorrelation characterized by the persistence of a random shock from one observation to the next. By convention, these parameters are represented as (p, d, q) in an ARIMA model.

The first component, trend, is the motion in a specific direction, usually upward or downward, within a series, or, more specifically, any systematic change in the level of a time series (McCleary & Hay, 1980). McCleary and Hay also distinguished between trend and drift:

> The real difference between trend and drift is that trend is deterministic behavior while drift is stochastic behavior. . . . A time series can drift for extremely long periods of time due only to random forces. Unless there is a strong theoretical basis (or empirical evidence) for assuming that a time series process trends deterministically, there are great advantages to be gained by modeling it stochastically. (pp. 35–36)

Most of the time series used in the social sciences do have systematic trends and are therefore nonstationary in the homogeneous sense. Almost every time series can be made stationary by differencing; that is, by subtracting each observation from the one that follows; for example, the first observation from the second, the second from the third, the third from the fourth, and so on. Sometimes a second differencing may be required, but this is extremely rare in the social sciences. First-order differencing accounts for the linear trend in the time series; second-order differencing accounts for a quadratic trend. Differencing does not affect the deterministic components of the time series process (McCain & McCleary, 1979). An appropriate differencing procedure always results in a constant series that is represented mathematically as:

$$Y_t - Y_{t-1} = \theta \text{ (a constant interpreted as the slope of the series)}$$
$$\text{or, } Y_t = \theta \tag{4}$$

Finally, although homogeneous-sense stationarity is a necessary condition of an ARIMA model, it is not a sufficient condition. An ARIMA model must also have a stationary variance. A process that is stationary in variance will have a single constant variance throughout its course; a series that is not stationary in variance may be made so by transforming the series (e.g., performing a log transformation) after any necessary differencing is implemented (McCleary & Hay, 1980).

The structural parameter p indicates the autoregressive order of an ARIMA (p, d, q) model. Some time series are characterized by a direct relationship between adjacent observations (McCain & McCleary, 1979). The most typical autoregressive process in the social sciences is the first-order autoregressive process, which is represented by an ARIMA (1, 0, 0) model, or if differenced once by an ARIMA (1, 1, 0) model,

$$Y_t = \theta y_{t-1} + a_t \tag{5}$$

where θ is a correlation coefficient that describes the magnitude of the dependency between adjacent observations and a_t is the error term, or white noise of the process. It is helpful to think of the ARIMA (1, 0, 0) model as an ordinary least-squares (OLS) regression model in which the current series observation is regressed on the preceding time series observation. Unlike the OLS regression model, the parameter $\theta 1$ must be constrained to the following interval:

$$-1 < \theta_1 < +1 \tag{6}$$

which is termed the *bounds of stationarity*. The principles of autoregression can also be applied to higher order processes, such as an ARIMA (2, 0, 0) model, which is a second-order process where the current observation is determined in part by the two preceding observations (McCain & McCleary, 1979).

The white noise, or stochastic component, is the driving force of all ARIMA (p, d, q) models. Integrated (trend) processes are the sum of all the past shocks, or errors, and are well represented by ARIMA $(0, d, 0)$ models. Autoregressive processes are an exponentially weighted sum of all past shocks, and are represented by an ARIMA $(p, 0, 0)$ model. The unifying feature between integrated and autoregressive processes is the persistence of random shock. Each shock persists indefinitely, but for the autoregressive processes the impact of the shock diminishes geometrically.

The final parameter, the moving average process, is characterized by a finite persistence in the random shock. A random shock enters the system and then persists for no more than q observations before it vanishes entirely (McCleary & Hay, 1980). Moving average processes are represented by ARIMA $(0, 0, q)$ models:

$$Y_t = a_t - \theta_1 a_{t-1} \tag{7}$$

where θ is a correlation coefficient and a_t is an error term. The general principle of the moving average process is that a random shock persists for exactly θ observations and then is gone. In moving average process, θ must be constrained as follows:

$$-1 < \theta < +1 \tag{8}$$

which is called the *bounds of invertability* (McCleary & Hay, 1980).

In theory, a time series can have both an autoregressive and a moving average term (McCain & McCleary, 1979). For example, an ARIMA (1, 1, 1) describes a differenced model where the current observation, Y_t, is predicted from both the preceding past observation, Y_{t-1}, and the preceding random shock, a_{t-1}.

In addition, a series can have seasonal components in the ARIMA model, or seasonal cycles that must be incorporated into the stochastic component. As an example, there are two types of autocorrelation: regular autocorrelation, described earlier as the structural dependency among adjacent observations; and seasonal autocorrelation, described as the structural dependency among observations separated by one period or cycle, such as an annual cycle or 6-month cycle (McCain & McCleary, 1979). The seasonal structural parameters are denoted by uppercase letters: P specifies the number of seasonal autoregressive terms; D specifies the number of times a series must be seasonally differenced; Q specifies the number of seasonal moving average terms; and S denotes the length or order of the period or cycle. The conventional means for specifying a seasonal model is ARIMA (p, d, q) (P, D, Q)s (Gonzenbach, 1995; McCleary & Hay, 1980).

ARIMA Modeling and Agenda-Setting Research

ARIMA modeling is a relatively new methodological approach in agenda-setting research. Currently, only a few studies have employed this method, such as Rogers, Dearing, and Chang's (1991) examination of the AIDS issue (also see Dearing, 1989; Gonzenbach, 1992, 1995).

The study by Rogers et al. (1991) examined the relationships among five agendas over 91 consecutive monthly time intervals: the polling agenda, as represented by the number of polls about the issue; the science agenda, as represented by the frequency of monthly articles in four leading medical journals; the real-world cue measure, which has the number of monthly AIDS cases; the media's agenda, comprising the monthly frequency of stories from the *New York Times, Washington Post, Los Angeles Times,* and the three networks' evening news broadcasts; and the policy agenda, which was the average monthly federal expenditures for AIDS research, education, and testing created from the annual expenditures for the years of the study.

Each of the univariate series was modeled with ARIMA modeling, and then the modeled series were used in a Granger causality test to determine whether causal relationships existed between each of the 10 possible pairs of relationships (Rogers et al., 1991). Granger causality is frequently used to determine over-time causality in longitudinal data. As K. A. Smith (1987) noted, X is a Granger cause of Y when Y is better predicted by incorporating X's past history over and above the influence of Y's past history on itself.

Rogers et al. (1991) specified the following possible conclusions for the Granger causality test:

1. A one-way causal relationship is determined when one time series explains the other, but the reverse does not occur.

2. A feedback, or reciprocal causal relationship, occurs when two time series contribute equally to explain each other's variance when they are included in the regression equation of the other.

3. An instantaneous causal link occurs when the present and the past history of one time series contributes to increase the other variable's total variance explained.

4. The absence of Granger causality is assessed when neither of two series increase the other's variance by including their past histories for the other. (pp. 26–27)

Four of the possible 10 pairs showed one-way causality over the 91-month time series: The science agenda predicted the media agenda; the number of AIDS cases predicted the media agenda, the science agenda predicted the polling agenda, and the policy agenda predicted the polling agenda. One pair, the media and polling relationship, showed a reciprocal, two-way relationship. The five significant bivariate relationships had two common dependent series, the media agenda and the polling agenda. The significant predictors from the bivariate analyses were then used to test two multivariate models, one with the media agenda as the dependent series and the other with the polling agenda as the dependent series. This analysis utilized multivariate transfer function analysis (Cuddington, 1980).

The first model indicated that the media agenda was predicted by itself, the science agenda, the polling agenda, and the number of AIDS cases. The second model indicated the polling agenda was predicted by itself, the media agenda, and the policy agenda. Finally, Rogers et al. (1991) repeated the steps of the aforementioned analysis for each of the four eras of the AIDS issue, which they had determined from a content analysis of the issue: the initial era (23 months), the science era (26 months), the human era (19 months), and the political era (23 months). This analysis may be suspect given the very low number of time intervals used in these four separate analyses (see McCleary & Hay, 1980).

NONLINEAR APPROACHES

The findings of panel and time series designs have raised questions about some of the linear assumptions of previous agenda-setting research. Research that explores the nonlinear relationships of agenda setting follows research in many fields that questions the basic assumption of linear causality in fields from physics to economics to psychology (Gaustello, 1995). The apparent presence of cycles (Neuman, 1990), time lags (Kessler & Greenberg, 1981), and time series interactions (Gonzenbach, 1992, 1995) provides reason to investigate the nonlinear relationships of agenda setting. This section reviews linear and nonlinear assumptions and some methodological techniques for empirical analysis of nonlinear relationships.

Linear statistical measures are designed to produce a two-dimensional view of a relationship. They have an independent variable that becomes one axis and a dependent variable that represents the other axis. By plotting points extended from the two variables (axis), a picture of their relationship is developed. This is true for even the most sophisticated multiple regression methods where the dependent variable is graphed in relation to a weighted value derived from several independent variables. To make predictions from the relationship, the slope of the line formed by the points predicts the expected value of the dependent variables. This method has value when the results can be seen as a straight line on a graph.

The validity of linear analysis becomes problematic in the presence of three factors that are important in this discussion of agenda-setting methods. First is nonlinear or curvilinear correlations that are seen in cycles and seasonal changes. The second occurs when two or more variables interact dynamically as seen in the influence of the public agenda on both events and the media agenda. The last factor that is discussed is the practical application of the central limit theorem to processes that change over periods of time.

Following the central limit theorem, if you find all of the relationships that determine weather and measure them precisely then you should be able to predict the weather well into the future. In a series of landmark papers, Lorenz (1963a; 1963b; 1964) described the problems of the linear method in analyzing weather data. He found that the rounding error of measurement and computer calculations eventually produced chaotic results. In short, he found a formula to explain why the weather is deterministically unpredictable.

The Lorenz principle is one part of what is called chaos theory (Yorke & Li, 1975) and has influenced the quantitative study of turbulence and change in many fields (Casti, 1989). Mathematically the equations seem simple but when graphed they produce surprising and intricate models out of apparent randomness. This structure allows prediction of order but not for any particular moment in time. The heart of chaos theory is that very small differences in initial conditions are exaggerated by iterations so that what seems to be natural randomness is in reality deterministic order and structure (Cohen & Stewart, 1994).

Agenda-setting research offers many of the same characteristics as the flow processes studied by Lorenz. Its methodology has sought to overcome seasonal patterns and dynamic interactions. This chapter has highlighted many of the equations that have been used to model shifting agendas. Mathematically they resemble the models that are being used in many areas of nonlinear dynamics to describe natural flow and turbulence. One path for future agenda-setting research is to further develop a methodology that seeks to model the complexity rather than add complexity to the model.

Methods of nonlinear analysis offer provocative alternatives and provocative names. Chaos, complexity, catastrophe, self-organizing science, synergetics, and nonlinear dynamics are all approaches that seek to combine holistic and reductionist perspectives. Communication fields have been slow to adopt these methods but there is some preliminary research that uses statistical procedures developed from these approches. The remainder of this chapter looks at some of the research and the underlying method of analysis.

There is research that focuses on interaction effects at the expense of analysis of causality. The work of Fan (1988; Fan & Elketroussi, 1989; Fan & McAvoy, 1989) is of particular significance in this area. Fan brought a background in biological research into the field of public opinion and has developed a method to measure and predict swings of public opinion based on difference equations. Fan used the basic assumptions of most agenda-setting research. He began with a content analysis of the wire copy from the Associated Press. The wire copy was coded for all issues mentioned in a story and an assessment of the positive or negative connotation of the material. The content analysis values were used as the basic unit for a comparison using difference equations to make predictions about changes in public opinion. By differencing the data, Fan demonstrated the impact of stationarity on efforts to predict changes in public opinion and the applicability of differential equations to iterative, qualitative data.

Difference and differential equations are used to plot the value of a function of a variable after successive iterations. The result of solving the equation for Time 1 is used as the starting point for the following solution. The independent variable, the number of iterations, does not explicitly bear on the dependent variable. The results are determined by the function of each iteration. The basic equations are similar to those used in analyzing the seasonal change in the size of animal populations (Aoki, 1995; Kocak, 1989). All of the equations in this chapter have been either in the form of difference equations or initial values of a difference equation.

The use of difference equations is the important step in this kind of analysis. Difference equations predict future values based on a known relationship. When there is a linear correspondence, simple multiplication is enough to provide that kind of prediction. When the relationship is nonlinear, difference equations solve the problem using a sequence of calculations. A two-dimensional result uses the number of iterations as one axis of the graph and the calculated value as the other (Haken, 1988; Hofstadter, 1985). The procedure could be seen as analogous to the correlation coefficient of linear data as it establishes the slope or slopes of nonlinear data.

Further research using the Fan approach has addressed the linear statistical problem that arises from using a limited number of issues to establish correlations between media and public agendas. The zero sum approach that has been used in most agenda-setting research acknowledges that there is a limit to the number of issues that can maintain importance at one time. The Fan method focused on a single issue and therefore lost the importance of the relationship of issues to each other. Zhu (1992) offered an improvement to the Fan equations to correct for issue interaction. Zhu's equations make use of time lags as an additional correction to the difference between media coverage and public response.

Zhu used a second-order difference equation to factor in time lags. The equation used by Fan, and updated by Zhu, offers the ability to analyze data in relation to different cycles and the time lags simultaneously. Difference equations depend on the number of iterations. Iterations can represent different media cycles. Fan used wire copy to make calculations based on a shorter interval of chronological time. The use of wire copy is based on two assumptions that difference equations are well suited to measuring. The first is that the wire services are sufficiently general in their coverage to provide a sample of the issues on the media agenda. The second is that the time lag for different media outlets will be different. Using the wire services loses issue salience comparisons but gains in the accuracy of the estimate of time lags. It also permits the calculations to be based on iterations of a duration that can be set by the researcher. In this case the nonlinear calculation allows prediction when the length of media cycles is not directly correlated to the length of public response cycles. By using second-order equations, Zhu was able to model the time lags of the interaction effects.

Research that has shown indications of a seasonal factor that influences public salience also suggests the validity of a nonlinear method. Neuman's (1990) calculation of the seasonal change of public opinion is a version of the same logistic equation (Kocak, 1989; Smith, 1968) used by Fan and in ecological research. By analogy, competing issues are similar to predators and prey sharing an environment. Comparing the ebb and flow of issue salience to the ebb and flow of the physical size of populations has intuitive merit.

The importance of the research of Fan, Zhu, and Neuman is in the application of nonlinear analysis. The results will need further testing and refinement of the algorithms before any attempts can be made to look for chaotic determinism. Brown's (1991) research in voting has indicated turbulence in voting patterns that may be chaotic. Coleman (1993) found similar suggestions in his study of Alabama voters. These studies are not measures of the same effects that are studied in agenda setting. Both studies point to the use of election results as a major weakness because the measurement points are a year or more apart. Application of similar techniques to agenda-setting research should provide better results by using more points of measurement.

A PRACTICAL EXERCISE

A complete discussion of the statistical procedures and mathematical proofs for this approach is beyond the scope of this chapter. What follows is a description of the basis for this kind of analysis. The modeling used here has all been done with Phaser, a computer program designed to model difference and differential equations (Kocak, 1989). Computer modeling allows visualization of more than two dimensions.

The linear relationship that is being described to varying levels of complexity in agenda-setting research is the relationship of issue salience and media salience. The equation for the basic relationship is:

Public salience = a function of media salience on public salience.   (9)

Previous research has shown that this is an incomplete picture. First, there is a an influence on both the media and public that comes from a combination of outside events and news makers. These two will be considered as one variable for the first level of analysis even though the nature of the influence is not the same. Second, previous research has also shown that the initial equation is nonlinear (Neuman, 1990). The actual relationship is curvilinear and dependent on time lags and seasonal variations. The equation can be restated to include these variables:

Public salience = a function of (a function of outside events on media salience), (on public salience, as a function of, (a function of media content on outside events)).   (10)

Expressing this equation in words is awkward at best so the math may lack eloquence as well. The improvement needed is to state the relationship of the variables as a differential equation.

Public salience now = a function of media content and outside events on public salience at a previous time.

Media salience now = a function of public salience and outside events on media salience at a previous time.

Outside events now = a function of public opinion, media content, and seasonal change on outside events at a previous time.   (11)

By plotting these three equations on the x, y, and z axes, a three-dimensional view of the relationship would be developed. This is a step in determining the presence of attractors. An attractor is a point of convergence in the time series (Haken, 1988; Johnson & Dooley, 1995). It is an indication that a deterministic structure is present. Linear methods would view the same results as error variance or noise.

The development of a method that uses some form of a three-dimensional model is something that may be in the future. The immediate future of agenda setting seems to follow the lead of Fan and Neuman into difference equations in a more linear fashion. The presence of attractors can be indicated in difference equations through the use of one-dimensional stair step maps.

Figure 9.3 shows a stair step graphing of the logistic equation. The stair step graph shows the curve of the calculated values and a method of calculating the iterates. The two axis represent the current value of a variable and the next value of the variable. The 45-degree line is drawn as a reference. The stair steps proceed from the initial value of the variable vertically until it intersects with the function curve. This is the point of the variable and its next iteration. The horizontal step is drawn to the intersection with the diagonal to reposition the initial value for the next calculation. The vertical line intersects the curve at the second iterated value.

Figure 9.3 shows the stairs descending into the unity position of the graph. Figure 9.4 shows the stair step converging on a single point. This graph used the same logistic equation but a higher value for the functions parameter. The value where the iterations converge is an attractor. In a nonlinear relationship, the presence of an attractor is an indication of a deterministic structure. Linear methods would view the same data as indicating error variance.

Time series methods depend on the linear restriction of stationarity. Corrections for stationarity that rely on normal distributions lose reliability when the data produces nonlinear results (SAS Institute, 1993). A possible alternative is to use attractors (Guastello, 1995; Johnson & Dooley, 1995). An attractor provides a deterministic value that can be used in corrections for stationarity.

The challenging part of this method is that small changes in the parameters of the function can cause the attractors to shift or disappear altogether. The

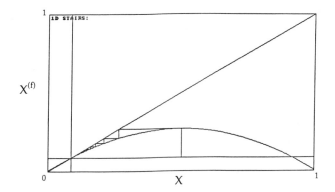

FIG. 9.3. Iterated function of the logistic equation in a stair step graphing.

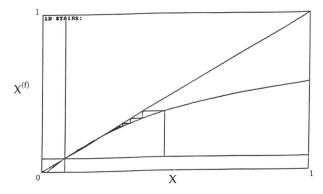

FIG. 9.4. Iterated function of the logistic equation in a stair step graphing.
As the value of the parameter increases, an attractor is indicated.

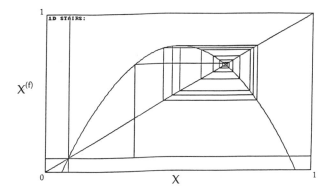

FIG. 9.5. Iterated function of the Neuman (1990) curve. An attractor is indicated
as the paramenter is increased to 1.

values of the parameter that cause these shifts are called *bifurcation points*. Figure 9.5 shows the Neuman equation as a difference equation. The point of convergence shown in this figure does not occur until the value of the parameter is greater than 0.9. If the parameter was a correlation coefficient, an attractor would appear when the correlation was high.

It is necessary to point out that this graphing of Neuman's equation is only an example. It is done to illustrate how difference equations can be used in the analysis of time series data. Based on the present research, there are interesting suggestions of attractors but nothing of substance. In fact, there is disagreement over the issue of using dynamic systems methods in social science research because attractors have not yet been proven to exist outside of natural phenomena (Guastello, 1995; Haken, 1988). Deterministic chaos focuses on natural systems without conscious efforts at self-monitoring. Applications to social science research will require a method of mathematically addressing the influence of reflexive adaptations on a dynamic system (McGavin, 1996).

CONCLUSIONS

The progress of agenda-setting methods and techniques may not be any less confusing after this review of statistical procedures and algorithms but the research is moving into the most sophisticated methods of analysis. The cross-sectional studies that provide a snapshot of the effect lead to trend analysis and panel studies. The lack of precision in trend analysis leads to time series (ARIMA and ARMA) procedures. Panel studies demonstrate the need for delayed cross lags that suggest second- (or higher) order analysis.

The progression of methods has led the field to the edge of self-organizing science. The methods of the nonlinear approaches can already be seen in the equations and analysis of agenda setting. The methods of future research can be informed by using more of the tools of nonlinear dynamics to enhance each of the methods that have been discussed here. There may or may not be attractors in agenda-setting data sets but searching for them offers the possibility of solving many of the problems that have been discussed.

It is interesting that two areas of communication research have begun to explore nonlinear dynamics as a methodological approach. Agenda setting has already been mentioned and the other is in organizational communication (Comfort, 1994; Guastello, 1995). Agendas and the metaphor of agenda setting share the need to be analyzed as a change process. It is the need to be analyzed as a process of iterations that has made the McCain and McCleary (1979) view that second-order processes are rare in the social sciences somewhat problematic. It may be that the most significant contribution of agenda-setting research is taking a leading role in reexamining our assumptions about linear methodologies.

10

The Messenger and the Message:
Differences Across News Media

Wayne Wanta

Marshall McLuhan said it first three decades ago: The medium is the message. In his controversial book *Understanding Media,* McLuhan (1964) argued that each medium has fundamental and unique characteristics. The information distributed by the media was much less important—actually, insignificant—compared to the medium itself. According to McLuhan, "the personal and social consequences of any medium—that is, of any extension of ourselves—result from the new scale that is introduced into our affairs by each extension of ourselves, or by any new technology" (p. 7).

Given the current explosion of new technologies in mass communication, the technical aspects of mass communication deserve closer scrutiny. The medium, then, although it may not be the message in and of itself, certainly plays a role in the mental processing of the information it delivers.

Other scholars have argued similarly that the mental processing of information varies across medium. Reading newspapers indeed is a very different cognitive task than viewing television.

Researchers have proposed two basic arguments regarding information-processing differences across media. The two approaches are based on (a) receiver characteristics, namely the mental effort involved in processing messages, and (b) medium characteristics.

MENTAL EFFORT DIFFERENCES

The mental effort approach argues that the amount of information people learn from individual media is dependent to a large degree on the amount of effort they must exert in processing this information. That is, the greater the effort individuals put forth, the more information they will gain.

Clearly, newspaper reading takes a great deal more effort than television viewing because reading is a more difficult task than television viewing. Individuals watching television news passively watch as someone else reads them the news, whereas newspaper readers must actively determine which newspapers stories they will read and which stories they will not read. Thus, individuals should learn more from newspaper reading than from television viewing.

Salomon (1979) took the mental effort argument one step further, arguing that expectations play a role in information processing. People expect reading will be more difficult than television viewing. Thus, preconceived notions about the amount of mental effort come into play: Readers expect reading to be more difficult, so they put more effort into reading than television viewers put into viewing television. Learning, therefore, is enhanced.

Salomon argued that the expected mental effort that individuals hold influences how they process information. People tend to allocate more mental effort to reading than to watching television. Thus, memory of content is often superior in reading compared to television viewing.

According to Salomon, the amount of mental effort allocated to a task is a function of perceived task difficulty. In the absence of other cues, preconceptions about the relative difficulty involved in processing information from print versus television impels the receiver to allocate more mental effort to a printed versus a televised message. It follows, then, that if individuals allocate more mental effort to reading printed words, they also will learn more.

The mental effort arguments have significant implications for agenda-setting research. If these arguments of mental effort are true, we should find stronger agenda-setting effects for newspapers than for television. Because agenda setting is a form of social learning, individuals should learn more about the relative importance of issues through newspapers than through television news because reading issue information in newspapers is a more difficult task than viewing issue information on television. In addition, besides more efficient learning of the salience of issues, newspaper readers should also demonstrate more efficient learning of the salience of how the issues are framed, as well.

MEDIUM DIFFERENCES

In contrast to the mental effort model of information processing, McLuhan (1964) took an entirely different approach to discussing differences between media. McLuhan categorized media based on the involvement each medium demanded from individuals. Television and newspapers were at opposite ends of McLuhan's spectrum.

McLuhan called television a *cool medium* because it provides little detail, but extends several senses. A cool medium requires the receiver of messages to have high involvement with the message. Without high involvement, an individual would not be able to process information efficiently from television, because television requires viewers to fill in many missing details.

Newspapers are *hot* because they provide a great deal of detail and leave the reader with little to add from her or his own experiences or knowledge. A hot medium extends a single sense in "high definition," but requires the receiver to have low involvement with the message.

However, McLuhan did not use *data* to mean information, but rather the physical impact of the medium on an individual's sense organs. Thus, as one critic noted, McLuhan argued that:

> Television is the "coolest," most involved of media, not because of any show or program that might be offered on it, but because of the operation of the picture tube, whatever the program. The onlooker is involved to the depths of his being without knowing it, because the picture on the tube is really a "mosaic " of tiny dots, which the observer must put together without knowing it. (Finkelstein, 1968, pp. 82–83)

Although McLuhan met with widespread criticism—authors in such hot media as *Life* magazine (Howard, 1966) and the *New York Times* (Cort, 1966) criticized his work—some of his ideas, at least on the surface, seem pertinent still today. Although the different media, contrary to McLuhan's argument, may not be more important than the messages they convey, newspapers, magazines, television, and radio nonetheless are different from each other. Each has its own strengths and weaknesses. More importantly, individuals process information from each differently. And, of course, if individuals process information obtained from various media differently, the effects of the information logically will also differ.

McLuhan would argue that a cool medium such as television requires more "physical filling in" by the audience than a hot medium such as newspapers. Television requires more concentration than mere looking because the dots on the screen offer only outlines of figures. Thus, viewers learn to fill in the characters on the screen—in a sort of Gestalt process—to complete the communication process. Thus, television viewers must have high involvement with the televised message. If this is true, the overall impact of television on individuals should logically be stronger. With more types of information impacting on a viewer, television inundates individuals with visual and verbal information. As McLuhan said, "TV engages you." Television viewers must actively fill in details around televised information.

The more detailed newspaper accounts of news, on the other hand, require less involvement from the reader, according to McLuhan. There is less "filling in" for readers to do, because newspaper accounts address fewer senses.

In sharp contrast, Krugman (1965, 1966) proposed the exact opposite of McLuhan's involvement argument. Krugman, through a series of experiments examining how individuals learn from advertisements, found support for the notion that individuals have low involvement with the broadcast medium.

Krugman found that involvement with advertising was higher for magazines than for television. Individuals did still learn some information from television ads, but this learning was passive and "characterized by an absence of resistance to what is learned" (Krugman & Hartley, 1970, p. 184).

Singer (1980) similarly argued that humans are active processors of information. They make use of schemata, memory, and imagination to decide what information should be screened out and how to organize and use information.

According to Singer, the characteristics of the print media allow readers to take full advantage of this cognitive potential. Television, on the other hand, has much different characteristics. Its rapid pacing makes television such a powerful medium that the information-processing activities that typically occur in newspaper reading—use of schema, memory, and imagination—are unlikely to occur, or are impossible to be executed. Singer concluded that newspaper readers will always process information more thoughtfully and thoroughly than will television viewers. Singer argued that the amount of information presented on television can tax processing capacity to the extent that viewers may not encode important information, especially when the televised content is complex.

The pacing of information transmitted by television is not controlled by the viewer. Singer (1980) claimed that rapid pacing of complex television content means television stimuli are perceived as a blur, because viewers "cannot make precise discriminations between the sights and sounds presented" (p. 39).

Singer also claimed that rapid pacing contributes to passive information processing, because information is presented and changes so quickly that viewers have little time to process and comprehend the incoming information. Thus, because of this rapid pacing, viewers have no time to elaborate or integrate television content with information stored in memory. As a result, cognitive operations that help move information from short-term to long-term memory cannot occur, leading to difficulty later when an individual attempts to retrieve information.

Singer argued that this superficial processing of information from television leads to stronger recognition but poorer memory recall. Reading, on the other hand, allows for more focused concentration because readers are relatively free of other visual or auditory distractions.

The process of reading necessarily involves the execution of more complicated cognitive operations: reading and translating words, in addition to making use of imagination to "see and hear" action depicted in a text. Print "requires us to draw upon our own memories and fantasies, to take the time to try to follow the drift of the writer and to conjure up by ourselves exotic settings, sights and sounds suggested in the text" (Singer, 1980, p. 48).

Because television supplies audio and visual information, Singer argued, this same type of imagining does not occur, because television visuals substitute "an external image that one can passively lean on, rather than forming one's own" (p. 57). Thus, Singer claimed, reading "engages the brain in a more complex way than does the more passive television viewing" (p. 57).

Singer (1980) argued that reading advantages are particularly apparent when complex material is being processed because the printed word is "critical for adding a logical direction to thought" (p. 59). Therefore, he argued, reading is a superior medium for enhancing recall, particularly when comprehension requires logical organization and thought.

PROCESSING PRINT
AND BROADCAST INFORMATION

Several differences between television news and newspapers affect how individuals process information transmitted by the two media. Generally, television news has an advantage in that it is more visually oriented and it employs more types of information—that is, sight, sound, and motion. Newspapers, on the other hand, have an advantage in that individuals can process information contained in them when it is most convenient for the reader and at a pace that is best suited for the reader. Both of these factors are important.

The Case for Stronger Broadcast Effects

Some evidence exists that visual information is more easily processed than verbal information. Son, Reese, and Davie (1987), for example, found that visuals can improve recall of television news stories. Culbertson (1974) found that photographs were rated as more emotional than verbal descriptions, indicating that visual information has a more powerful emotional impact on individuals than the written word. Nickerson (1968) also found that visual information is processed more efficiently than verbal information.

The physiology of the processing of visual information offers one clue why visual information has such a strong effect on individuals. Lester (1995), in *Visual Communication: Images With Messages*, provided a detailed explanation of the physiological effects of visual information on individuals. As Lester noted, processing of visual information is extremely complex, involving several stages. The brain cells in the visual cortex respond to four elements: color, form, depth, and movement. Newspapers typically can utilize two of these elements: color and form. Television, however, can utilize three: color, form, and movement. Thus, adding the third element of movement to information further stimulates the visual cortex, which may in turn increase the overall effect of the information.

Moreover, television utilizes the additional element of sound. Of course, under certain circumstances, the use of visuals and sound can be a liability. Brosius, Donsbach, and Birk (1995), for example, found that routine pictures, those that are constantly used in news bulletins but do not correspond to the information in the story, do not facilitate the retention of news content. That is, pictures that do not depict the action of a news story precisely can interfere with the mental processing of information. The visuals and sound in newscasts need to be well coordinated to enhance information processing.

However, by employing sound, along with its other visual stimuli, television provides viewers with a greater variety of information than newspapers. Thus, because television has more types of information to process than newspapers, information from newscasts may have a more profound effect on viewers than newspapers have on readers.

Applying this notion to agenda setting, then, one would expect stronger agenda-setting effects for television than for newspapers. Because television provides color, form, and movement—all of which stimulate the visual cortex—as well as sound, television viewers are inundated with a much wider variety of information than are newspaper readers. This diverse information, therefore, should have a strong influence on viewers. In other words, the color, form, movement, and sound of television should provide viewers with information about issues that is more memorable than the information contained in newspapers. Television news, then, should have a stronger agenda-setting effect on individuals.

In addition, Neuman, Just, and Crigler (1992) found that audiences judged television coverage as more attention grabbing, interesting, personally relevant, emotionally involving, and surprising than newspaper reporting. They also found that individuals reported a greater sense of attachment to issues presented by television than to issues presented by newspapers. They concluded that the visual characteristics of television are one reason for these differences.

The Case for Stronger Print Effects

Although television inundates viewers with several types of information, newspapers nonetheless offer one significant advantage over the broadcast media—namely, newspapers are a more permanent source of information. Television provides viewers with sight, sound, and motion, but newspapers offer readers a source of news that is readily available for use at any time of day. The permanency of newspapers is important for two reasons:

1. Readers can process information contained in newspapers at their own pace. Few individuals tape news broadcasts. Thus, viewers must watch and process the evening news while it is being broadcast. If a news segment is paced too quickly, a viewer may not have time to digest and process the information contained within it. A reader, on the other hand, can read a story, stop, contemplate the significance, and return to the story for additional information. If readers want to stop and contemplate the significance of a story, they can do so at their own pace.

Thus, whereas television news may be a "blur," individuals control the pacing of information when reading newspapers. With the ability to stop and contemplate the full significance of a story, an individual should be more strongly influenced by newspaper content than by television content. Thus, newspapers should produce stronger agenda-setting effects than television.

2. Readers can return to newspapers at more than one point in time. Again, viewers must watch and process information from the evening news only while it is being broadcast. If a viewer is distracted, even for just a moment, he or she cannot return to the broadcast at a later time to review the story. The missed segment is gone forever. Readers, however, can skip stories or even entire sections and return to them whenever they want.

Because the information contained in television news stories has only one chance at influencing viewers, newspapers have the potential to provide readers with an agenda of issues that is much more easily accessible. Thus, again, we would assume that newspapers would produce stronger agenda-setting effects on individuals than would television newscasts.

Research suggests these two factors are significant advantages in the agenda setting process.

Newspaper research suggests that readers read the newspaper at various times during the day—whenever it is convenient for them (see Stone, 1987). Because readers read the news when they want to, at the pace they want to, the information contained in the newspaper may have a more powerful effect than television news.

Television research suggests that, although viewers now have more potential news sources than ever before (CNN, Headline News), most continue to view the evening news at traditional times. Thus, viewers demonstrate little control over when they watch the news or how the news is paced. Broadcast news, then, may have less of an effect on individuals than the print media.

The Case for Similar Effects

Of course, a third possibility is plausible—namely, that print and broadcast media produce similar agenda-setting effects.

Indeed, both print and broadcast media do cover the news of the day. Because many—if not most—print and broadcast journalists are products of journalism programs, they should have similar concepts of what constitutes news. Thus, because of the socialization of the news (see McCombs, 1987), we could assume that the news products of the print and broadcast media should be similar.

Moreover, certain media do play a role as agenda setters for other media. As Winter and Eyal (1981) noted, the *New York Times* often sets the national issue agenda that other media—both print and broadcast—follow.

The processing of information across the two media may be similar as well. Meadowcroft and Olson (1995) found no differences in knowledge recall regardless of whether the information was printed and read or broadcast and viewed. Thus, the possibility exists that newscasts and newspaper coverage will function similarly in the agenda-setting process.

THE NATURE OF NEWS IN THE PRINT
AND BROADCAST MEDIA

Previous research, then, is inconclusive regarding the processing of information among print and broadcast news consumers. A case can be made that television news should be more efficient in transmitting information, that newspapers should be more efficient in transmitting information, or that there is no difference between television and newspapers.

Beyond the type of processing involved by print and broadcast news users is the question of the nature of the news in the two media. The types of stories reported in newspapers and on network news are vastly different.

Newspapers have several advantages over television news, as McClure and Patterson (1976) argued. Newspapers can clearly demonstrate the significance they attach to a given story through traditional means of indicating emphasis and significance. Readers, for example, know that long stories are more important than short stories. Similarly, readers understand that other factors indicate the relative importance of stories: stories with pictures versus stories without pictures; large headlines versus small headlines; front page versus back page; above the fold versus below the fold. Thus, the print medium gives readers a strong, lasting visual cataloging of the news.

Television news, according McClure and Patterson (1976), gives limited coverage to a large number of stories, rather than providing in-depth reports, as newspapers do. Newscasts provide "little hard issue content, little information about the positions of candidates and almost no background or contextual information to give the voter perspective" (pp. 25–26).

True, the lead story on a network news broadcast gives a strong indication to viewers that the issue covered in the story is important. However, because of the rapid pace of the telecast, viewers likely have a difficult time differentiating between stories beyond the lead story. For example, is the third story, which might be only 20 seconds long, more important than the fifth story, which might be 2 minutes long? From a news director's standpoint, yes; but the evidence from a news consumer's standpoint is less clear.

Furthermore, what about the closing story, which could involve an in-depth analysis that might last 4 or 5 minutes? Certainly, a news consumer would believe that an issue addressed in such a fashion must be highly important. However, would viewers believe that an issue touched on earlier in a broadcast is more important? Not necessarily.

Of course, this does not mean that the broadcast medium is ineffectual in the agenda-setting process. McClure and Patterson (1976) noted that television can have a strong impact in some instances. For example, if television news breaks into regular entertainment programming, this break in routine can greatly affect viewers. Television, however, is dependent upon exciting and directly relevant visual presentations.

McCombs (1977b) similarly argued that the medium shapes the message. McCombs believed that newspapers perform an initiating role in the public opinion process. Because newspapers have greater "channel capacity" with their dozens of pages in contrast to a half-hour for television news presentations, newspapers can pick up public issues earlier than television. Occasionally, an emerging issue might receive coverage on the back pages of a newspaper. Television news, however, is more like the front page. "Only when issues have achieved prominence are they likely to rate TV news time or front page space" (McCombs, 1977b, p. 98).Thus, newspapers play an important role early in an issue's life cycle because of their ability to begin tracking and reporting public issues earlier than television.

Television, on the other hand, plays a different role in the agenda-setting process. Television has a more universal appeal, drawing a larger audience than newspapers because of its broad appeal. Thus, television makes politics salient to many members of society who are not reached by newspapers.

AGENDA SETTING AND THE MEDIA

The preceding discussion leads to the obvious and logical conclusion that individuals learn information from television and newspapers in vastly different ways. Thus, television and newspapers should play different roles in the agenda-setting process. Few agenda-setting researchers, however, have examined differences between media.

McClure and Patterson (1976), in the most comprehensive study examining contrasts across media, discovered several differences between print and broadcast media. In their study conducted during the 1972 election, they found that heavy television news viewers on the whole were not more susceptible to agenda-setting effects than light viewers. On the other hand, newspaper exposure was strongly related to agenda-setting effects. Thus, they concluded that television news "is not an efficient communicator of everyday political information" (p. 25).

Tipton, Haney, and Baseheart (1975) also found supporting evidence that newspapers correlate better than television with voter agendas. In their study of a local election, they found an agenda-setting effect for area newspapers but not for television and concluded that television news may actually have little effect on focusing public attention on issues in local election campaigns

McCombs (1977b) argued that television news might have a stronger short-term impact, but newspaper content may have a more consistent effect across longer periods of time. He concluded that the broadcast media are better at adjusting their agenda to fit the agenda of their audience. Moreover, data from the classic Charlotte study of the 1972 election suggest a two-stage agenda-setting process. Newspapers acted alone as an agenda-setting influence early in the 1972 campaign. However, as the campaign period progressed, newspapers shared their agenda-setting influence with television. Thus, newspapers may have a stronger long-term effect, with broadcast news having a stronger effect in the short term.

Zucker (1978), on the other hand, argued that at the national level, the public may be more influenced by the three networks' newscasts than by newspapers because of television's wider accessibility. Differences between newspapers and television, however, should extend far beyond mere accessibility. Differences should also exist because of the different processing necessary to make sense of the issue information transmitted by newspapers and television.

EVIDENCE OF AGENDA-SETTING DIFFERENCES ACROSS MEDIA

As the preceding discussion has shown, several differences exist in both the nature of the news product provided by the print and broadcast media and the type of information processing that consumers of the two media undergo.

Of concern here is an examination of differences in agenda-setting effects across the print and broadcast media. If the processing of issue information differs across the two media, a comparison of the two media should uncover several differences in agenda-setting effects. Three potential differences are discussed here.

1. The magnitude of agenda-setting effects. Previous research suggests that newspapers have a stronger agenda-setting influence on individuals than television (McClure & Patterson, 1976; Tipton et al., 1975). Thus, we would expect a comparison of print and broadcast media to reveal a stronger agenda-setting effect for newspapers than for television.

2. The optimal time lag. Previous research suggests that television may have a stronger initial agenda-setting effect, but that newspapers will have a stronger long-term effect (McCombs, 1977b). Thus, we would expect agenda-setting effects to appear more quickly for television than for newspapers.

3. Decay of agenda-setting effects. Because previous research suggests that individuals are more active processors of newspaper information than television information (Salomon, 1979; Singer, 1980), we would expect that the agenda-setting effects will decay much more slowly for newspapers than for television because the active processing of information should enhance long-term recall.

These are important questions for agenda-setting research.

First, an examination of differences across print and broadcast media should provide insights into how individuals learn about important issues based on their involvement in the mental processing of issue information. If newspapers demand higher involvement from readers, the magnitude of agenda-setting effects may be higher as well. Thus, the information processing inherent in the agenda-setting process is worthy of further investigation.

Second, because information processing is potentially different for broadcast and print media, the time-lag for agenda-setting effects to occur likely will differ also. Thus, an examination of differences across media will be important for agenda-setting researchers.

The time frame is one of the most important considerations agenda-setting researchers must address in their analyses. A message transmitted through the news media needs some sort of repetition before it can fully influence an individual. Determining the optimal time lag for this repetition of issue information to have the greatest magnitude of influence is a key consideration.

Chaffee (1972) argued that time lag selection is especially important in agenda-setting research because studies in this area investigate a causal hypothesis. A time lag that is too short will not capture the causal relationship, Chaffee argued, but a time lag that is too long is also a serious matter because "there is always the danger that a causal effect will 'dissipate' over time if the researcher waits too long to measure it" (p. 8).

Salwen (1988) believed the time lag question is important because researchers need to confine their measures of media coverage to as short a time period as possible because "any time discrepancies in the measurement of the public agenda may affect the public's evaluations of issue salience" (p. 101).

Finally, memory decay also is an important consideration across the two media. Watt, Mazza, and Snyder (1993) found agenda-setting effects varied across different issues, but these same effects could also vary across media. Tracing the time frame when the repetition of news reports no longer has an influence on individuals would provide important guidelines for future agenda-setting researchers.

The results presented here come from five studies that specifically dealt with the time lag question in agenda setting. Obviously, other studies have produced findings that would be pertinent here, but these five studies offer excellent opportunities to compare media differences because of their comparable methodologies. In brief, the studies are:

- Winter and Eyal (1981), which examined the *New York Times*. This longitudinal study concentrated on one issue (civil rights) across 22 years.
- Zucker (1978), which examined the three national networks. This longitudinal study compared the agenda-setting process across six individual issues over 8 years.
- Salwen (1988), which examined three local and regional newspapers. This study again concentrated on one issue (the environment), but investigated the agenda-setting process for subissues, such as water pollution and air pollution. This study was a three-wave panel survey, with media coverage analyzed for 239 days.
- Wanta and Hu (1994), which examined five news media. This cross-sectional study used an index of issue concerns and compared these concerns with coverage in a regional newspaper, a local newspaper, a national network newscast, a local newscast, and a national news magazine.

- Wanta and Roy (1995), which examined three news media. This cross sectional study also used an index of issue concerns and compared these concerns with coverage in a national newscast, a local newscast and a local newspaper. One other methodological difference should be noted: This study took into consideration memory decay. The issue coverage was weighted by the distance in time from the survey period. Thus, coverage just prior to the survey period was weighted more heavily than coverage months before the survey period.

The results of the five studies are compared in Table 10.1.

STRENGTH OF AGENDA-SETTING EFFECTS

All five studies found strong support for the agenda-setting hypothesis. Correlations varied from $r = .58$ to a near-perfect correlation of $r = .98$. The strongest correlation found by Winter and Eyal (1981) was .71. The largest correlation in Salwen's (1988) study was .98. Zucker (1978) found a correlation of .80 for one of his issues. The median correlations were .68 for Winter and Eyal, .76 for Salwen, and .59 for Zucker.

In the Wanta and Hu (1994) study, the largest correlation was produced by the national network newscast (.92), followed by the local newscast (.91), the regional newspaper (.88), and the local newspaper (.60). The news magazine produced the weakest agenda-setting effect correlation (.58). The median correlations were .68 for the national newscast, .67 for the local newscast, .73 for the regional newspaper, .57 for the local newspaper, and .53 for the news magazine.

Wanta and Roy (1995) found the strongest correlation for the local newspaper (.81). The national network newscast (.68) and local newscast (.67) produced very similar results. The median correlations were .54 for the local newspaper, .64 for the national newscast and .53 for the local newscast.

Taken as a whole, the results of these studies are inconclusive. The strongest correlation was produced by Salwen's regional newspapers and the weakest by Wanta and Hu's local newspaper and national news magazine. The local newspaper also produced the strongest correlation in the Wanta and Roy (1995) study. However, newscasts, both national and local, produced correlations larger than those produced by newspapers in the Wanta and Hu (1994) study. Thus, no clear trend emerges from the comparison of the studies on the magnitude of agenda-setting effects across media.

Time Lag

Winter and Eyal (1981) found that the optimal time lag for agenda-setting effects to occur for the *New York Times* was 4 to 6 weeks. According to Salwen

TABLE 10.1
Comparisons of Results of Five Studies

Study	News Medium	Largest Correlation	Optimal Time Lag	Effects Decay	Lag From Peak to Decay
Winter & Eyal (1981)	*New York Times*	.71	4 to 6 weeks	3rd month	2 months
Zucker (1978)	Network Newscasts	.80	2 to 4 weeks	suggests 6 weeks	2 to 4 weeks
Salwen (1988)	3 local newspapers	.98	7 to 10 weeks	25 weeks	18 weeks after peak
Wanta & Hu (1994)	National newscast	.92	1 week	8 weeks	7 weeks after peak
	Local newscast	.91	2 weeks	12 weeks	10 weeks after peak
	Regional newspaper	.88	3 weeks	26 weeks	more than 22 weeks
	Local newspapers	.60	4 weeks	26 weeks	more than 22 weeks
	Newsweek	.58	8 weeks	26 weeks	more than 22 weeks
Wanta & Roy (1995)	National newscast	.68	4 to 5 days	14 days	10 days after peak
	Local newscast	.67	6 to 7 days	14 days	7 to 8 days after peak
	Local newspaper	.81	15 days	28 days	13 days after peak

149

(1988), the optimal time lag for three regional newspapers was 7 to 10 weeks. Zucker's (1978) study found the optimal time lag for network news was 2 to 6 weeks.

Results from Wanta and Hu (1994) show the national newscast had the shortest time lag (1 week), followed by the local newscast (2 weeks), the regional newspaper (3 weeks), and the local newspaper (4 weeks). The national news magazine's optimal time lag was 8 weeks.

The optimal time lags found by Wanta and Roy (1995) were 4 to 5 days for national newscasts, 6 to 7 days for the local newscast, and 15 days for the local newspaper.

Overall, then, the optimal time lags varied greatly—from 4 or 5 days to 8 or 10 weeks. One trend was constant, however: National newscasts produced agenda-setting effects much earlier than newspapers. National media also appear to have shorter time lags than local or regional media.

Accumulated Learning and Decay of Effects

The correlations in Winter and Eyal (1981) show a significant drop off during the third month. Thus, the agenda-setting effects shown in the first 4 to 6 weeks dissipated 2 months after their peak.

The correlations in Salwen, although reaching the $p < .001$ level in Week 7, dropped to the $p < .01$ level at Week 25. Thus, the agenda-setting effects apparent in Week 7 dropped a level 18 weeks later.

The time period for agenda-setting effects to decay was not readily apparent in the Zucker (1978) study. Zucker did conclude, however, that "news of more than six weeks ago is considered old or is already forgotten" (p. 238). Thus, he argued that agenda-setting effects decay an extremely short time after peaking.

Four of the media in the Wanta and Hu (1994) study did not drop below the $p < .05$ statistical level in any of the 26 weeks examined. However, the national network newscasts (in Week 8), and the local newscasts (in Week 12) dropped from the $p < .001$ level to the $p < .01$ level. The regional paper did not drop below the $p < .001$ level in the 26 weeks examined. The local newspaper, which only reached the $p < .05$ level, did not drop below this level throughout the entire study. Thus, the lags from the strongest correlations to the points at which the correlations dropped a level were 7 weeks for the national newscasts, 10 weeks for the local newscasts, and more than 22 weeks for both the regional and local newspapers.

Because the Wanta and Roy (1995) study took into account memory decay, their results were substantially different from the other studies cited. They found agenda-setting effects decayed after 14 days for the national newscasts, 14 days for the local newscasts, and 28 days for the local newspapers. Thus, the time periods between the optimal time lag for agenda-setting effects to occur and for the agenda-setting effects to disappear were 10 days for national newscasts, 7 to 8 days for local newscasts, and 13 days for local newspapers.

Overall, then, another consistent trend emerged. Agenda-setting effects for newspapers decayed much more slowly than agenda-setting effects for the newscasts.

FINAL COMMENTS

As the studies mentioned here demonstrate, the agenda-setting process is not uniform across different news media. Broadcast media produce agenda-setting effects earlier than the print media. Agenda-setting effects, however, decay much more slowly for newspapers than for newscasts. The magnitude of the agenda-setting effect across media is not clear.

The trends in these studies also offer some explanations for previous research findings. For example, perhaps the limited support for an agenda-setting effect by television found by Tipton et al. (1975) and McClure and Patterson (1976) could be due to the fact that the researchers were examining a time frame that was too long for the optimal agenda-setting effect to occur. Perhaps the agenda-setting effect occurs relatively quickly—in a week or so—and dissipates shortly thereafter. Thus, it was not so much that television has a weaker agenda-setting effect than newspapers in these studies, but the time period used by previous researchers was too long. This is a methodological question that certainly can be addressed in future studies through the use of a more appropriate time lag.

The differences found for the decay of agenda-setting effects were expected based on previous research dealing with information recall research. Newspaper reading requires more active and complex processing of information, which aids long-term memory recall. Thus, the active processing of newspaper information enhances recall of the social learning of issue concerns that is the basis of the agenda-setting process. Individuals, then, retain information about important issues for longer periods of time if they gained this information through the print media.

The results of the strength of agenda-setting effects, on the other hand, were inconclusive. Two explanations are plausible here. First, perhaps it is as Meadowcroft and Olson (1995) found: Learning of information is very similar across print and broadcast presentations. Thus, individuals did not learn more from newspapers than they did from television; they just learned the issue information faster from television and recalled the issue information for longer periods from newspapers.

Second, the similar magnitude of agenda-setting effects could be due to the fact that the studies examined here are not very comparable because of their differing methodologies. Indeed, the five studies discussed here employed single-issue, multiple-issue and issue concern index designs. They employed longitudinal and cross sectional surveys. The methodological differences, then, may have influenced the measurement of the agenda-setting effect. Still, all were concerned with the temporal aspects of agenda setting and allowed for a relatively accurate assessment of the trends in the agenda setting process.

III

NEWS AGENDAS
AND SOCIAL SYSTEMS

11

Media Agenda Setting and Press Performance: *A Social System Approach for Building Theory*

Dominic L. Lasorsa

In democracies, the decisions of individual reporters and editors combine to create media content (newspapers, newscasts) and somehow these psychological processes of individual media practitioners converge to create a sociological product, the media agenda. The responses of individual community members to those media products work together to create public concern, and somehow these psychological processes of individual community members converge to create another sociological product, the public agenda. If we are to get closer to a general understanding of how media agenda setting works and of its political importance to society, we need to understand how the psychological activities of individuals generate these sociological outcomes. We need to examine how the media claim to operate in different types of societies and how the media actually do operate in different types of societies, as well as how audiences claim to react to those operations and how audiences actually do react to them. We must be prepared to deal with both sociological and psychological theory, and with both theory and practice.

One way to get closer to a general theory of media agenda setting is to view agenda setting as a sociological process that incorporates psychological sub-processes. This view of agenda setting combines what we know about how the media operate in society (from sociological theory) and what we know about how media producers and consumers process information (from psychological theory). According to this view, agenda setting operates at the level of the community, but to understand it we need to examine some of what goes on within individuals. In other words, the effect of agenda setting is felt on the community as a whole, but some of the important steps leading up to the effect occur within the minds of individuals.

In every community, including those predating mass media, methods are devised by which the community decides which concerns are to be addressed. If the community is unable to find efficient mechanisms for doing this, it cannot survive for long. Methods for deciding which problems need attention have become more sophisticated, and one method—polling—has evolved into an industry itself. Regardless of how technologically advanced such methods become, in some societies the process of deciding to which problematic stimuli to react may still be simple and uncomplicated. In a dictatorship it may not be necessary to know much about what problems the rank-and-file members of the society think are important. Such input may even be undesirable (from the point of view of the dictator). On the other hand, if a community is structured such that the thinking of the general populace does matter—that is, if it is a relatively democratic state—then the processes by which community members decide which problems need to be addressed may be important to the survival of that community. In most modern democracies, the mass media produce products for the community that somehow influence the public's notions about which issues are more important than others. That is the agenda-setting hypothesis.

Precisely how these signals influence audience members is not clear. To understand the process of agenda setting requires us to understand how individual community members make sense of media products. It should be recognized that media practitioners are individual community members, too, and that unless we can uncover some reason why media practitioners should be immune somehow to the effects of the products they create, they too will be affected by the psychological subprocesses that affect other community members. Furthermore, when individual media practitioners help generate the media agenda they too are engaging in certain psychological subprocesses unique to their profession. In this view of agenda setting, psychological subprocesses occur at both ends of the agenda-setting process, among those producing media messages and those consuming them. These psychological subprocesses need to be taken into account when trying to explain how the media agenda and the public agenda are created in a society, and how one influences the other.

THORNY QUESTIONS:
COMMUNICATION IN A DEMOCRACY

We begin with the thorny question of how to regulate communication in a democratic society. Then we briefly compare and contrast the major ways that societies have chosen to think about regulation—that is, their normative theories of mass communication. We then attempt to move closer to reality by examining the actual functions that the media may serve in society. Putting these ideas together, we attempt to show how agenda setting is an important media function, particularly in democratic societies.

When democracy was still a relatively new idea, many great thinkers grappled with the practical question of what laws and regulations to enforce regarding the transmission of messages from one person to another. In describing the necessary conditions for the good state, Plato (370 B.C.) showed his concern for the need of a mechanism to regulate communication in society: "Then shall we simply allow our children to listen to any stories that anyone happens to make up, and so receive into their minds ideas often the very opposite of those we shall think they ought to have when they are grown up? . . . It seems, then, our first business will be to supervise the making of fables and legends, rejecting all which are unsatisfactory."

Democratic theory as espoused by the ancient Greeks is clear about its essential requirements. Primary among these is the need for an "informed" electorate, a public of adults capable of governing itself because it knows enough about what can be done and, ultimately, what to do. The ancient Greeks would marvel at the methods for communicating that are available 23 centuries after Plato's death, but they would understand the discomfort of the seemingly paradoxical desire of wanting to allow people to communicate freely but only within limits (Corbett, 1991). Democracy has such a mass appeal that even those who do not desire to practice it may identify with it. The Somali Democratic Republic, for example, was ruled for 22 years by dictator Mohammed Siad Barre, who rose to power in a military coup in 1969. After Barre was deposed and fled into exile in 1991, more than half a million Somalis starved to death as warring clans struggled for power in this "democratic republic" (Schwab, 1995). A better way to tell the difference between democratic and undemocratic regimes is to examine how they behave, not what they call themselves. Especially enlightening is a careful examination of how the society regulates communication among its members.

This is easier said than done. The regulation of communication in any society may be complex and involve both overt laws and covert actions. Take the case of comic book publishers, artists, and writers in the 1950s in the United States. They were forced to conform to a capricious industry-devised code of content or lose their ability to have their comics distributed by wholesalers to stores. Described as the comics industry cleaning itself, the actions were not self-censorship at all. One of the targeted publishers, William Gaines, said, "I will no longer publish horror and crime comics because of a premise—that has never been proved—that they stimulate juvenile delinquency. We are not doing it so much for business reasons as because this seems to be what American parents want, and the parents should be served." Although Gaines implied that he chose to go along with most of the major comic book publishers, later he explained what really took place: "I later found out that it was because the word was passed by the wholesalers, 'Get 'im!' So they got me. . . . I'd been told that if I continued publishing my magazines, no one would handle them. I had no choice" (Savage, 1990, p. 98). This demonstrates the complexity and subtlety of the regulation of communication in society and the difficulty we may have in uncovering and understanding it. It also shows how an agenda can be limited, even in democratic society.

COMMUNICATION AND IDEOLOGY: HOW MEDIA SHOULD BE

In the mid-1950s, about the same time that Wertham (1954) was leading the crusade against comics with his influential book *The Seduction of the Innocent,* a group of four other scholars of mass communication published *Four Theories of the Press,* in which they attempted to show that there were four basic ways that the mass media operate in society. They called them the authoritarian theory, the libertarian theory, the Soviet-totalitarian theory, and the social responsibility theory (Siebert, Peterson, & Schramm, 1956). In an *authoritarian* society, the mass media are supposed to serve the ruler. Messages that support the ruler are transmitted, and those that oppose the ruler are not. Machiavelli (1532/1995) encapsulated the meaning of the authoritarian theory of the press when he instructed leaders of state: "A prudent prince cannot and should not keep his word when to do so would go against his interest" (p. 18).

In a *Soviet-totalitarian* type society, the mass media are supposed to serve the state. Messages that support the state are transmitted, and those that oppose the state are not. Lenin (cited in Seldes, 1967, p. 768) encapsulated the meaning of the Soviet-totalitarian theory of the press when he said, "The press should be not only a collective propagandist and a collective agitator, but also a collective organizer of the masses." In a *libertarian* society, the mass media are supposed to serve as a plane of discussion on which ideas battle for acceptance. The superior message will win adherents and the idea it defeats will lose support. Milton (cited in Seldes, 1967, p. 345) encapsulated the meaning of the libertarian theory of the press when he said, "Let her (Truth) and Falsehood grapple: whoever knew Truth put the worst in a free and open encounter?"

In a *socially responsible* society, the mass media are supposed to ensure that all members of society have access to the plane of discussion. The superior message, even if held by someone without much power, will win adherents and the idea it bests, even if it is held by someone with much power, will lose support. The Commission on Freedom of the Press (1947) encapsulated the meaning of this theory when it said of the press: "It must be accountable to society for meeting the public need and for maintaining the rights of citizens and the almost forgotten right of speakers who have no press. It must know that its faults and errors have ceased to be private vagaries and have become public dangers" (p. 131).

The approach taken by Siebert et al. (1956) to the understanding of how communication works in different types of societies is helpful in its attempt to focus on how societies intend to use mass media in different ways, but it also obscures some of the commonalities across these different systems. These normative theories of the press may tell us how the mass media should operate in society but do not tell us how the mass media actually do operate. As Altschull (1984) pointed out, regardless of how press systems theoretically work, in practice all press systems—more or less—are agents of those in power, with implications for the agenda-setting power of the press.

NEW MEDIA STIR CONCERNS ABOUT EFFECTS

Concerns about the effects of the mass media on society and its members rise and fall over time and from place to place, but one would be hard pressed to find a time and place when mass media operations have not been worrisome to at least some members of society. The introduction of a major new mass communication technology in society almost always raises concerns and hopes about that technology. From the printing of books to the Internet, history is filled with guesses about the effects of the introduction of a new technology. Books, magazines, radio, movies, comics, television, and video games all have been charged with changing society and its members, often negatively. Sometimes the introduction of a new technology has an effect on one society much different from its effect on another society. Copy machines changed the way business was conducted in the United States, but copy machines were used in the Soviet Union to reproduce underground newspapers called *samizdat*, which—because they were so difficult to control—helped topple the government. Audiotapes circulated in Iran before the revolution there.

Because it is difficult to imagine how a new technology will be used, its introduction always poses opportunities and risks. The mass-produced automobile was viewed as an extension of existing transportation technologies, the "horseless carriage." Who, for example, would have imagined that the automobile would result in drive-in theaters, where young adults could escape the control of their parents. The automobile may not have caused the sexual revolution, but it certainly contributed to it. The automobile proved to be more than a carriage without horses, just as television proved to be more than radio with pictures. No one can know for sure how new media will change what "old" audiences will think, feel, and do. During the first half of the 20th century, the power of radio to affect was demonstrated time and again. The amazing success of advertising on radio, although making many quite happy and rich, made others concerned—and not rich. The panic created by "The War of the Worlds" broadcast in 1938, Franklin D. Roosevelt's "fireside chats" in the United States, and Adolph Hitler's equally effective use of radio in Germany before and during World War II convincingly demonstrated the power of radio over its audiences (Severin & Tankard, 1992).

VOTING STUDIES USHER IN LIMITED
EFFECTS ERA

In this early period, Lazarsfeld and his colleagues decided to study the effects of the mass media on voting. They studied the U.S. presidential elections of 1940 (Lazarsfeld, Berelson, & Gaudet, 1948), 1944 and 1948 (Berelson, Lazarsfeld, & McPhee, 1954). They were surprised to find that the mass media seemed to have little direct effect on people. Their work ushered in the "limited effects" era that guided mass communication research for years (Klapper, 1960).Yet, even as concerns about the effects of the mass media waned during this period, some were acutely unsatisfied. Later researchers argued that the findings might have been relevant in the 1940s but that times had changed. They argued that television, which was not a factor in the 1940s elections, has since become a major political force. In the 1940s, those who were not interested in politics could escape mass political communications more easily than they could in the era of television. According to this reasoning, selective exposure to mass media political information, which could have limited the effects of the mass media in the 1940s, would be much more difficult to overcome in the TV world. Other researchers argued that the methods used by Lazarsfeld and his colleagues were not designed well enough to uncover media effects. Still others argued that the original results did show media effects on certain subgroups or at certain critical times during the campaign but that these results were lost or neglected in the overall findings (Chaffee, 1975). These arguments did make it easier to bridge the gap between the scientific findings and people's gut feelings, but the 1940s election studies were troublesome for a whole generation of mass communication scholars whose instincts and experiences seemed to be telling them one thing while theory and research seemed to be telling them something else. How could such a powerful set of agenda issues have so little effect?

ATTENTION SHIFTS FROM ATTITUDINAL
TO COGNITIVE EFFECTS

Meanwhile, another phenomenon resulted in a breakthrough in the thinking about media effects. Academic departments in mass communication and, in particular, journalism were developing, and they accepted into their graduate programs promising young journalists interested in studying the industry with which they were most familiar. Whereas the major centers for the study of psychology and sociology were accepting the limited effects conclusions and moving on to what appeared to be more promising areas of research, these mass communication scholars were less accepting of the explanations for limited effects—personal influence, group dynamics, selective exposure, and reinforcement. Social psychologists and others concluded that the field of mass communication was no place to tarry, but these journalists turned scholars believed that the mass media—evidence notwithstanding—were too important to ignore.

One of the first major contributions of this new group of researchers was to redirect attention away from the persuasive effects of the mass media to cognitive effects. Researchers such as Chaffee and McCombs, who were trained in the social psychological traditions at Stanford University, were unsatisfied with a preoccupation with attitudinal effects. They reasoned that the primary purpose of the mass media is to provide information, not influence people's attitudes or behavior. They and other scholars, particularly those at the University of Wisconsin and the University of Minnesota, began to carefully consider the cognitive effects of the media.

One of the first results of this new way of thinking was McCombs and Shaw's (1972) modern formulation of the agenda-setting phenomenon. These scholars argued that the mass media, through their news coverage, convey to their audiences information about which political issues are most important. The press agenda influences the public agenda. As Cohen (1963) said of the press: "It may not be successful much of the time in telling people what to think, but it is stunningly successful in telling its readers what to think about" (p. 13). At a simple cognitive level, the press agenda did matter.

McCombs and Shaw referred to this media effect as a "function" of the press. It is ironic that although agenda setting has subsequently captured the attention of a whole generation of mass communication scholars and has become one of the most researched concepts in mass communication history, the original notion of agenda setting as a function has not been much developed. Much of the meaning of agenda setting as a political process is tied to this view of agenda setting as a function of the press.

FUNCTIONS OF THE MEDIA IN SOCIETY

All press systems can be examined for the ways and the extent to which they fulfill a function. Wright (1959) identified one important function of the mass media: entertainment. The mass media provide their audiences with a wide array of dramatic and comedic messages. Such media content may have political effects, but content often lacks much direct political relevancy. A considerable amount of mass media content seems to serve mainly the purpose of amusing the audience. Lasswell (1948) identified other important functions of the mass media. The mass media transmit the social heritage from one generation to the next. They do this by telling stories about holidays, holy days, historical figures, and cultural events that keep our social memories alive. Through such media content, audiences learn and rehearse the traditions that make us what we are, whoever we are. Another major function of the mass media is to survey the environment for their audiences. As the extension of our senses, the media convey to us what is going on in places beyond our touch, sight, hearing, smell, and taste. The media inform us about how safe, for example, is the world, continent, nation, region, state, county, city, village, neighborhood, family, and self. The media give their audiences the news, all the relevant facts they can muster—and find space for. Surveillance is regarded as the reporting function of the mass media.

Lasswell also cited as a major function of the mass media the correlation of the parts of society in responding to the environment. By disseminating commentaries, editorials, news analyses, and other interpretations of the news, the media tell their audiences how to react to what is going on around them. Correlation is often regarded as the editorializing function of the mass media. For Lasswell and others, the press agenda was related to social functioning.

Where Agenda Setting Fits In

Although many media practitioners spend much or all of their time engaged in the entertainment and surveillance functions of the media, media scholars have given much attention to the correlation function of the media, perhaps because they were especially concerned about deliberate attempts to persuade. As performers tried to entertain their audiences and as journalists informed their audiences, communication scholars studied the persuasive effects of the media. This was because much of the fear about the media concerned their ability to change people's minds and behaviors, as opposed to informing or amusing them. Researchers found few media effects on attitudes and behaviors, mainly because there are other powerful forces at work to neutralize the media. The media in the United States and other researched countries were found to do a relatively poor job overall of persuading their audiences, of making them take position X on issue Y. When we shifted attention to the surveillance function of the media, their informing role, we began to find greater media effects.

Somewhere between the function of informing (reporting the facts) and persuading (selecting certain facts that support a particular argument) is an area in which we find the agenda-setting role of the press. Although the media profess to publish all the news of the day, audiences know that the media do not; the media are selective. There are droughts and floods, warfare, and who knows what else going on around the world that the mass media are not covering. We are not aware of these events as a result. Audiences know this, and audiences also know that among all the news that gets reported, the media give more attention to some issues and events than to others. From this awareness of reality and knowledge of cues, the audience senses what issues the media consider to be most important, and that realization powerfully affects them. Unless the audience member already has other sources of information about the issue, he or she is likely to add a prominent media issue to the agenda of his or her concerns, thereby pushing out some other previously important issue, or to move such an issue lower on the agenda. No one can consider too many issues at one time.

Even though many researchers seem to have abandoned the original notion of agenda setting as a function, the idea remains thought provoking and may lead us closer to a theory of agenda setting—that is, to a full explanation of how the process works. Shaw and Martin (1992) found that very different types of people who share a medium also share a media agenda. This view of agenda setting helps resolve one of the nagging puzzles of agenda setting. For years, scholars have been grappling with the unsatisfying categorizing of agenda setting as a purely cognitive effect, some arguing that it clearly also has an attitudinal component. The clear distinction that Cohen (1963) made between what we think (attitudes) and what we think about (cognition) has always seemed too clear. The journalist surveys the environment and reports the news as best he or she can to the audience. The journalist selects certain of these facts and organizes them into an argument to inform or to persuade the audience. Are there not properties shared in these two activities that newsrooms try hard to separate?

In most U.S. newsrooms, attempts are made to keep these operations as distinct as possible so that the audience will believe that the editorial operations are not seriously affected by the advertising sector. For example, efforts are made to label advertising so that audiences can tell the difference between advertising and the editorial side of the operation. Some advertisers attempt to make their advertising seem like editorial content by presenting it in the format that editorial content traditionally takes. Of course, the law requires advertising to be so labeled, even if with small type.

U.S. newsrooms (outside the advertising sector) generally are concerned with two major functions: surveillance and correlation. Editors and reporters do the jobs of conveying to us what is going on out there (the reporting function) and of interpreting that (the editorial function, using the term in its more specific sense). Because U.S. journalism is based on the premise that news should be unaffected by outside forces, newsrooms try to protect their credibility by separating surveillance functions from correlation ones. As with advertising and editorial content, efforts are made to label the products of these two functions—news versus editorial—so that audiences will not confuse the two. But the media may perform another important sociopolitical function, one that is not deliberate and planned. We call it agenda setting.

CONDITIONS FOR AN AGENDA SETTING EFFECT

If this view of agenda setting is correct, then certain conditions need to hold. A first step toward strengthening the theory is to provide evidence supporting these conditions, or at least to suggest ways to gather such evidence where none now exists. One of the major assumptions of this view of agenda setting is that in a democratic society there is such a thing as a media agenda that has a general sociological effect across society. If we find that the mass media in a community have widely different agendas of issues, then that would seriously challenge the notion of an agenda-setting effect across society. Under such conditions one should expect effects to be audience specific. A media agenda would affect mostly its own audience and might be canceled out by the effects of a different media agenda attended to by the same audience member. The more unified the media products are in creating the agenda across the community, the greater we should expect agenda-setting effects to be across the community. Therefore, within a democratic community at any one time we should expect to find rather high consistency across the various media agendas as they converge to form an overall media agenda for that community. In fulfilling their surveillance functions, the media should agree generally about what is happening and what deserves the most attention now.

At the same time, however, we should not expect to find that the media agree nearly as much about how we should respond to those issues; that is, what position to take on each issue. In fulfilling their correlation functions, the media should not agree generally about how the public should respond to what is happening. This is another way of saying that the mass media should do a relatively good job of telling us what to think about, but not what to think.

How well do the media mirror this view of agenda setting? Evidence suggests that in the United States the news media agree on what events and issues deserve our attention (the media agenda), but they do not agree on how we should react to these events and issues (the correlating of the parts of society in their response to these stimuli). In 1986, an attempt was made to trace over time the agendas of four different news media and to see how consistent they were with each other (Lasorsa & Wanta, 1990). Compared were the *New York Times*, ABC News, *Newsweek*, and the Austin (Texas) *American-Statesman*. Although these four media outlets differ in size, modes of transmission, resources, influence, and audiences, they still retained remarkably similar agendas, and that may be because they shared the same general surveillance function.

It was found that the mass media agreed on what events and issues to publicize, but another study (Lasorsa & Reese, 1990) found that four different news media tended not to agree on how these events and issues should be responded to. Compared were the *New York Times*, the *Wall Street Journal*, *Newsweek,* and CBS News. All four of these major mass media outlets covered the stock market crash of 1987, but the coverage itself differed in terms of the causes they attributed to the crash, as well as in what they considered to be its effects. This makes perfect sense and explains why the media may have little effect on what people think, although they affect what people think about. This same procedure used to examine the media conditions that allow for agenda setting to take place can be used to examine the audience conditions at the other end of the agenda-setting process that also permit and facilitate it.

I worked as a newspaper gatekeeper for many years, and it always struck me as quite remarkable how often mass media would cover the same issue or event—but cover it in very different ways. The media in a community often do share the same agenda—so they do tell their audiences to think about the same things—but what they say about those issues and events can be very different. Two media in a community will cover the same events and issues, but the stories they tell—what they say about those events and issues—often differ significantly. That goes some way toward explaining why the media are good at telling us what to think about but not so good at getting us to think the same things about these events and issues. Let me give you some examples.

Sometimes, when competing media cover the same issue or event but produce different stories the reason is fairly obvious. On February 10, 1985, the two major Dallas, Texas, newspapers both covered an important libel case. The *Dallas Morning News* began its story this way: "A Huntsville jury has ruled that a former Texas prison official failed to prove his libel case against the Dallas Morning News and reporter W. R. Deener III." Its headline: "Jury finds The News did not libel official." The *Times Herald* covered the same story, but its story was very different. Its lead, from the Associated Press wire service, said: "HUNTSVILLE (AP)—The Dallas Morning News was ordered to pay $290,000 in punitive damages to a former assistant warden for the Texas Department of Corrections Friday. The award was assessed by a state District Court jury that found that a reporter falsely attributed a statement to the former assistant warden." Its head: "'Dallas Morning News' assessed $290,000 for false statement." This is the same topic from two very different perspectives.

Neither the major local daily newspaper nor the local college daily newspaper were directly linked to the quality of the Texas mental health system but on September 14, 1988, both interpreted the results of a major study comparing states' public mental health systems differently. The Austin (Texas) *American-Statesman* began its story this way: "A new consumer rating of the quality of public mental health systems ranks Texas 31st among the states, up from 47th place 2 1/2 years ago, but still in the bottom half nationwide." Its headline: "Texas mental health system rises to 31st in national ranking." The University of Texas *Daily Texan* reported on the same event. Its lead began: "An evaluation issued Tuesday of mental health care in the United States ranked Texas 49th in spending and was received with lukewarm enthusiasm by the commissioner of the Texas Department of Mental Health and Mental Retardation." Its headline: "Texas ranks 49th in mental care spending."

Sometimes, it appears to be a matter of seeing the glass as half empty while some other medium is seeing it half full. On February 17, 1985, the *American-Statesman* ran an Associated Press version of a major report based on U.S. Census Bureau data: "WASHINGTON (AP)—Private health insurance protects nearly three-quarters of all Americans, with the share covered highest in the Northeast—the region which also reports the longest average hospital stays in the country." Its headline: "85% of Americans have health insurance." the *New York Times* ran its own story: "WASHINGTON, Feb. 17—A new study by the Census Bureau says that 15 percent of all Americans, 35 million people, lack any kind of health insurance." Its headline: "15% OF AMERICANS LACKING INSURANCE; Census Study Finds 35 Million without Health Coverage—Rise From Late '70s." Again, the same event was reported but decidedly different interpretations of the event were presented.

Here is another example where a Census Bureau study leads to one impression in one newspaper and to a totally different impression in another. When the Census Bureau released a report in December 1984 on "latchkey children," the Scripps Howard News Service offered this report: "WASHINGTON—Stories of young 'latchkey' kids roaming the streets after school while their mothers are at work may be exaggerated, the Census Bureau says."

"A survey released today of families with children ages 5 to 13 found that only one child in four has no parent at home after school, and only one in 14 is left without adult supervision." The headline over this story in one newspaper said: "Study finds few 'latchkey' kids." Another story about the same study, same day, in a different newspaper read: "WASHINGTON—More than 2 million U.S. youngsters spend at least some time unsupervised after school, with the largest share in white, upper-income families, according to a Census Bureau study."

"Known as latchkey children, about 2,065,000 youngsters are left to care for themselves after school—about 7.2 percent of all youngsters ages 5 to 13, the Census Bureau study stated." The head over this story: "Count 'em: 2 million latchkey children."

When U.S. President Ronald Reagan went to Moscow in 1988 for a summit meeting, the *Houston Chronicle* front-page story on May 31 was decidedly upbeat. Its headline read: "Reagan tells dissidents future looking brighter." Its crosstown rival, the *Houston Post*, however, was less optimistic in its front-page headline: "Things aren't better, refuseniks tell Reagan."

Even the same story can be given a different twist, just with its headline. Both the *American-Statesman* and the *Daily Texan* ran the same Associated Press story about the likelihood of a postal rate increase but whereas the *Statesman* headline said, "Postal rates may rise in April," the *Texan* headline said, "Postal rate increase delayed." In all of these cases, the newspapers covered the same event or issue, but the ways these events or issues were covered were different. One can ask where the surveillance function ends and the correlation function begins.

CONCLUSION

The challenge of assembling these various "levels" of press performance is the heart of building theory. As an illustration, one might imagine starting with a general national classification, for example, a libertarian type press context. Next one might consider which is the broad function of a particular story, say surveillance, and then examine how the story is framed. As we have seen, media

PRESS SYSTEM

↓

BROAD FUNCTION

↓

EVENT/ISSUE FRAMING

↓

SOCIAL GROUP LEARNING

↓

INDIVIDUAL AGENDA

FIG. 11.1. Building a general theory of agenda setting.

can differ when presenting the same story or issue. We ask what the collective group learns. Most agenda-setting studies focus here, matching story with group learning (using content analysis and survey techniques). There is another key step: How and what does an individual learn, a much less studied aspect of agenda setting (usually requiring the tight controls of an experiment)? Figure 11.1 sketches the building process. The distance from libertarian press system to individual learning—each "step" operating as a sort of gate—is great conceptually. That is the challenge of assembling a broad agenda-setting theory, one exciting challenge for communication scholars of the 21st century. Level 2 agenda-setting studies that focus on attributes of messages and not just the broad subjects of the messages suggest the press, on occasion, can tell people how to think about an issue.

Many years ago, Cohen and Nagel (1934) demonstrated that the scientific method is nothing more than applied logic. So let us imagine: If the press (under some conditions) can give us a topic to think about, and how to think about that topic, does the press also sometimes tell us what to think, just as people suspected before the Lazarsfeld studies? Probably not.

12

An Agenda-Setting Perspective on Historical Public Opinion

Edward Caudill

Public opinion is an enduring and important problem for students of the past because it is a critical part of any history involving democratic institutions. Past public opinion will never be "discovered" in a trunk of old letters and documents. Historians have worked around this problem by compiling evidence from sources as disparate as presidential letters and newspaper cartoons, and deducing a public temperament. Whether right or wrong, conclusions based on such an approach are even more risky than usual for historians.

Agenda setting, however, provides a unique tool by which historians, like paleontologists reassembling fossilized bones, can reconstruct an extinct creature; in this case, historical public opinion. Like paleontologists, historians will never see the complete animal in its natural environment, but they can learn more about the dimensions and life of the creature with disciplined, systematic research and logical deduction from existing evidence. Such logic requires an empirical foundation and a framework to guide the research questions, as well as provide the parameters for sound generalizations from the data. Agenda setting can provide these for historians by virtue of an extensive body of empirical research that shows a relationship between media content and public opinion.

This chapter outlines some challenges and possibilities associated with adopting agenda setting in historical studies. The fundamental challenge for historians is one of appropriate generalization, which is addressed in the first part of the chapter. Next, the relevance of agenda setting is outlined in a review of studies that are conceptually and methodologically useful for historians. Finally, a proposal is put forward for how one might adapt agenda setting to the study of historical public opinion, avoiding the problems that have plagued historical generalization.

THE CHALLENGE OF HISTORICAL
GENERALIZATION

A critical issue in using agenda setting to answer historical questions is one of generalization, which seems so often to frighten or appall historians, as they go about their business with a perspective deeply influenced by statistical reasoning, frequently without statistical evidence. History as written, for example, is full of quantitative generalizations, expressed in squishy fashion as "more than," "most," or "less than." The issue is not whether historians should generalize—because they must—but avoidance of drawing the incorrect conclusions from correct particulars (Fischer, 1970). The agenda-setting hypothesis is a useful generalization for historians who are willing to accept its constraints and risks in exchange for the sharper definitions and a clearer understanding of the dynamics of past public opinion.

Even as historians recount unique events and individuals, they generalize in order to make comprehensible and meaningful the vast varieties of human experience. The result would be moral and philosophic anarchy if the experiences of others, past and present, had no meaning for anyone else. However, generalization often intimidates rather than inspires historians. The problem is not with generalizing, which is unavoidable if one is to make sense of or learn from any problem, but the extent or the level at which one generalizes. At some levels, historical generalization is absurd, and even contrary to evidence. At other levels, generalization can work, true in both its particulars and broad conclusions. Agenda setting, properly applied within the limits of evidence and generalization, can serve historians well.

Although there are countless ways to organize history, generalizations in the field can be grouped conveniently into four broad categories.

- First, there are patterns so general as to be useless; for example, we live and die; cultures rise and fall.
- Second, there are attempts to describe patterns that are so specific the generalization fails scrutiny of its supporting evidence—Schlesinger's 30-year cycle in U.S. politics, for example.
- Third, there are patterns that appear to be appropriately general, but turn out simply to be wrong. Marxism is prominent in this category.
- Fourth, there are patterns appropriately general and specific that seem to have been correct. Kuhn's argument about scientific revolutions is one.

The last category's value is twofold. First, it is correct by virtue of fitting the historical facts. Second, it is useful because it makes history more comprehensible. In a subject as far-flung and complex as public opinion, the ability to make it even slightly more comprehensible is a major accomplishment.

There are countless ways to classify historical generalizations, and my purpose is not to challenge other historians' taxonomies, but merely to organize the generalizations conveniently for immediate purposes. Gottschalk (1963), for example, found at least six types of generalizations, which I draw on for my four categories. I am dismissing the first type of generalization, those that are true but uselessly broad (we live and die; graduate school was tougher in the old days), in order to proceed to the more substantial problems and possibilities associated with the other categories.

The second type of generalization—a pattern so specific that it fails—is simply a historical conclusion that outruns its data. Schlesinger's (1986) 30-year cyclical hypothesis posits that U.S. politics alternates between periods when problems demand public action and periods when they demand private action. The Reagan 1980s were a replay of the Eisenhower 1950s, which were a replay of the Harding–Coolidge 1920s. On the other side of the cycle, 1992 and the election of a Democratic president occurred a predictable 30 years (approximately) after Kennedy's election of 1960, which was about 30 years after Franklin Roosevelt's election, which was about three decades after Theodore Roosevelt championed public action against the monopoly problem, among others. Schlesinger was, perhaps, on to something, but the 30-year cycle is problematic when one brings to light the data he conveniently ignored. Where do Woodrow Wilson (1912, 1916), Richard Nixon (1968, 1972), and Jimmy Carter (1976) fit in the cycle? More striking, how does the 1994 Congressional election fit the cycle? This is not to deny any pattern to variations in beliefs about solutions to problems, but it is to challenge the neat packaging into three-decade units and offering the simple dichotomy of public–private solutions.

The third generalization is one that is appropriately general in describing broad social or economic movements, but is wrong. Marxism comes first to mind, but it has been an extremely influential idea. Marx's social theory was based primarily on class struggle, a conflict that he believed was irreconcilable. Marxism is the belief that material conditions determine social change—economic determinism, in other words. Therefore, the evolution of human society is driven by development of material goods. Given this axiom, and the evolutionary perspective that he adopted from Darwin, Marx asserted that society moved through stages of development: As humans increased control over nature and factory power grew (which is what he observed in an industrializing Europe), then society changed from a slave system to a feudal system to a capitalistic system to socialism and, finally, to communism. Marxists have insisted on operating at the macro, rather than micro, level of analysis, which leaves the idea conveniently untestable in any empirical fashion.

There are a number of useful ideas in Marxism that might help explain history: that society evolves (but by itself, a Type 1 generalization, so broad as to be useless); that class conflict exists (which appears to be true in different times and places, but to widely varying degrees, but with "conflict" so loosely defined that almost anything can be interpreted as a manifestation of class conflict, from beheading monarchs to writing comic strips); that people react to economics and material needs (obviously). However, a logical explication of Marxism as a historical explanation reveals some problems. A syllogism of Marxism is the following:

Statement 1: Society evolves.
Statement 2: Materialism drives social evolution.
Statement 3: Greater control is developed over nature, material goods and means of production.
Conclusion: Society will evolve in this fashion: slavery to feudalism to capitalism to socialism to communism.

The conclusion is the capstone of Marxist thought, but it does not follow logically from the preceding statements. It is an assertion, not a deduction, that social evolution will have this direction. Nothing in the statements suggests directional evolution. In Statement 1, both the terms *society* and *evolution* are difficult to define, and, therefore, hard to systematically assess. In Statement 2, it is highly questionable that people are motivated solely by material goods, and that materialism is the only variable in social evolution. It is quite easy to find other motives in human behavior, such as love and hate, or the lust for power. Statement 3 might be acceptable, but it is merely a rewording of Statement 1, and does little, if anything, to clarify or advance the terms society and evolution. Thus, Marxism is a generalization that defies systematic analysis of historical evidence.[1] It has no empirical foundation.

The fourth type of generalization, which is apparently correct, is demonstrated by Kuhn's (1970) paradigmatic explanation of the history of science. His key concepts—paradigm, anomaly, crisis, and normal science—are used to explain and make clearer the nature of scientific revolutions. For Kuhn, the purpose was to offer a general framework that made the history of science more comprehensible. Kuhn showed how successful theories establish themselves as the paradigm for scientific activity; they define not only acceptable techniques for tackling problems, but also which problems even are considered. In addition, the loyalty of scientists to a paradigm is so great that scientists may refuse to admit anomalous facts and will try to pretend that the old system is still functioning smoothly. Only when the anomalies become unbearable will a crisis state emerge, and younger, more radical scientists will cast around for a new theory. The history of several fields have fit Kuhn's pattern over the last 150 to 200 years, including physics, biology, chemistry, and psychology. Kuhn suc-

---

[1]In fact, recent events in the former U.S.S.R. and Eastern Europe would suggest that social evolution is moving toward capitalism and socialism and away from communism. Even when the U.S.S.R. existed, it had not evolved through the prescribed stages of political and economic development, as it went from feudal directly to communist, skipping altogether the capitalist and socialist stages.

cessfully explained how certain issues and questions were addressed or dismissed in the history of science. Another reason for the success of Kuhn's generalization over Marx's is that the latter stresses the normative, whereas the former stresses the objective. Thus, Kuhn can be held to standards of evidence shared across individuals, groups, and even cultures.

The challenge to historians, then, is to have the successful generalization and specificity of Kuhn, avoiding the pitfalls of the Schlesinger and Marx examples. Agenda setting can work as a historical generalization because it is objective, like Kuhn, rather than normative, like Marx. In addition, agenda setting has several other attributes that make it likely to succeed as historical generalization, attributes that are found in Kuhn. The first is the discipline of definition, which Kuhn was careful to do in dealing with such ideas as normal science, anomalies, and crisis states, and which is critical to studying such an amorphous field as public opinion. Marx's key concepts, especially society and conflict, are dauntingly difficult to operationalize. Like Kuhn's paradigm, agenda setting is a limited generalization, not pretending relevance to all people in all of time, in all social systems, as Marxism has done. Kuhn was talking only about the history of science, not all of history. Agenda setting would be useful in societies in which there is a more or less open press, in which people are free to select their media, and in which the press reaches a substantial part of the population. In would not be useful, for example, in totalitarian systems or primitive, illiterate societies.

The Agenda-Setting Model for Historians

Because agenda setting is a communications process, the historian cannot dwell on public opinion independent of the agents of communications that are accessible for study, and these are usually magazines and newspapers. In addition, the depth of public opinion will remain evasive within the confines of the agenda-setting model, which measures presence, not intensity, of issues.

It is not an original observation that mass communications theory has something to offer historians. Nord (1982) stated, "Mainstream American history is often simplistic, even naive in its understanding and portrayal of the process of mass communication" (p. 56). He observed that few historians have looked at the communications process, and either assumed that newspapers reflected public sentiment because the public read them, or that papers did not reflect public sentiment because they were produced by editors with special interests. He said there were several areas in which researchers and journalism historians seemed to be making progress in making media more scrutable for historians generally, and agenda setting was one of them.[2] Thanks to agenda setting, he said, it is no longer necessary to argue that newspapers reflect public opinion in order to argue that newspapers bear some relation to the consciousness of the audience.

---

[2]The other four areas are diffusion, organization theory, economics, and socialization studies.

However, historians need to consider several conceptual problems before they use agenda setting, the major issue being the idea of public opinion. The social scientists' practice of defining, and thereby restricting, terms is by itself quite useful to historians, especially to those studying such broad fields as public opinion. Benson (1967) proposed that historians confine the term to opinion pertaining to political issues, but said it was not the only possible way of defining the term. The other half of the term, public, might be those "of a specified political entity having the right, or claiming the right, implicitly or explicitly, to influence government actions, directly or indirectly" (p. 524). Benson proposed a typology of formative agents of opinion that would include government officials, political leaders, mass media directors, leaders of nonpolitical formal organizations, pressure-group leaders, and "influentials."[3] Among the types of media that would be useful in the study of opinion, he included prestige and large-circulation newspapers and magazines as well as those devoted to class, section, and ethnic groups, which he called "representative media."

A STRATEGY FOR STUDYING HISTORICAL PUBLIC OPINION

If historians adopt the agenda-setting perspective for discovering past public opinion, they may benefit from considering several preliminary issues outlined here. First, how is the statistical reasoning of agenda setting fitted to history? Second, how is public opinion defined? Finally, issues also must be clearly defined and relationships understood among variables in the opinion-formation dynamic—particularly the press, its readers, and policymakers.

Benson, noting that historians have been rather haphazard in studying public opinion, proposed a three-step research strategy:

1. Reconstruct the distribution of opinion on specified issues over time.
2. Reconstruct and explain the formation of opinion.
3. Reconstruct and explain the impact of opinion upon policy.

The traditional agenda-setting model would be most applicable to Step 1, but research on influence agents on the media agenda would be useful in Step 2. With respect to Step 3, reconstructing and explaining the impact of opinion on policy, Baumgartner and Jones (1993) showed how media play a role in policy formation by directing attention to different aspects of the same issues. They found that with nuclear power, pesticides, and smoking, there were waves of enthusiasm or apprehension, and issues seemed during these times to be entirely positive or negative. They also found media attention to issues to be fitful, not

---

[3]Benson's use of leaders and groups, and his concern with quality of opinion suggests the historical application of other concepts that are prominent in communication theory: two-step flow of information, opinion leaders, and knowledge gap.

sustained, and associated with how it was discussed: "As an issue surges onto the media agenda, so does it lurch onto the agendas of federal and state agenices . . ." (p. 104). They stopped short of implying causation, but pointed out that government and media affected each other with reinforcing patterns of positive feedback and "punctuated equilibrium" in their attention to issues. The "bottleneck of attention" they cited also is useful for historians as the idea applies to both media and political systems. It implies narrowness in the range of issues media or government can deal with simultaneously, and it explains why only a single dimension of a multifaceted issue will receive attention. It also means individuals have a limited ability to attend to multiple issues simultaneously. The historian would be supported in limiting the issues pursued in the study of public opinion, and in presuming a rather simple definition of the issue by the public.

Benson (1967) concluded by pointing out that the search for opinion, like the search for any history, is never done under ideal conditions with all possible sources available. Because so much documentation of the past is lost through purposeful concealment or destruction or technological interference (telephones have virtually destroyed what used to be available in letters), historians are left with the results of "involuntary sampling," fragmentary records that may or may not allow reasonable generalization about the past. Therefore, history (or the search for public opinion) becomes the search for the best indicators, not perfect ones. Here is the implication of statistical reasoning in history: One is minimizing error and finding the best "fit" for the data; and the historian, like the social scientist, cannot expect to explain 100% of variance, but explains as much as possible within the limits of the evidence. Benson's call for historians to generate data and develop long-term trend analysis is suggestive of the agenda-setting setting hypothesis, in which time is a critical variable. In addition, the approach demonstrates the intrinsically historical nature of research into agenda setting, inasmuch as it has been a study of events and agendas of the recent, not distant, past, and of the process of agenda building over time.

Boyce (1978), like Benson, said historians have had problems defining public opinion. Boyce criticized the impulse to give public opinion a mystic quality, disapprovingly citing Lasswell and Kaplan's definition (cited in Boyce, 1978) of public opinion as a "deeply persuasive organic force ... which somehow integrates and momentarily crystallizes the sporadic sentiments and loyalties of the masses of the population" (p. 216). To combat such fuzziness, he said, historians might abandon private letters and go to the opposite end of the spectrum. If public opinion is public, then he believed it made sense to turn to the press, where opinions are expressed "in leaders, in readers' letters, and here the opinions are public" (p. 217).

Although agenda setting would not provide a definitive answer to whether opinion flows from press to public or vice versa, it would provide that which Benson sought: the beginning of a classification system for studying public opinion, clarification of terms, and understanding relationships of variables. Boyce (1978) pointed out that public opinion does not mean everyone's ideas about all issues: "Since the historian invariably studies public opinion with reference to specific issues (the Boer War, the New Deal, or whatever) he can use the press and the other organs of communication to discover how issues were first identified, defined and treated" (p. 221).

Just as historians must restrict the meaning of public opinion, so must they put limits on the issues to be studied. When it came to whether the press leads or follows public opinion, Boyce (1978) quoted the sensible comment of the 1949 Royal Commission on the Press in England: "A paper can be a little ahead of its readers, but not far" (p. 222). This is a useful idea for historians even if it skirts the causal question because a historian can at least proceed to discerning the nature of public opinion even if he or she cannot explain its origins.

In order to restrict public opinion to methodologically manageable proportions, Harding (1937) delineated what he called "the range of permissible opinion," which is similar to Boyce's idea that a newspaper cannot be too far ahead of its readers' opinions. Harding's range has four characteristics: it must be affirmed before other people; the holders of the opinion must recognize it to be in some degree relevant to their interests; they must claim, or admit to possessing, some degree of competence to accept or reject it; and they must regard the opinion as having some claim on them for consideration—not reject it as axiomatically wrong. He contended that opinions expressed by a newspaper will be within the public's permissible range of opinion because a newspaper cannot isolate itself from its audience, and it must take care to remain fairly central in the field of public opinion on a major issue.

In addition, he said, newspapers are compelled to come into line with every important change that they see no chance of successfully resisting. Harding believed this applied to only relatively important issues, but this usually is not a problem for historians because the issues of interest tend to be the major ones, and subsequent studies by Shaw and McCombs (1977) and Shaw and Martin (1992) suggested that the public agenda will be limited anyway. Harding dismissed what he deemed eccentric campaigns or minor issues because he believed newspapers could be far removed from the majority view of the audience without loss of circulation. However, assessment of opinion based on newspapers, Harding said, must involve more than measurement, counting, and classification. It also demands subjective interpretation, knowledge of events, and insight into contemporary institutions, which are the ingredients of good history anyway.

Neuman's (1990) research could be adopted by historians who are working with another issue Benson raised, that of distinguishing among types of phenomena. Neuman said there was a pattern to evolving public awareness, and that a critical mass or threshold developed to move an issue from private concern to public issue. He proposed that researchers ask both what types of audiences are most likely to be influenced (demographic and behavioral categories; typologies of informational "need orientations"), and whether different types of issues may be characterized by unique agenda-setting dynamics. On the nature of issues, he usually distinguished between obtrusive and nonobtrusive issues, but he categorized them along another dimension and identified the four types as crisis, symbolic, problems, and nonproblems. Neuman suggested a general pattern of responsiveness of public and media to the different types of issues, and that is an S-shaped logistic curve as a model of the shape of the agenda-setting function. He argued that public perception of crises is operating not in response to real conditions as much as it is to a systematic cycle of interest followed by saturation and boredom and decline of attention. Neuman drew on media indices (the *New York Times,* the *Reader's Guide to Periodical Literature*, and the *Vanderbilt Television News Archive Index*) and Gallup's most important problem (MIP) question to arrive at a list of 10 issues (including crime, drugs, energy, inflation, pollution, racial unrest, Vietnam). For Vietnam and urban unrest, which he called crisis issues, the peaks of the attention curves from media and the MIP response were found to be to be highly correlated. For these types of issues, Neuman said, there was consistent evidence of a curvilinear relationship between volume of media coverage and level of public concern. Curvilinearity was not dramatic and in most cases could be approximated by linear models. For other issues, he found the relationship roughly linear. Evidence of a linear or near-linear relationship simplifies the task of the historian attempting to compare the relationship of media coverage and public opinion, and especially for crisis issues.

In bringing the problem of public opinion closer to the study of the press, history, and agenda setting, Mayer's (1992) research into the sources of attitude change is important. He found four sources of attitude change: generational, demographic, external events, and media. He said four groups played a role in the process of public opinion formation: political leaders, political parties, interest groups, and mass media. Like Boyce and Benson, he provided possible parameters for the study of the press and public opinion, but Mayer is closer to what is recognized as the agenda-setting hypothesis itself. Historians have relied on all of these sources, although political leaders have received by far the most attention. He said mass media have an impact on mass attitudes in two major ways: They inform the public about events, and they help shape the way the public understands and interprets those events, what McCombs and Evatt (1995) called the second level of agenda setting, which focuses on the role the media play in framing issues in the public mind. The media succeed not only in telling the public what to think about, but they are also successful at telling people how to think about those issues.

A classic study in symbol analysis that demonstrated the limits and potential of social scientific methods was quite suggestive of the potential for agenda setting in historical issues. Merritt's (1965) *Symbols of American Community 1735–1775* explored the separation of the colonies from England and the process of political disintegration and integration. Merritt said his approach was useful for fitting single pieces of information to a continuing pattern, as well as enriching the study of patterns in history. The analysis of political symbols in colonial newspapers was especially useful for focusing attention on years or months of particular importance in the long-run processes. This reasoning would fit just as well with agenda setting, which, like Merritt's symbol analysis, relies on content coding in order to discern media content. Like agenda setting, his method was useful for dealing with questions that were quantitative in nature: how much, how often, and with what variability. Both agenda setting and Merritt's symbol analysis are a study of media content over time.

Funkhouser (1973) used agenda setting as a guide for inquiry into past public opinion, as he demonstrated a media–public opinion relationship over an extended period of time in the past. He used Gallup polls from 1964 to 1970, asking about the MIP facing America, and he used the *Reader's Guide to Periodical Literature* (1960–1970) for major topics in weekly news magazines, including Vietnam, race relations, inflation, crime, urban riots, campus unrest, the environment, drugs, sex, mass media, population, poverty, smoking, science, and women's rights. He found the three most important problems in terms of national news magazine coverage were Vietnam, race relations, and campus unrest. These and other issues correlated significantly (.78) with the importance given them in the Gallup surveys. However, he said the MIP question could be an indirect content analysis of news media because the amount of media attention given an issue strongly influences its visibility to the public. He also used a reality index, which measured the actual rates of crime, drug use, inflation, and the rise and fall of Vietnam and urban riots. Funkhouser said the media did not give an accurate picture of what was going on in the nation because most attention was given to people and agencies rather than issues, but he did show a strong relationship between the media and public agendas.

Winter and Eyal (1981) used an approach similar to Funkhouser, but narrowed the research to a single issue—civil rights. Looking at 27 years, 1954 to 1976, they found "it has not been necessary to extend the media agenda beyond two months in order to predict public salience" (p. 381), even though numerous other studies had shown the optimal span to be from 2 to 5 months. They believed recent, rather than cumulative, media emphasis led to public salience for civil rights. For historians, this supports studying recent rather than cumulative issues, and the latter is easier to measure than the former. The shorter time period they found for public salience may simplify the task of relating media attention to public events and policy actions.

Gallup's question on the MIP has itself generated a number of studies, among them Smith's (1980) trend analysis for the years 1946 to 1976. The trend analysis is a valuable methodological concept for historians because the idea is not only inherently historical, but it is systematic and suggestive of causation, which could take the historian beyond description. Smith said, "The MIP question documents not only the shifting concerns of post-World War II American society, but also the general ebb and flow of recent American history. . . . The MIP question also shows how major social groups perceived events" (p. 177). One aspect of his research may be of special interest to historians concerned about subgroups, those outside or on the margin of mainstream groups, and the press. Smith concluded that the MIP question showed major social groups tended to have "small and trivial" differences on the whole, but that notable differences occurred under certain circumstances, such as Blacks and civil rights. However, this would not be problematic for historians because the finding concurs with common sense, and helps historians because it provides empirical support for the received knowledge that U.S. politics, as Hofstadter (1957) argued, has a history of strong centrist tendencies, largely shunning radicalism.

In a second study on the MIP question, Smith (1985) said that "perhaps no other single item gives us as deep an understanding of American history over the last five decades. The most important problem question provides a grand overview of social change, describes history from the perspective of the participants, and helps to define distinct historical periods and identify turning points" (p. 264). In the article, Smith showed MIP responses paralleled significant events, such as the emergence of energy as a national concern at the time of the Arab oil boycott in 1973 and 1974, or how government as a problem reached its peak just before Nixon's resignation in 1973, and the decline of economic worries in the wake of World War II.

Other Studies Useful to Historians

There are many agenda-setting studies, of the hundreds over the past several decades, that are not immediately historical in their applications, but that are valuable to historians because the social-scientific findings have implications for both the concepts and methodologies associated with studying past public opinion. Shaw and McCombs (1977) found that the public agenda typically included five to seven items, which is evidence for the the practical necessity of a historian limiting study to major public issues. Miller (1956) estimated that in terms of "distinguishable alternatives" the information-processing capacity for people was about 6.5, and that 4 and 10 were the limits of a single standard deviation. In other words, there were limits to people's carrying capacities. He called it the magical number 7, plus or minus 2. In limiting the agenda to a historigraphically manageable size, the findings of Shaw and Martin (1992) provided further support for excluding marginal issues. They theorized that the press pulled divergent parts of the collective social system together, and in doing so the press was in effect accomplishing a "democratic averaging out of agenda differences" (p. 913). The press agenda was not simply a White upper class agenda, or that of the predominant power structure.

The historical ramification is that the press agenda might be a reasonable guide to opinion beyond the immediate audience of the newspaper or magazine, a conclusion that also could be inferred from Boyce (1978) and Harding (1937). The media, they found, lined up social issues for collective identification and social discourse, to the extent that even White upper class males brought their agendas in line with other demographic groups. However, Hill (1985) showed limits on the impact of agenda setting among groups because there is substantial evidence that audiences with higher education levels are more susceptible to agenda-setting effects.

These limits on the size of the public agenda also were reinforced by McCombs and Zhu's (1995) research on the number of responses to the MIP question: "The number of issues nominated in response to the MIP by the average American has varied in a narrow range between .82 and 1.34, with the mean being 1.07" (p. 506). They stated that the relative stability in the number of issues was consistent with the zero-sum perspective of agenda setting. This is encouraging for the historian not only because it means a very clearly defined agenda, but also because it suggests that items enter and exit the public agenda in a fairly orderly fashion. They found no increase in the public's collective carrying capacity over time, which for historians means a stable, predictable, limited agenda. However, they did find strong evidence for both agenda diversity and issue volatility, which means the historian could not be presumptuous about the nature of the specific items even though he or she could work within an agenda-setting framework in order to define, limit, and describe the public agenda.

USING AGENDA SETTING IN HISTORICAL STUDY

Two scholars provide examples of the fruitful use of agenda setting to guide inquiry into 19th-century public opinion. Ellegard used the English press to understand opinion about Darwin's theory of natural selection in the 1860s. Nord looked at agenda setting as a political process in showing how newspapers were a part of the reform politics in St. Louis and Chicago. On the issues of utility regulation and street–railway regulation, Nord (1981) showed how reformers and newspaper allies built a successful campaign in Chicago, but reformers in St. Louis failed, lacking cooperation from newspapers in that city. Ellegard (1958) did a detailed content analysis of British periodicals from 1859 to 1872. He concluded that the general public remained ignorant of the principles of Darwin's natural selection, and instead focused on the religious implications of the theory, with predictable differences showing up in different demographic groups. For example, the appeal to those in lower education groups was more likely to center on the "missing links" argument. Attitudes were determined, he said, by religious, political, and ideological allegiances, as well as by attachment to a social group. In charting the course of opinion, Ellegard analyzed newspapers for political and religious orientation, educational appeal, estimated circulation, the amount of information provided on Darwinism, and the attitude toward Darwinism.

Because agenda setting has been demonstrated under a variety of conditions in the 20th century, it should be present under similar conditions in the 19th century. Historians must consider numerous important changes, such as literacy rates, mobility, transportation and communications systems, social and political issues, and changes in the press itself.

The test of agenda setting as a historical generalization could be done in two parts. The first part would be a systematic comparison of the differences found in public opinion as it is derived from polls and the press. Pollsters define public opinion in a statistical, aggregated fashion. The historical method proposed here would be systematic, but dependent on a different data set—the periodical press. If relations between the two are constant, then one can be inferred from the other. The studies by Smith (1980, 1985) and Funkhouser (1973) approximate the type of study I propose for Stage 1, but they do not explore systematic differences between the two kinds of public opinion. Such a study would have to be done in a period in which public opinion data are available, probably no earlier than the 1930s, when Gallup began asking the MIP question. The opinion data would be correlated with the media agenda at various appropriate intervals. Depending on the strength of the correlations in the first part, the strategy for the second part of the study would be to move back in time, when there were no scientific opinion polls, but at which point newspapers could be content analyzed, and done so with some knowledge of the readership (whose agenda is being set). Using the knowledge from the first part about the systematic nature of the differences in the two kinds of public opinion, a content analysis would provide a picture of public opinion, from which an estimate of statistical, poll-type public opinion could be inferred.

The media agenda revealed in the content analysis could be historically "tested" for valid generalization to an audience by use of other historical sources concerning the public agenda, including legislation, letters of individuals, literature, and public or political events. In addition, Part 2 would be most effective if using the same newspapers and magazines, or at least similar ones, as used in Part 1. This would minimize the error associated with introducing different variables into the research design, such as audience demographics. Along these same logical lines, it also would be most effective, defined here as minimizing error, to use the same or similar geographic regions and to focus on the same kinds of issues.

The parameters of applicability of such research are narrow in terms of time, place, people, and issues. In the United States, such an approach definitely is plausible for periods since the 1890s, when a true "mass press" emerged in a few places, and probably since the 1830s, when the "penny press" expanded the reach of newspapers. Going further back in time is complicated by a press of more limited circulation and the difficulty of defining the audience of the newspaper. There is no definite cutoff point, but it remains for the historian to decide when the data about audience are unacceptably vague, and weigh that cost against the risk of having virtually no information on public opinion.

The places about which such research would seem most logical are democracies with more or less open press systems, which obviously include the United States, Great Britain, and Western Europe. The reason is simple: In a totalitarian system, or closed political system, there is no assurance that the press reflects concerns of the audience. It may be offering an agenda, but there is nothing to support the idea, as we have in agenda-setting research in the United States, that the audience is adopting the agenda in any appreciable fashion. Another limitation would be the opinion holders under study, who would necessarily be the reading public; and using ideas from the two-step flow of information theory, could tentatively extend opinion downward. However, it obviously excludes some segments of the public, such as illiterates, recluses, or people who simply do not read about or participate in the normal flow of politics and the economy (chronic know-nothings).

HISTORICAL LOGIC
AND AN AGENDA-SETTING PERSPECTIVE

By assuming some of the good habits of social scientists, especially those of definition and precise measurement, historians could know more about public opinion, but in doing so may need to abandon any pretense of knowledge about the lowest strata of society, people who are unlikely to use media or who may well be incapable because of higher illiteracy rates. Exclusion grates on libertarian impulses, even though it might enhance knowledge. Historical agenda setting means limiting oneself to readers of particular newspapers and magazines and generalizing to demographically similar groups.

A similar discipline would be necessary in selecting topics for study, for reasons both practical and demonstrated in earlier research. No historian can write about an all-inclusive public agenda in which all subjects are given a hearing. The research has also shown a limited carrying capacity on the public agenda, which also is constrained in its relationship to the press agenda to only certain kinds of issues. It also appears that the press is going to be more useful as a guide to public opinion in certain times, or "climates" of opinion, than others. For example, Boyce (1978) said there is reason to believe that in times of crisis people turn, more than usual, to newspapers for guidance. Linking this to Harding's idea of a permissible range of opinion, it is a reasonable assumption that the press is more useful as a guide to public opinion during times of stress, and only within a moderate range of opinion for a selected number of issues.

Historians, however, should remain alert to leveling effects of social-scientific generalizations, which at their best provide elegant explanations and substantial data, but which should not replace that which makes history so alluring, the uniqueness of individuals, places, events, and eras. The historian would not be relieved of the responsibility of knowing the broad outlines of social and political history, of sorting through the morass of causes, of appreciating the individuals who drive events, or of caring about the consequences for people then and now. Individual people, places, and events are unique, as all of us know, not just historians.

13

Cultural Agendas: *The Case of Latino-Oriented U.S. Media*

América Rodriguez

Mass media are not monolithic. Newspapers not only differ from television, but also among themselves. Despite wide agreement on the major items of daily news, media differ in the placement of that news and in the details included. If you look closely, you can find traces of differences resulting from different regions, gender perspectives, and unique publications. At broader levels, there are nuances of cultures that are evident in the media of different minorities that attempt to both reflect the larger culture and serve specialized audiences. This is true of a growing segment of the United States, the publications of U.S. Latino citizens.

The U.S. Census Bureau predicts that by 2020, Latinos will make up the nation's largest minority group, some 30 million people, 22.5% of the U.S. population (U.S. Bureau of the Census, 1993). The media that target these communities—television, radio, magazines, and newspapers, both English and Spanish language—comprise the fastest growing segment of U.S. media (Stein, 1994). Park (1922), in his landmark study of the immigrant press, concluded that the principal social function of foreign-language newspapers was to ease the transition to U.S. society. More recently, Riggins (1992) and Subervi-Velez (1986) argued that ethnic media have a dual role, simultaneously assisting in the adaptation to the majority society, and encouraging the distinctive identity of the ethnic community.

These studies reflect the emergence of a new U.S. immigration paradigm. Since the last large wave of European immigration to the United States in the first decades of this century, most immigration has originated in Latin America and in Asia. These immigrants have challenged the myth of the "melting pot" and spurred appreciation of the complexity of cultural adaptation. Today, when U.S. Latino "ethnics" far outnumber Latin American immigrants, study of contemporary U.S. Latino-oriented media reveals the tangled, often contradictory elements of the ongoing social adaptation of Latin Americans and people of Latin American descent to the United States.

Consumers of U.S. Latino-oriented news media have pictures in their heads (Lippmann, 1922)—pictures of the world and the nation—that are significantly different from those presented in the general-market media. Most U.S. Latino journalists were educated in U.S. journalism schools, and the general form of the pictures they learn is readily recognizable, yet much is tailored to the perceived interests of the ethnic minority audience. Latino news media are constructed from a global point of view that prominently includes Latin America—as well as a national mapping that features the east side of Los Angeles, the south side of San Antonio, and Spanish Harlem.

Although Latino-oriented media cover Congress and city halls (as well as general-market sports and entertainment), they also, unlike most general-market media (Martingale, 1995), commit considerable resources to issues such as legal immigration and the environmental disasters along the U.S.–Mexico border, as well as U.S. Latino and Latin American sports and entertainment news. The repeated selection and salience of these topics constructs the predominant frame of U.S. Latino media, one that depicts—both symbolically and substantively—the ongoing relationship of U.S. Latinos with Latin America. U.S. Latino media are audience centered; the distinct and particular interests and needs of the presumptive audience of U.S. Latinos (or Hispanics) motivate their production.

This chapter, which is intended as a call for further research and not a definitive analysis, examines the framing of contemporary U.S. Latino-oriented news, analyzing dominant patterns as well as variations across genre (e.g., print vs. electronic), and national origin of the targeted Latino media audiences. One overriding theme is that of cultural duality and ambiguity—the desire of U.S. Latino-oriented news media to preserve distinctive Latin American ethnic ties, and also fully participate in "American," or U.S. society. The framing of U.S. Latino-oriented news media is considered an element of the dynamic social processes that transform "immigrants" into "ethnics."

Framing in this essay relies on Entman's (1993) definition, which emphasizes selection and salience, as well as Gitlin's (1980) less cited one, which stresses the active, repetitive process of framing: "Media frames are persistent patterns of cognition, interpretation and presentation, of selection, emphasis and exclusion, by which symbol handlers routinely organize discourse, whether verbal or visual" (p. 7). Before turning to examinations of contemporary Latino-oriented news media, this chapter attempts to avoid mediacentric distortions by contextualizing U.S. Latino-oriented media with brief histories of U.S. Latinos and media institutions, including advertisers. These are the social formations that underlie the framing of contemporary U.S. Latino news media.

A BRIEF HISTORY OF U.S. LATINOS

Collectively, U.S. Latinos are among the poorest members of society, with a median family income of $23,900, compared with $37,000 for non-Hispanic families (U.S. Bureau of the Census, 1993). Although represented in all income levels, as a group, Latinos have the lowest educational achievement levels of all U.S. groups, with less than half (44%) having completed high school, compared to 88% of the general population (U.S. Bureau of the Census, 1993). The 1990 census reported more than half (53.7%) of U.S. Latinos speak Spanish at home. Spanish is, by far, the most frequently used language in the United States other than English (U.S. Bureau of the Census, 1993). These statistics are just broad demographic markers: Latinos are multiracial and multinational. A consideration of U.S. Latino immigration history reveals profound differences in Latino groups' orientation to the dominant society.

Mexican Americans, the largest of the national origin groups, comprise about two-thirds of all U.S. Latinos and have perhaps the most contentious U.S. immigration history. Originally, Mexicans were not immigrants to the United States, but rather a conquered people after the 1846–1848 Mexican-American War, when the United States annexed half of Mexico. A significant portion of Mexican immigration to the United States has been agricultural and periodic, with periods of recruitment by U.S. employers, followed by mass deportations. This pattern slowed, and permanent, urban-oriented immigration increased markedly after the world wars (Cornelius, 1992) . Today, Mexican Americans are a social and political presence throughout the southwestern United States. However, with the majority U.S. society at times welcoming and at times shunning, the foundational ambiguity of Mexican immigration and ethnicity remains, creating what one historian called "an ambivalent Americanism" (Sanchez, 1993, p. 13).

After Fidel Castro's rise to power in the early 1960s, Cuban immigrants—largely middle class and professionals—were enthusiastically welcomed to the United States as political refugees, and given extensive resettlement assistance by the U.S. federal government. More recent waves of Cuban migration (the Mariel boatlift of 1980, and the "rafters" of the mid-1990s) have not received an official welcome, but many of these Cuban immigrants have benefited from the resources of the thriving Cuban American community, concentrated in south Florida. Cubans make up less than 10% of U.S. Latinos, but their wealth and political activity have given them disproportionate power in U.S. Latino media circles.

Puerto Ricans, who have held citizenship since after the United States annexed the Caribbean island in 1898, are not technically U.S. immigrants. Beginning after 1950 and with increasing frequency for the next several decades, Puerto Ricans relocated and took mostly menial, yet relatively better paying jobs on the mainland, largely in New York City. They are the poorest of Latino groups, representing about 10% of U.S. Latinos.

In sum:

> Under the same label we find individuals whose ancestors lived in the country
> at least since the time of independence and others who arrived last year; we find
> substantial numbers of professionals and entrepreneurs, along with humble farm
> laborers and unskilled factory workers; there are whites, blacks, mulattos and
> mestizos; there are full fledged citizens and unauthorized aliens; and finally,
> among the [recent] immigrants are those who came in search of employment and
> a better economic future and those who arrived escaping death squads and
> political persecution at home. (Portes & Truelove, 1987, p. 360; see also Nelson
> & Tienda, 1985)

The immigration histories of Latino groups (which in the last 20 years have
been joined in the United States by other Latin American immigrants, princi-
pally from Colombia, the Dominican Republic, and El Salvador) comprise their
collective memories and community identities.

Powerful evidence of these clear identities is found in the results of a 1992
survey in which Latino citizens and legal residents were asked to identify
themselves. Only about one in five chose a general panethnic label such as
Latino or Hispanic. The remainder chose a national origin identifier; for
example, "I'm Puerto Rican," "I'm Cuban," or "I'm Mexican." Only about 10%
chose American (de la Garza, 1992).

The persistence of national origin identification among Latinos, despite the
uniform adoption by government agencies and the media (both general-market
and national U.S. Latino-oriented media) of the label Hispanic, is significant.
It points to the persistence of residential and occupational segregation of U.S.
Latinos within U.S. society. Additionally, it highlights the geographic concen-
tration of Latino subgroups—for example, Cubans in south Florida, Puerto
Ricans in New York, and Mexicans and Mexican Americans in the Southwest.
As a national public service announcement commemorating the 1995 Hispanic
Heritage Month put it, "One Language, Different Rhythms."

A BRIEF LOOK AT THE U.S.
SPANISH-LANGUAGE PRESS

The first general circulation Spanish-language newspapers linked workers on
either side of the U.S.–Mexico border with their focus on the lives and
livelihoods of these transnational communities. Eighteenth- and 19th-century
U.S. Spanish-language newspapers demonstrated the porousness of the
U.S.–Mexican border through their role as organs for Mexican political parties
and labor unions. The fluidity of this political demarcation can be seen in
newspapers such as *Regeneración* and *El Heraldo,* which although published
in the United States, also had significant readership in Mexico (see the articles
collected in Gutiérrez, 1977).

In the early 20th century, several Spanish-language newspapers that are still published today, including *La Prensa* of San Antonio and Los Angeles' *La Opinión*, were founded with the stated purpose of defending and promoting Mexican American communities in the United States. Through their publication of poetry and literary essays, these newspapers sought to maintain ties to Mexican culture. These newspapers also were fierce advocates for Mexican labor in the United States, exposing and publicizing worker exploitation by U.S. employers.

By mid-century, *La Prensa* and *La Opinión* became public voices for emerging Mexican American political power, endorsing candidates and drawing up legislative agendas. The shift in focus to political concerns, however, did not mean that these newspapers turned their backs on Mexican and Latin American politics. Political and cultural events south of the border remained a daily, prominent feature of the U.S. Spanish-language press.

The early U.S. Spanish-language press was supported by fraternal organizations and advertising from immigrant enclave businesses. Later, these media, although still dependent on local immigrant-oriented businesses, became early participants in the development of a national Hispanic advertising market.

History: U.S. Spanish-Language Radio and Television[1]

The foundational framing of the U.S. Spanish-language press, a perspective that straddled the U.S.–Mexico border, and so the binationality of their immigrant audiences' lives, was also apparent in early U.S. Spanish-language broadcasting. The first Spanish-language radio programs in the 1920s and 1930s (there were no U.S. Spanish-language radio stations until mid-century) were produced by members of the immigrant community. Radio station owners would lease unprofitable hours (usually midnight to 7 a.m.) to immigrant producers. Soon, the radio station owners found that the live music and *novela* (soap opera) programming was attracting new advertisers to previously "dead" airtime (Fowler & Crawford, 1987; Gutiérrez & Schement, 1979).

With the development of sound recording, Spanish-language radio quickly expanded, becoming one of the first entrants in the transnational media marketplace. Emilio Azcárraga, the William Paley of Mexican broadcasting, who had transformed his theater and musical performance troupes into Mexico's first radio network, soon exported his commercially successful "conservative nationalism" north of the border (Hayes, 1993). Azcárraga never owned a radio station in the United States, but programming from his Mexico City radio station, as well as several border stations before long dominated U.S. Spanish-language radio.

---

[1]For a more complete treatment of these issues, see Rodriguez (in press).

In the early 1960s, when Azcárraga might have been content with his binational radio empire, he again looked north and saw a ready market for his fledgling television network, Televisa. He founded the Spanish International Network (SIN, today called Univisión), as the U.S. subsidiary of Televisa. From 1961 to 1981, SIN's programming was identical to the Televisa programming available in Mexico: *telenovelas* or soap operas, sports, variety shows, and uncritical news programming that reflected Televisa's close relationship with the Mexican government.

In the early 1980s, after completing a national affiliate expansion that allowed it to reach nearly all of the United States with repeater and UHF stations, SIN began producing limited U.S. programming, largely news and public affairs. At the same time it was building its technological infrastructure, SIN began promoting the concept of a national panethnic Hispanic market, the commercial foundation of contemporary U.S. Latino-oriented media.

The nexus of the notion of a unitary Hispanic market, and so a national U.S. Hispanic audience, has two interconnected elements: language and ethnicity. The Spanish language is understood in this marketing stratagy as being so powerful as to blur, if not eliminate differences in race and national origin among U.S. Latinos. In order to reach Hispanics, specially tailored advertising, preferably in Spanish, was required. This, not surprisingly, was the conclusion of the first Hispanic marketing research, entitled "Hispanic USA," commissioned by SIN in 1982.

Initially, Madison Avenue resisted portions of this homogenized Latino audience concept, opting to produce three treatments of Spanish language spots, particularly crafted for each of the major national origin subgroups, with particular Spanish intonations and nationality-specific music and landscapes. By the mid-1980s, the panethnic model, utilizing a "Walter Cronkite" Spanish and similarly denationalized music and geography, had gained ascendancy in national broadcast and spot advertising. (Many local Spanish-language advertisers continue to be attuned to their communities' national origins). The Spanish language became, in commercial terms, a proxy for race, class, and national origin and the symbolic core of the transformation of Latinos into a national ethnic "Hispanic market."

CONTEMPORARY U.S. LATINO MEDIA: LANGUAGE AND PANETHNICITY

In addition to the strictly communicative attributes of language there is the functional appeal of the Spanish language for those U.S. Latinos who do not speak English. Consider the symbolic aspects of the Spanish language in U.S. Latino-oriented media. Sociolinguist Fishman (1989) wrote: "language is more likely than most symbols of ethnicity to become the symbol of ethnicity. . . any vehicle carrying such precious freight must come to be viewed as equally precious in and of itself. The link between language and ethnicity is thus one of sanctity by association" (Fishman, 1989, p. 32). What Fishman called the "symbolic boundary function" (p. 34) of language is activated by the interaction of the ethnic group with the dominant society. The production and consumption of Spanish-language media then is an activity of ethnic U.S. Latino expression, a declaration and reproduction of a distinct ethnic identity. Along with that, of course, comes a distinct public agenda.

The Spanish language is representative of a particular worldview. Latino news media's focus on Latin America, of the Spanish-speaking part of the globe, in contrast with the dominant society's Eurocentric view, is an ethnic point of view. For most U.S. journalists (and other cultural producers) the world rotates on an east–west axis, with Europe at one pole and Asia the other. One origin of this perspective is clear: Most U.S. residents trace their ancestry to Europe.

For Latino journalists this cognitive global map has a north–south axis, one that runs through the United States and then Central and South America. Or, as Univisión Vice President for News Guillermo Martinez (personal communication, Dec. 6, 1990) said, describing his presumptive audience's worldview, "They are first interested in *su patria chica* [their hometown], *su nacción* [their nation], and *su patria grande que es el continente* [their larger country, which is the Latin American continent]. A Salvadoran is more interested in whether there is corruption in Mexican government or not than they are in the fact that Margaret Thatcher fell in London." The domestic equivalent of this defining panethnic frame holds that Puerto Ricans are more interested in news of Mexican Americans in Texas, than say, German Americans in the Midwest. With variations of style and emphasis, this worldview is shared by other Latino-oriented media.

The role of the Spanish language in Latino-oriented media has several interacting dimensions. It is central to the commercial conceptualization of the Hispanic market: The Spanish language is the key to the definition and targeting of U.S. Latinos. The Spanish language has a more diffuse yet sustaining role. It is the vehicle and emblem of a point of view that characterizes U.S. Latinos as an ethnic minority group. There exists in U.S. Latino-oriented media a tension between definitions of Latinos as a distinctive ethnic group and their positioning as just another U.S. community with needs and desires not substantively different from those of the mainstream.

Contemporary Radio and Television

Latino-oriented radio and television have carved out a relatively small, but commercially feasible niche in the media marketplace. Both Spanish-language radio and television have benefited from new audience measurement methodologies specifically tailored by Arbitron and A. C. Nielsen for the Hispanic audience. These techniques allow the Hispanic audience to be commercially visible and increase its market value (Barnes & Thomson, 1994). Both radio and television have deepened the economic and structural ties to Latin America that characterized their early years.

The United States' 150 Spanish-language radio stations (out of some 10,000 radio stations nationally) are tightly formatted; for example, Spanish International, Tropical, Norteña, and Tejano. Many of these musical selections are recorded in Latin America, but many of the recording labels are U.S.-owned and marketed throughout the Spanish-speaking world. U.S. Spanish-language radio exemplifies the panhemispheric marketing ideal. In Los Angeles, Miami, and San Antonio, Spanish-language radio stations are the top rated stations in their respective markets. As with most U.S. radio stations, since the late 1980s deregulation, news and public affairs programming is minimal (there are no Spanish-language news-talk stations). Spanish-language television has also secured its market niche.

Spanish-language radio is predominantly controlled by U.S. investors, but Spanish-language television has significant Latin American capital behind it. A 25% share of Univisión (formerly SIN) is owned by Televisa, the Mexican entertainment conglomerate, which is the largest producer of Spanish-language television programming in the world. However, Televisa's minority ownership stake in Univisión understates Televisa's interest in the largest U.S. Spanish-language television network.

Televisa owns PanAmSat, the satellite that transmits its Mexican-produced programming to the United States, as well as other Televisa and Univisión programming to Latin America. Televisa also produces more than half the programming Univisión transmits to its 600 stations. Half of Telemundo, the smaller U.S. Spanish-language television network, is owned by a consortium of Venezuelan and Colombia broadcast companies.

Although Univisión and Telemundo rely heavily on imported *telenovelas*, sports, and variety programming, both networks have concentrated domestic production in news and public affairs programming. Telemundo, from its Miami headquarters, produces Telenoticias, a 24-hour news service. Telenoticias, which was purchased by CBS in 1996, originally was created with the stated goal of competing with CNN's Spanish-language service in Latin America. Many of Telemundo's 400 U.S. affiliates are airing Telenoticias in the overnight hours. Thirty-minute segments are broadcast by most affiliates as traditional nightly news programs. According to A. C. Nielsen's fall 1995 report, Telenoticias has not helped Telemundo close its U.S. ratings gap with Univisión. Telemundo attracts about 15% of the U.S. Spanish-language television audience and Univisión about 85%.

Univisión's nightly national newscast, the *Noticiero Univisión*, is arguably the premier example of contemporary U.S. Latino-oriented news media, with a nightly audience of about 1.2 million viewers (Rodriguez, 1995). About half of each newscast is made up of Latin American news; about a fifth is taken up by news of U.S. Latino communities. The remainder of each *Noticiero* is much like general-market nightly national television news programs, with coverage of the White House, Congress, and other U.S. governmental activities. In contrast,

ABC's *World News Tonight With Peter Jennings* gives less than 1% its airtime to news of Latin America and U.S. Latinos and 40% to "Beltway" news of the U.S. federal government. (A detailed explanation of the methodology and results of this comparative content analysis can be found in Rodriguez, 1993.)

The panhemispheric worldview of the *Noticiero* is constrained by the traditional U.S. training of its journalists. Univisión journalists shun the advocacy label often associated with ethnic minority journalism, embracing instead professional objectivity,using government sources and presenting two sides of each public issue. What distinguishes these journalists from their general-market counterparts is their insistence on the inclusion of Latin Americans and U.S. Latinos as legitimate news actors in a national news program.

The *Noticiero* closely follows immigration legislation in Congress and U.S. Latino candidates throughout the country. One telling example of a Latino angle on an otherwise predictable story concerns President Bill Clinton's failed attorney general nominee Zoe Baird. Univisión covered the scandal by following the revelation that Baird did not pay Social Security taxes for a Latino couple in her employ. Univisión interviewed the couple and then used the controversy as a "peg" for a week-long series on U.S. Latino domestic labor. From its Mexico City and other Latin America bureaus, Univisión journalists produce reports on the politics and economics of countries seldom featured by other U.S. news organizations.

A comparative content analysis of *Noticiero Univisión* sound bites with those of ABC's nightly news program highlights the differences—and similarities—in the two U.S. journalistic points of view. Both ABC and Univisión news rely heavily on government officials as newsmakers: 41% of Univisión sound bites are from government officials and an identical percentage of ABC sound bites are. Both networks also used what Gans (1979) called "unknowns," or ordinary people, for 27% of their sound bites.

These similarities between the leading national English-language national television newscast and its Spanish-language counterpart speak to the formulaic nature of U.S. television news—a ratings-validated commercial broadcasting formula that stretches across language and ethnic differences—a formula that Univisión journalists admit they mimic. According to the *Noticiero* executive producer, "The American [meaning U.S. English language] newscasts are the best in the world" (Calle, 1995, personal interview).

Evidence of the distinct worldview generated by the self-consciously U.S. Latino ethnic point of view of the *Noticiero Univisión* is found in an analysis of the race and ethnicity of the sound bites of the two national newscasts. There is a larger representation of people of color overall on *Univisión* than on ABC. Not unexpectedly, 35% of Univisión sound bites were from Latinos, as compared with less than 1% of ABC sound bites. Yet, news actors who are African American or Asian American are 50% less represented on *Univisión* than they are on ABC. In other words, the *Noticiero Univisión*, although modifying the White ethnocentrism of general-market news, is shaped by its own Latino ethnocentrism. Other "minorities" are excluded, or at least deemphasized.

Other Univisión news and public affairs programming is also modeled on successful U.S. commercial formulas. *Primer Impacto* (First Impact) is a somewhat sensational "tabloid TV" program. *Cristina*, a daily talk show, is much like *Oprah* or *Donahue*. *Temas y Debates* (Themes and Debates) is a Sunday morning political talk show. Despite the format similarities, however, the framing of these programs is clearly oriented to the U.S. Latino ethnic minority audience, featuring Latin American entertainers and movie and sports celebrities, U.S. Latino transvestites, Latin American natural disasters, and U.S. Latino domestic violence, kidnapping, and government officials.

On one level, these programs are Spanish-language translations of proven U.S. commercial formulas. Univisión, for all its cultural differences, is an audience-maximizing, advertiser-supported enterprise, like other U.S. networks. Considered as cultural products, these programs are examples of U.S. Latino cultural adaptation to the dominant society. These programs are produced by, and for, an audience-centered, U.S. Latino ethnic minority. As such, these cultural producers are securing a niche, a corner within, not apart, from U.S. society and claiming it for U.S. Latinos.

The United States is, according to Latino advertisers and marketers, home to the hemisphere's wealthiest (although not the largest) Latino media and consumer market. Univisión exports *Cristina* and *Primer Impacto* to Latin America, along with other U.S.-produced entertainment and sports programming. Currently, MTV, NBC, CBS, ESPN, and CNN produce Spanish-language programming in the United States for broadcast here, as well as export to Latin America. These are yet more examples of the growth of a panhemispheric media market, a melding of Latin American and U.S. Latino cultural production.

Newspapers and Magazines

Contemporary U.S. Latino-oriented print media exemplify the economic and structural integration of Latino-oriented media into U.S. general-market media. Latino-oriented newspapers and magazines target a higher income, more "assimilated" audience than do radio and television, but their general framing, a framing that constructs both a substantive and symbolic ongoing relationship between U.S. Latinos and Latin America, is the same as that of their electronic counterparts. There is also a print Latino agenda.

Currently, three Spanish daily newspapers are published in the United States. Peter W. Davidson bought New York's 82-year-old *El Diario-La Prensa* from Gannett in 1989. *El Diario-La Prensa* is the centerpiece of what Davidson described as a "Hispanic marketing company," which includes a magazine distribution firm, an advertising agency, and weekly Hispanic newspapers in San Francisco and Chicago. *El Diario-La Prensa* relies heavily on translated wire service copy and emphasizes news of Puerto Rico, Colombia and the Dominican Republic, the primary countries of origin of the New York metropolitan area's Latino communities.

Los Angeles' *La Opinión,* founded in 1915, is now 50% owned by the *Los Angeles Times,* the flagship newspaper of the Times-Mirror Co., and 50% owned by the founding Lozano family. Latinos are by far the largest minority group in Southern California, and are predicted to make up Los Angeles' majority population early in the 21st century. In its regular editions, the *Times* gives considerable coverage to U.S. Latino communities as well as Latin America, with an emphasis on Mexico and Central America. This practice is expanded in *La Opinión.*

In Miami, *El Nuevo Heraldo* recently suffered staff cutbacks, but continues daily publication. This Spanish-language publication of the *Miami Herald* has both the highest circulation and the highest amount of advertising of the nation's Spanish-language dailies, a reflection of the high income levels of south Florida's largely Cuban-origin Hispanic market. Meanwhile, weekly community-based Latino-oriented newspapers, many of them publishing bilingually, with some articles in English and some in Spanish, continue their (sometimes sporadic) publication, largely in major metropolitan areas.

Other U.S. Spanish-language newspapers have not fared as well. In Los Angeles, Fort Worth, Chicago, and New York, weekly and daily Spanish-language editions, published by those cities' major newspapers, including New York's *Daily News* (called *El Daily News*) have folded. According to their publishers, although circulation was at acceptable levels, they never gained enough advertising to be profitable. According to market analysts, this can be attributed to many advertisers' conviction that relatively higher income Latinos can effectively and efficiently be reached through English-language general-market media, or in the case of lower income Latinos, through Spanish-language radio and television (Myerson, 1995).

The search for vehicles with which to target U.S. Latino middle-class audiences continues with Spanish-language magazines, which are published—with special U.S. Latino-oriented framing—in the U.S. for distribution here and in Latin America. These include *Vanidades* (similar to *People*), *Buen Hogar* (a version of *Good Housekeeping*), *Cosmopolitan*, and *Deportes Internacionales*, a monthly sports magazine, published by Televisa, the Mexican entertainment conglomerate, and minority owner of Univisión.

The newest, fastest growing segment of Latino-oriented media is English-language magazines. These target upper income (family incomes of $50,000 and above) U.S. Latinos, presumably assimilated and either bilingual or English dominant. In these glossy monthly publications such as *Hispanic, Hispanic Business*, and *Latina* (from the publishers of *Essence*, an African American monthly), the Spanish language is present, but sparingly, as an ethnic emblem.

For instance, a regular column in *Hispanic Business*, which reports on promotions of U.S. Latinos in the corporate world is, like the rest of the magazine, written in English, but entitled "Avanzando," Spanish for "getting ahead." *Hispanic*, a feature and entertainment monthly, calls its national U.S. Latino restaurant and music reviews "Vida," or "Life." These Spanish-language words, embedded in English-language text, signal a minority ethnic affiliation that has not been eliminated by the professional and material successes of this segment of U.S. Latino audiences.

CONCLUSION

This analysis of U.S. Latino-oriented media brings into question traditional notions about the inevitability and totality of U.S. immigrant cultural assimilation (Handlin, 1941/1979; Higham, 1955/1988). Almost 150 years, roughly seven generations, after the conquest of much of Mexico by the United States, the Spanish language itself and the U.S. Spanish-language media, fed by Latin American immigration, continue to thrive, albeit in a relatively small percentage of the population. What is not clear is whether or how Latin American immigration to the United States will change. U.S. federal legislation may significantly curtail Latin American (and Asian) legal and illegal immigration, thereby depriving Spanish-language media of a sustaining audience. It also is not clear whether or to what extent U.S. Latino residents will continue to maintain their use of Spanish. Some earlier U.S. groups, such as the Germans, dropped their language after a generation or two.

The Spanish language plays an important symbolic (as distinct from communicative) role in media that target today's English-dominant, "assimilated" U.S. Latinos. These English-language Latino ethnic media suggest that although the Spanish language is a key ethnic indicator, a worldview that includes Latin America and U.S. Latino communities may become a more important defining element of contemporary U.S. Latino media. Yet, unlike several U.S. Spanish-language media, which are commercially established in the "narrowcasting" of the U.S. media market, these U.S. Latino English-language media have yet to prove themselves. The future of these and other U.S. Latino media are intertwined with the dynamism of the social movements of Latin American immigration and adaptation to U.S. society. Within the general media agendas that characterize the United States there are a variety of smaller, dynamic, specialized agendas. In a sense, the richness of the large public community springs from the richness of the small groups that make up the whole.

14

Setting the Agenda for Cross-National Research: *Bringing Values Into the Concept*

Holli A. Semetko

Andreina Mandelli

The concept of media agenda-setting has moved media effects scholarship away from the "limited effects" model that emerged from studies of voting behavior in the United States in the early post-World War II period. Agenda setting provides a perspective on the role of the news media in the political process as influential in a variety of ways. The strength of the agenda-setting hypothesis is that it has been supported by evidence from more than 20 years of studies drawing on a range of methodological approaches (see McCombs, 1992; McCombs & Shaw, 1993). Support for media agenda-setting effects on public opinion has been found using different research designs (cross-sectional surveys, panel studies, and experimental studies), in many countries, during and outside of election campaigns. The fact that a range of methodological approaches point to the same theoretical conclusion further strengthens the validity of the concept (see Hovland, 1959).

These studies are discussed at length in Semetko (1996a), with special emphasis on the methodological and theoretical developments stemming from the concepts of agenda setting, priming, and framing. Here, we assume that readers are somewhat familiar with the agenda-setting literature. We focus on a cross-national comparative perspective in media effects research. This perspective is shaped by an understanding of the institutional, historical, political, and media system contexts in which media agendas are formed and media effects occur on public opinion. A cross-national comparative perspective provides an opportunity to escape from the ethnocentrism common in most research (see Blumler & Gurevitch, 1995; Kohn, 1989; Prezworski & Teune, 1970; Swanson & Mancini, 1996). It provides an opportunity to examine how those involved in the political communication process—publics, political parties, and media—behave when operating under different institutional constraints and to consider the consequences of this for democracy (see, e.g., Semetko & Borquez, 1991).

There is a rich and varied literature in comparative political science from which scholars of comparative communication research benefit, although the comparative paradigm in political science itself has come to be reconsidered (Almond, 1990). Blumler, McLeod, and Rosengren (1992) argued that comparative communication research is best characterized as "exploratory" and that we need "(1) more theories specifically fashioned to guide communication analysis across spatial and temporal boundaries, and (2) more evidence of cumulativity in findings and their interpretation" for there to be a "formed genre of comparative communication research" (p. 4). Swanson (1992) argued that theoretical diversity is characteristic of cross-national comparative communication research. The most common approach is the case study. This may involve a case of a process, issue, or media or political institution in one, two, or several countries. The volume edited by Swanson and Mancini (1996) takes this approach with many countries, each discussed individually in single chapters, and the editors synthesize and integrate common themes in the introduction and conclusion. Another common approach in cross-national survey research involves comparing relationships between variables based on nationally representative samples in a number of countries, such as the pioneering work of Almond and Verba (1963, 1980) in *The Civic Culture* and the debate it generated resulting in *The Civic Culture Revisited.*

In this chapter, we discuss the system characteristics that provide a context for cross-national variation in media content and effects research. We sketch examples from previous and ongoing research projects to illustrate the value of and potential for future cross-national comparative research. We consider possible cross-national differences in news "frames" and the potential influences of political culture on news content and effects. We discuss the usefulness of bringing values into the concept of agenda setting. A better understanding of the dynamics of public opinion and political and social change can be gained by bringing together the media effects literature with that on political culture, as political agendas never exist in a vacuum.

SYSTEM CHARACTERISTICS

Political Systems

The idea that the press or news media take different forms in different countries, of course, is not new (Siebert, Peterson, & Schramm, 1956). But the consequences of this for the range and quality of political information in the news media during periods of routine governance as well as during election campaigns deserves more attention. Certain macrolevel characteristics should be taken into account when considering cross-national visibility of political information and political actors in the news media and its potential influence on public opinion. The types of political and electoral systems are important. Presidential systems such as that in the United States or most Latin American countries would be more candidate-driven and candidate-centered in comparison with parliamentary systems where a broader range of party elites may be visible. A simple plurality electoral system will further emphasize the individual, whereas the party counts for more in a proportional representation system. The party system—the range of political parties and their relative strength—is also important for the visibility of political elites and the treatment of political issues in the news (see also Seymour-Ure, 1974).

Media Systems

There are a number of aspects of the media system that could have a bearing on the way in which politics and elections are presented. One is the balance of public service versus commercial broadcasting, and the extent of competition in the broadcasting system. In Britain during an election campaign we expect greater emphasis on politics, the election, and the substantive issues on the public service channel with the commercial channels reserving less space for political and election news with more time given to topics that would maintain audience interest—the polls and horse race, or the personalities and private lives of the party leaders, for example (Nossiter, Scammell, & Semetko, 1995; Semetko, Scammell, & Nossiter, 1994). As media systems become more competitive, election broadcasting may also adapt to maintain audiences (Semetko, 1991).

Competition has altered the landscape of European broadcasting (*European Journal of Communication*, 1992). The balance between public and private broadcasting has changed in most countries over the past decade as new channels have entered the marketplace and competition has intensified. In the late 1970s and early 1980s, we could speak of broadcasting systems that were entirely public service. In Europe many of these were financed by license fees (Belgium, Denmark, Norway, Sweden), so-called *pure public* systems, whereas others were financed by a mixture of state funds and advertising revenue (Austria, Finland, France, Germany, Greece, Ireland, the Netherlands, Portugal, Spain, Switzerland), so-called *mixed revenue* public broadcasting systems (Brants & Siune, 1992). Commercial or private broadcasting was well established by this time in the United Kingdom and Italy—so-called *dual systems*—in which public service channel(s) competed with private channels. Other long-standing dual systems include Australia, Japan, and the United States, as well as many Latin American countries in which the broadcasting systems were based on a U.S. model. By the 1990s, the few pure public systems left had introduced competition and/or shifted to an advertising-based form of finance. Today, Germany might be described as a dual system with an increasingly equal share of the audience among public and private broadcasters. In Spain, new private channels financed entirely by advertising were launched in the late 1980s and are rapidly taking audiences from the public service monolith (Diez-Nicolas & Semetko, 1995; Lopez-Escobar, 1992; Lopez-Escobar & Faus-Belau, 1985). The more public service dominant the system, the more likely it is that prime time includes a broad range of political news and current affairs programs. The more commercially driven the system, the more market pressure for ratings and hence the more reluctant prime-time television is to replace popular entertainment programs with political informaion (Blumler, Brynin & Nossiter, 1986; Blumler & Nossiter, 1990).

Another important characteristic of the media system is the degree of political autonomy of broadcasting from government and political parties (see Smith, 1979). The more pure public the broadcasting system, the more likely it is that government or political parties influence the broadcasting organziations. As competition increases along with the number of channels, there is a diversification of income sources and this diminishes the control of political authorities (see Brants & Siune, 1992). The more pure commercial the broadcasting system, the less opportunity there is for government or political parties to exert direct influence over broadcasting organizations.

Even in countries where there continues to be a substantial public service component to the broadcasting system, the forms of control exerted by political parties or government varies. Public service broadcasting is not always equated with a progovernment stance. In Germany, there are advisory boards overseeing the two public service channels in which all parties represented in the state parliaments participate. In France, Greece, and Spain, the party in power appoints key people in the public service broadcasting organizations. Although Prime Minister Margaret Thatcher arguably ended the tradition of appointing nonpartisans to the BBC's Board of Governors, the BBC has nevertheless distinguished itself by often being on the receiving end of government criticism for its investigative and news reporting. The BBC can bite the hand that feeds it, so to speak.

There are traditions and practices surrounding party access to the public via broadcasting and the press. At least one democracy—Israel—actually prohibits television from broadcasting news about the politicians or parties in the weeks preceding the vote. The severe restrictions on the visual appearance of politicians in news and current affairs programs in the weeks before election day stem from the country's unique historical circumstances. As a result, viewers have witnessed some bizarre news clips in which the most important person in the story is missing—Egypt's Anwar Sadat meeting with Israel's Menachem Begin's empty chair in the 1981 campaign is just one example (Cohen & Wolfsfeld, 1995). The edited volume by Kaid and Holz-Bacha (1995) reviews restrictions on political advertising in Western democracies, as well as contents and effects. Some countries limit the presentation of poll results as the election nears.

Access can include the rules and regulations governing the purchase of airtime on electronic media as well as the availability of free airtime to broadcast advertisements or, as they are known in Britain, Party Election Broadcasts (PEBs) during campaigns, or Party Political Broadcasts (PPBs) in noncampaign periods (Scammell & Semetko, 1995). According to the 1990 Broadcasting Act in Britain, political parties are prohibited from purchasing time on commercial channels but continue to receive free airtime to present a handful of PEBs during a campaign or PPBs during the year, although these may be no less than 5 minutes or longer than 10 minutes. In Germany, the parties are permitted to purchase time on the private channels and the ads broadcast in the free time made available on the public channels are no more than 2 to 3 minutes (Schoenbach, 1987). Parties may pay to advertise directly in newspapers, but other forms of relationships between parties and the press—such as ownership or subsidization of the newspaper by a party, business, or union—may also influence access.

Political culture, historical context, and traditions surrounding political broadcasting are also considerations. Why is it, for example, that in parliamentary democracies such as Germany, Britain, and Spain, the range and quality of political information available to viewers of main evening news programs in the final weeks before election day varies so much from country to country? Politicians in these and other countries rely on similar sorts of campaigning styles aimed largely at television news deadlines (Swanson & Mancini, 1996). Television news reporters operate under similar kinds of production constraints in each country. These factors are not alone in shaping the key characteristics of election news. Culturally relevant definitions of balance influence the content of political news (Semetko, 1996b). There is considerable cross-national variation in campaign reporting on political parties and actors in recent election campaigns in these countries (Semetko, Diez-Nicolas, Schoenbach, Scammell, & Nossiter, 1994). The essays spanning 25 years of political communication research in Britain and the United States by Blumler and Gurevitch (1995) illustrate the persistent importance of political culture in comparative communication scholarship.

CROSS-NATIONAL DIFFERENCE IN NEWS "FRAMING"

Gitlin (1980) argued that frames make it possible for journalists to deal with large amounts of information rapidly and routinely, and package it for audience consumption. These frames provide a way for audiences to interpret events. According to Kosicki (1993),

> We make interpretations based on abstract and conceptual reasoning, and accommodate new information into our existing frames. These frames may be thought of as a type of schema, similar to scripts, prototypes, categories, and so on. That is, they help structure our everyday experiences and basically facilitate the process of meaning construction. These frames allow us to understand issues in particular ways, and also guide news work and audience responses to media content. (p. 115)

The way an issue or problem is framed—as urgent or negligible, for example—could shape public perceptions of the salience of that issue (Schoenbach & Semetko, 1992). McCombs (1996) called this a second level of agenda setting, where the attributes of a particular message may be as important as the broad subject of the message.

In-depth interviews have been used in the United States to understand how audiences frame issues and how that is influenced by news frames presented. These studies suggest there are important divergences between the discourse of journalists and politicians on the one hand, and viewers and readers in the mass public on the other (see, e.g., Gamson, 1992; Graber, 1988). This disjuncture between publics and elites led Neuman, Just, and Crigler (1992) to conclude: "The disjuncture in conceptualization also underscores the disconfirmation of the agenda-setting hypothesis. People think for themselves, and media and official versions of problems and events make up only part of their schema for public issues. The disjuncture in public and media frames demonstrates that alternative frames are out there in the public discourse on issues" (p. 112). Different frames allow a "freedom" in interpretation, in other words.

Going deeper into audience members' private thoughts and discussions about political issues, Neuman et al. (1992) provided evidence of individuals' abilities to draw on their own personal experiences, and stores of knowledge and to discount or disregard media issue "frames." However, it is worth noting that the gap between the public's rank order of the media's most common media frames identified in chapter 4 of *Common Knowledge*—conflict, economics, human impact, moral values, and powerlessness—is not as great if the frame of conflict, which is one of the most important features of news stories, is omitted. The Spearman's Rho is +.20 when the rank order of all five frames is compared between the public and media agendas, but if the conflict frame is removed from the list the correlation between public and media agendas is +.80.[1]

---

[1]This information was provided to the author (M. McCombs, personal communication, May 1996).

How the Media and the Public Frame the Daily News

	Media		Public	
Frame	%	Rank	%	Rank
1. Conflict	29	2	6	5
2. Economics	16	4	21	3
3. Human impact	18	3	36	1
4. Moral values	4	5	15	4
5. Powerlessness	33	1	22	2

To what extent do the media agenda and the public agree on their picture of the world? For all five frames the correlation is +.20. For four frames (omitting conflict) this is +.80 Spearman's Rho (Neuman et al., 1992).

In his Foreword to *The Formation of Campaign Agendas* (Semetko, Blumler, Gurevitch, & Weaver, 1991), framing is described by McCombs as a useful way to understand the impact of journalists' professional ideology on the news agenda.

> A news story is not a random set of facts. A news story differs significantly in style, for example, from a world almanac entry. Even though both represent a set of facts, they are distinct genres of writing. A news story is exactly that, a story. It has an organizing theme that frames the facts. The difference between a hack and a professional journalist lies in the ability to discern an organizing theme in a set of facts. Note that the reference is to *an* organizing theme, not *the* organizing theme. Because there is no single compelling theme in most newsworthy situations, several questions must be pursued about the emergence of the central themes in election campaign stories.

> Who determines the frame of a campaign story? The candidates and the party organizations, or the journalists? In the response to this question lies the tension between enterprise reporting with the responsibility of the news media to present an independent picture of the day's events and reflective reporting with the responsibility to allow significant political groups access to present their views in the news media. Individual journalists and news organizations differ in their response to this question. . . . Cultural differences also exist between American and British journalists in the substantive frames of election stories. (pp. xvi–xvii)

An ongoing study of public opinion in the Netherlands aims to shed light on these cultural differences and provide refinement to theories of the effects of the news media as well as cross-national comparative theories of political and social change within an understanding of institutional contexts.[2] The Dutch study provides an opportunity to consider the importance of key institutional influences such as the parliamentary and coalition-based system of government and an increasingly competitive television news marketplace, on the frames presented in the news and among the public. As many continental European countries have similar institutional characteristics, the Dutch study will also generate hypotheses about news framing, media agenda setting, and priming in other countries where comparable research is possible or already underway (Diez-Nicolas & Semetko, 1995; Scammell & Semetko, 1995; Semetko & Schoenbach, 1994). The Dutch investigation uses content analysis to identify the prominent issues and the different frames represented in national television news and the major newspapers. Experiments provide a rigorous test of the impact of particular news frames on political attitudes of Dutch audiences. Survey data collected in collaboration with the Netherlands Institute for Public Opinion provide generalizable evidence concerning the effects of news on public opinion.

[2]Professor Holli Semetko and Dr. Patti Valkenburg at the University of Amsterdam are supported by the Dutch KNAW for this study of media influences on the Dutch public linking the concepts of agenda setting, priming, and framing in a multiple method research design.

It may be that political, economic, and social issues in the Netherlands are framed in similar ways as in the United States (see, e.g., Iyengar, 1990a, 1990b; Neuman et al., 1992) or Britain and that these frames have consequences for Dutch public opinion about issues, political parties, and political leaders. However, the multiparty coalition system of government (as opposed to a presidential system in the United States or an adversarial majority system in the United Kingdom) could mean there actually is less evidence of the "conflict" frame in Dutch political news. Different viewpoints within government and opposition groups could result instead in more emphasis on conflict in political news (see van der Eijk & van Praag, 1987; Kleinnijenhuis, Oegema, & de Ridder, 1995). There may also be different kinds of political conflict frames (such as government vs. opposition, or among the coalition parties of government).

The structure of the broadcast news media in the Netherlands is a consequence of the country's history and political culture, based on a distribution of power across various social groups or "pillars" in the society (McQuail, 1994). The relatively recent introduction of private TV (vs. public service broadcasting) in Holland may mean there are new presentation techniques aimed at increasing audience share, as evident in other European countries. There may be more political news on private channels framed in the context of "human interest," with an emphasis on individuals and personalities. This, in parallel with the decline of Dutch political parties (Andeweg & Galen, 1993), could potentially "prime" the Dutch public to alter the traditional criteria by which they evaluate parties, leaders, and issues, and draw instead on issues prominent in the news. We would benefit from similar studies conducted with other national systems.

Political Culture

There is much evidence in political science literature to support the inclusion of political culture as a variable in cross-national research. Scholarly interest has increased over the past decades, not least because of the work of Inglehart (1977, 1990), which emphasizes the development of so-called *postmaterialist* values—as opposed to traditional materialist values—in advanced industrial democracies. New postmaterialist attitudes, particularly among younger cohorts in the 1970s and early 1980s, encouraged the development of new political parties on the left in Europe, such as the Greens in Germany and elsewhere. Postmaterialist values are those associated with quality of life issues and individual freedom. These values have become more evident among publics in all Western democracies since the end of World War II and, at the same time, social cleavage politics has diminished and issue voting has increased in many countries (Dalton, 1988). This process sometimes has led to electoral realignment because the traditional political parties are organized around traditional social cleavages. These processes are generational and developmental in nature.

According to Dalton (1996), "public opinion surveys . . . document the slow and steady growth of postmaterial values in advanced industrial democracies. An evolutionary change in values is transforming the nature of citizen politics" (p. 97).

Nevertheless, there remains considerable debate within the scholarly community about this (see, e.g., Davis, 1996). There is also evidence that in the United States public opinion about the most important issues facing the country have become less "liberal" since the early 1970s (Smith, 1990). In addition, McCombs and Zhu (1995), in further analysis of trends in the U.S. public opinion agenda between 1954 and 1994 found that prior to 1970, there was a significant decline in concern about materialistic issues and a significant increase in concern about postmaterialistic issues, but that the trends essentially reversed course in the post-1970 era with materialistic concerns on the rise and a significant drop in postmaterialistic concerns.

Culture, according to Inglehart (1990) is a "system of attitudes, values and knowledge that is widely available within a society and transmitted from generation to generation. . . . Consequently action cannot be interpreted as simply the result of external situations: Enduring differences in cultural learning also play an essential part in shaping what people think and do" (pp. 18–19). Political opinion change is not due exclusively to an individual's cognitive capabilities, but rather: "Cultural men process experience into action through general cognitive, affective, and evaluative predispositions; the patterns of such predispositions vary from society to society, from social segment to social segment; they do not vary because objective social situations or structures vary but because of culturally determined learning" (Eckstein, 1988, cited in Inglehart, 1990, p. 19).

A political culture approach to understanding political opinion change has three important features. One is the inclusion of cultural-evaluative processes in the cognitive and affective phenomena related to public opinion formation. Because this process is normative and historically bounded, a second feature is that the specific political cultures and historical situations are crucial contexts for any analysis of political change and public opinion. A third is that social change is viewed as a long-term process: "These key postulates of the political culture approach have crucial implications for social change. Cultural theory implies that a culture cannot be changed overnight. One may change the rulers and the laws, but changing basic aspects of the underlying culture will take many years" (Inglehart, 1990, p. 19).

BRINGING VALUES INTO THE CONCEPT OF AGENDA SETTING

The political culture approach to understanding public opinion has reintroduced values into the study of political change, but the approach has paid little attention to the impact of media performance in this process. The media are considered to be socialization agents that foster the process of social development and political sophistication, and therefore also postmaterialism and "new" issue-based politics. Whereas the cognitive school in public opinion research puts less emphasis on the affective side phenomena, because it is primarily concerned with the cognitive mechanism that helps explain the short-term formation of public choices, Inglehart's perspective includes values in the analysis but does not consider short-term political change. A number of important research developments, however, have suggested not only that values may be the new structuring dimension of politics, but also that media framing of the symbolic issues may be at the origin of public opinion irrationality and volatility (Zaller, 1992), consistent with what Edelman (1964) wrote about the role of media in symbolic politics. The potential short-term influence looks quite different from the long-term socialization role of the media described by Inglehart (1990). In the latter, media effects on political culture are primarily described in terms of learning and cognitive sophistication. In the case of short-term influences, media may influence the opinion formation at the symbolic level. Here we need to know more.

How can this be integrated into agenda-setting research? The aim of Mandelli (1997) is to do just that, by addressing questions about the role of the mass media in a major scandal in Italian politics, drawing on survey data and media content analysis. Mandelli's case study of political corruption focuses on whether the media contributed to the direction (and the volatility) of radical opinion changes that occurred in Italy in the early 1990s. The study hypothesizes that the news outlets were particularly important in the process of building the new political-cultural environment that followed the disruption of the old ("corrupt") political system. In Italy, the inherent limits of a single-country case study are outweighed by the opportunity to study the complex dynamics of public opinion changes and interpret the data within their institutional, political, and cultural contexts. The Italian government has turned over many times in recent years. The problem of corruption in politics is not uncommon in most societies. Indeed, the way in which the news media influences public opinion about government and political leaders in the context of scandals is the subject of ongoing research in Spain and Britain.[3]

If, as Carmines and Stimson (1989) argued, symbolic issues are the most likely to influence mass opinion changes, then underlying values should be strong predictors of individual political opinions and voting intentions. Some scholars did not find that postmaterialist values had expected influences on Italian electoral politics, but this does not exclude the possibility that other values (or other combinations of the basic values) are important in the Italian political-cultural context (see Sartori, 1969, and Wildavsky, 1987, for arguments about beliefs and values as products of specific social and policy

---

[3]A cross-national comparative study of media coverage of political corruption in Spain and Britain is currently underway, involving Dr. Maria Jose Canel at the University of Navarra in Pamplona and Dr. Karen Sanders at Sheffield University in the UK.

contexts). Attention should be paid to specific historical circumstances of Italian political culture (particularly the emphasis on solidaristic and participatory values; see Putnam, 1993), which is not easily illuminated using Anglo-Saxon public opinion categories (La Palombara, 1987). But Mackie, Mannheimer, and Sami's (1992) results may also suggest that the transformations of the political culture are not rigid and highly predictable long-term processes, as those described by the postmaterialist hypothesis. They may also follow short-term patterns of change—that may even be in conflict with the long-term change—due to development of specific political-cultural situations.

Values among the Italian public may have changed not only because of changes in the generational cleavages (due to social change and different socialization processes), but also because of media framing of key historical and policy events. It is therefore important to include the intervening role of political values in the media influence process in the short term, and in the study of political-cultural change. Media influences on political socialization may help explain generational change in public opinion and long-term realignment. Media impact on political values, due to the framing of the issues in the agenda, may help to explain both cultural and political instability (and in the Italian case identify a possible role played by the media in the rise of new parties on both sides of the left–right continuum).

Mandelli's argument partly conflicts with the mainstream idea of the process of the development of political culture and its impact on public opinion for at least two reasons (Mandelli, 1997). First, if media content can influence political values, this means political culture is not only a stable and long-term generational phenomenon (as claimed in the political culture literature), but subject to short-term change. Second, if political values can be primed by media content, then not only are changes in postmaterialist and materialist values relevant, but the basic components of the culture (the priority assigned to order, to political egalitarianism, to economic concerns, and to individual freedoms) also need to be considered in the context of media content. The framework of the Italian case study is based on the view that there is an important political process at work in building the agenda of public sentiments as well as the agenda of political issues. In this process, media play a critical role, because the framing of political issues is a process in which news media may be particularly independent from the political reality, following news values external to the political debate (Gans, 1979: Neuman et al., 1992 ; Tuchman, 1978).

CONCLUSION

We began by emphasizing the wealth of evidence collected over more than two decades, based on a range of methodological approaches, that supports the idea that the news media shape public perceptions of the importance of issues. However, we should also mention that some recent studies in Europe found mixed or no support for the agenda-setting hypothesis. Panel studies conducted during election campaigns, for example, show fluctuation in Germans' opinions about the importance of issues that cannot be explained by the pattern of coverage in the news outlets to which the respondents were exposed (Semetko & Schoenbach, 1993, 1994), little or no correspondence between British television news agendas and individual viewers' agendas (Miller, Clarke, Harrop, LeDuc, & Whiteley, 1990), and the lack of any significant effect by a leading partisan British tabloid newspaper on the vote switching of its readers (Curtice & Semetko, 1994). However, the absence of evidence to support the agenda-setting hypothesis does not mean that other important media effects on the public were entirely absent. Significant media effects on knowledge and on public evaluations of political leaders were found in these German and British election studies—cognitive and affective, if not always a behavioral (i.e., voting change) effect.

It is important to consider how public priorities and political sympathies are shaped in nonelection (or routine) news periods. A 3-year panel study of Germans in the early 1990s in nonelection periods found significant media effects on individuals' feelings of political efficacy (Semetko & Valkenburg, 1996). Latin American research indeed suggests that in Brazil, preelection campaign news can play a major role in shaping a candidate's future (de Lima, 1993). Miller et al. (1990) revealed important biases in favor of the incumbent government on British television news, particularly in the period prior to the official campaign. Political change is ongoing, not just taking place at the time of an election.

Agenda setting and the related concepts of priming and framing are important bases for more coordinated cross-national research efforts. These studies should be considered from two angles—one concerns how the media agenda and story frames are formed and the relative contributions of politicians and journalists to the process; the other concerns the influences of the media agendas and story frames on public opinions about the salience of issues, the urgency of problems and the responsibility for solving them, and related evaluations of political parties and leaders.

Comparative political communication research would benefit from integrating a political culture approach to understanding political and social change with a more cognitive approach to understanding public opinion. Political culture helps to explain why a U.S. news story about poverty often is framed in such a way as to place the responsibility on the individual rather than on the system or state (Iyengar, 1991), whereas a story about poverty is likely to be framed differently in most European social welfare states. One can only speculate about the resulting influence on public policy.

The study of media influence on the dynamics of public opinion should be integrated with the study of the postmaterialist value changes that are evident in most Western societies (see Dalton, 1996; Inglehart, 1990). This is also relevant to societies in transition such as Russia or Latin America, where postmaterialist values are considerably less evident than are materialist concerns. By bringing public values into the concept of media agenda setting, research can provide a deeper understanding of the role and influence of the media in the development and dynamics of public opinion about important issues. This understanding is needed in all countries that seek to build equitable societies. Presumably we all want that—leaders, citizens, journalists, and scholars.

15

Agendas for a Public Union or for Private Communities? *How Individuals Are Using Media to Reshape American Society*

Donald L. Shaw
Bradley J. Hamm

There has been a disruption of American social union. There is little room for compromise on such public issues as abortion or gun ownership. Less extremely, men differ from women, and Whites from Blacks (and others) on quotas or affirmative action programs. In fact, men often differ strongly from men, women from women, and minority members from each other. From one point of view there is an erosion of social toleration. The "liberal" or "conservative" mass media have often been blamed for the state of society about which they bring us daily and hourly messages. From another, there is an absence of widely shared commitment to overcome social norms. We are seeing the loss of a core, resulting in a basic change in people.

The United States is no stranger to disagreements. The Civil War stretched over 4 years and resulted in more than a half-million men killed in battle or from disease. The late 19th and early 20th centuries saw violent disagreement between management and labor, along with the finally successful efforts of women to win the right to vote in elections everywhere. What is different about recent times is that—for the first time in U.S. history—people of like minds easily can find each other through specialized television, cable, or radio shows, or through use of "small" media of many kinds, from electronic mail to faxes to computer-generated newsletters. Social issues are no longer mostly confined to geographic areas, as with the Civil War, or even social class, as with labor–management disagreements. Today people can organize and influence political systems without even meeting face to face. A major magazine in 1995 described the politically disaffected this way: "(They) do not fit the media and political stereotypes: They include militia members and moderates, angry men and frightened women, liberals and conservatives, drifters and doctors" (see "Notes from underground," 1995, p. 25).

Newer communication technologies—faxes, e-mail, mobile telephones—now allow individuals to communicate directly with each other, or even to collect together into special interest groups, as a counter to the whole. Even the few major mass media are fragmenting into smaller, if often still large, units, as AM radio has spawned talk shows that attract millions of like-thinking audience members. These communication technologies are centrifugal in direction, pulling away from the core. Recent, smaller communication technologies have weakened the force of social gravity so that the centrifugal forces are slightly out of balance, and centripetal forces that pull us toward a common core are weakening.

The thesis of this chapter is simple—that the traditional mass media are in decline as audiences shift to more individualized media, and, partially as a result, the ability of leaders to hold large social systems together is also in decline because citizens are as likely to seek out messages from other individuals or groups who think like themselves as they are to remain committed to messages that represent the entire group. Further, this loss of community accelerates the decline of mass media, because people no longer have as strong a need for mass ties. As a result, national agendas are in danger of fragmenting. Thus, a downward spiral occurs in the use of mass media. Individuals who find their views reinforced through specialized programs such as talk shows or through their own electronic mail groups have the courage to stand against or ignore the masses if, for example, they are trying to save the whales in the Pacific Ocean, vote with presidential challenger Ross Perot, or live in what have been called electronic "virtual communities." Unfortunately those who are skinheads, bigots, or pornographers also can easily find each other. Like the Roman god Janus, communication technology has two faces.

Evolving technology has put into the hands of millions of ordinary people the capability of both gathering and, more significantly, reaching out. Historically we were accustomed to learning knowledge from permanent institutions such as the church, school, workplace, and government. These institutions, all triangular in organization, have treated knowledge as if it were relatively stable for all times and as if the structures that administer the knowledge were also fixed, even if people are exposed to competing information agendas.

These historic assumptions are questionable. Many churches, especially the ones that are established hierarchies, are struggling to maintain the faith in an age of unbelief or behavioral challenge. Governments are imperiled, as voters around the world turn the rascals out. Within the United States, many politicians and journalists have argued that we have hit a bad place in our democracy with distressed voters who are fed up with those who are running things. In fact, subgroups are so polarized and ensconced in private groups that our democracy itself may be imperiled. Each president seems to have about 2 years before powerful subgroups coalesce and sufficiently polarize to challenge the ability to build consensus. It is not a question of political ideology or even necessarily dissatisfaction with those who are in office. Regardless of who is in, individuals and groups will naturally gravitate to the opposition and, assisted by intercommunication, feel little need to carry on a dialogue with the larger social whole.

THE STATE AND MASS MEDIA

For nearly three centuries, the national state has dominated world politics. The modern mass media—large-circulation daily newspapers, general news magazines, network radio and television, and commercial films—helped consolidate the national state by focusing attention at the top, sometimes as a result of dictatorships, as in the former Soviet Union or contemporary Cuba, and sometimes as a result of widely shared news values, as in the United States.

Audiences have gathered around each mass medium in large numbers at the same time, as with network radio and television, or at approximately the same time, as with newspapers, magazines, or commercial films. Audiences are fickle, apparently because individuals seem to spend about the same about of money each year for the mass media, so a new medium gains audiences at the expense of older media. As audience members shift, faithful (and often aging) members of the audience remain committed enough to linger around the medium with which they are familiar. Others, who are less committed to established media, move to new media. The force of habit works in favor of the mass medium, as it does for any other activity.

The spread of communication technologies makes the threat of very large monolithic states less threatening than ever, and many national organizations, such as large armies, are increasingly anachronistic. Manufacturing and business interests have been international for decades. At the same time that large national boundaries are being pressured, communication has become a central force in the national life, where local structures are replacing large national ones—in some cases, literally, as in Bosnia, and in others metaphorically, as in the United States, where groups have moved inside of politically correct boundaries to live apart from the society as a whole.

We are becoming wired together as individuals and groups, not just in national systems, and it is not clear if we will learn to live in peace or in conflict. The centripetal forces of which the mass media are an important part are delicately balanced against the centrifugal forces, of which the small communication media are also very much a part.

A DISRUPTION OF SOCIAL UNION

Many—but certainly not all—individuals have collected in small, self-contained social units and, like termites, they are nibbling on the social wood foundations of our national union. This is not the fault of communication, and certainly the movement is too powerful for the declining mass media to "stop." Nor it is the fault of the groups, made up of individuals with real or imagined grievances. Those institutions that historically have attempted to nourish a common core—schools, mainline churches, government, and mass press—are all struggling. For years, the flow of mass media could be visualized like a pyramid, with a few leaders at the top and the masses at the bottom. Now horizontal communication is as or more powerful than vertical communication. In a way that philosopher Ortega y Gasset (1932) did not imagine, the masses are beginning to revolt—not as individuals but as hard-core interest groups, now that individuals can find each other.

As the mass media decline, the ability of national states to hold together also is declining because leaders are losing the power to control the spread of the national political, economic, and social agendas. One outcome of the mass media, it turns out, is that large numbers of people reading, watching, or listening to a common voice at the same time meant that at least some of the agenda was collectively shared. Agenda-setting research does strongly find that the mass media historically have had the power to tell people what to think about, even if the audience does not think about issues the same way. With the decline of mass media, that community-wide agenda-setting power is in decline, with implications for holding society together by consensus.

Although many, no doubt, may be delighted at the decline of "liberal" or "conservative" media, this erosion of national power should be of concern to all of us. One can watch some states, such as the former Soviet Union and the old Yugoslavia, fragment, and separatist feeling is strong in Quebec. The mass media for a half-century operated as a centripetal force to pull different parts of a nation together, but a declining mass media have also weakened the force of social gravity. Even a controlled press could not hold the Soviet Union together.

Like most people in history, we are not aware that we are passing from one era of history to another. It takes the work of historians, coming along later, to group years and provide convenient labels for periods of time so that our collective experience can be organized by times, like a shelf of library books are organized by subjects. Nevertheless we are leaving one era of history—the era of mass media—and passing into an era in which the mass media, although powerful and rich, are no longer strongly able to identify mass audiences and shape collective mass opinion along clearly defined boundaries, such as a national state or even a small, local city. Communication technology has made profound revolution possible.

FORCE CENTRIPETAL: A COMMON AGENDA

For nearly three centuries, certainly for the past half-century, the evolution of mass media has nourished the growth of coherent communities by focusing on common issues. Those media that challenged the larger community at times—for example, the Black-led abolitionist press in the United States—still sought to improve the larger society by addressing its social, political, and cultural injustices. However, media, schools, churches, the post office, and spreading transportation provided the centripetal forces of society. In the colonial years, churches and ministers were probably more important than small-circulation weekly newspapers with their (often) post-master editors.

As communication technologies developed—steam presses, inexpensive paper making, typewriters, telephones, photography—these were significantly employed to expand the power of the mass media as a national force. However, centrifugal forces also were developing. Communication is central to human activities, as it is to the lives of all other animals, and the technology that allowed development of sophisticated communication, such as television, radio, newspapers, magazines, and films, allowed humans to extend the range of their voices far beyond the local community.

Technological developments in themselves are neither good nor bad. Yet the results of technological change can be both, and one cannot predict what will happen, if anything, when a new invention is introduced to society. The printing press allowed manuscript books to be printed, which perhaps could have been predicted. The printing press eventually supported the publications of newspapers and magazines, which probably could not have been predicted.

Likewise, one could not predict that newspapers, and later, magazines and pamphlets, would range into the countryside beyond the borders of the places where they were published. With the spread of more dependable mail service, some publications were delivered to large regions. Until the 1840s, most citizens of the new nation thought in terms of their states or regions, such as the South or New England. Then historians such as Hildreth (1969) and Bancroft (1834–1875) began to write histories of about the entire nation, which was a new way of thinking—a nation with its own fixed boundaries.

Some evidence suggests that communication technology is an important part of that process. Merritt (1966) argued that colonial newspapers helped build a sense of American—as contrasted with British—community. Schlesinger (1958) argued that newspapers set up the basis of the American revolution by shaping men's minds long before the shooting started. The very concept of a nation as a distinct unity that stretched beyond local towns and villages seems partly to be the result of the ability of print media, books, newspapers, magazines, pamphlets, and brochures to send ideas across space, as one might throw a stone. A nation is, in a sense, a collective agenda.

If many people share the same ideas, expressed in common media, then they are better able to participate in a common political system. Knight (1960) argued that the press helped the United States stay a coherent nation during the 19th century as it spread west because so many people in the territories kept in touch with those back home via newspapers, however tardy in delivery, and later by telegraph. Communication technology first fixed communities in place and allowed those places to become quite large. In the early 19th century, political leader Fisher Ames (see Shaw, 1984) wondered how far a nation could spread without falling apart, as an iceberg crumbles at its edges, but the press of the period kept fences around the divergent populations. The newspapers of the period located people in place. The 1844 invention of the telegraph speeded up communication, but also did its part in keeping people in touch with each other.

Later communication technologies—the camera, radio, and television—extended the range of communities even further across space, but these media usually remained focused on communities in space for most of their subjects, relying on official sources who tended to be those leaders who were elected or appointed, in government, public service, education, or business.

COMMUNICATION TECHNOLOGY
AND NATIONAL POWER

Canadian scholar Harold Innis (1950) studied the relationship between communication developments and power and found a relationship between the ability to communicate and state power. For example, and probably too simply, if Roman legions could be moved around in response to easily transmitted orders, then the Empire would not need so many legions stationed everywhere. In modern times, some leaders in the economically developing world have complained about the control by developed nations over the world's information distribution system, such as the Associated Press (United States) or Reuters (England). The satellites that are so important to modern communication were hoisted by developed nations, a modern example of the direct relationship between technological capability and information power. Some have called for a new world information order in which all nations have more stake in the sharing of information.

Other Canadian scholars, McLuhan and Fiore (1967), found unanticipated effects from television. This medium required much from viewers who perceptually had to fill in the picture, thus becoming involved, according to McLuhan. Such media were cool, whereas print media brought the message relatively completed and were hot. By requiring involvement, McLuhan argued, cool media were causing people around the world to connect with each other—all shared the involvement of a cool medium—that accounted for the wide sharing of values about, for example, rock stars and jeans. Technology changed human perception. McLuhan argued that individuals were retribalizing as a result of exposure to mass media, particularly television. Based on history, the word *tribes* has a positive connotation. Tribes lived in particular locations and developed mechanisms to nourish and protect tribal members.

In Germany, Adolph Hitler and his Nazi Party showed the chilling power of the state to influence masses of people once the messages were limited and controlled at the top and the competition of alternative messages at the bottom was cut off. In those days, the telephone and telegraph were relatively easily controlled, unlike today's faxes, computer network messages, mobile telephones, transistor radios, televisions, and audio and video players. The mass media fit democracies such as the United States and England well, but it was clear that the mass media also fit the totalitarian state very well. The overlap between the dictatorship of Germany's Hitler and the Soviet Union's Josef Stalin—the most powerful and destructive dictatorships of modern times—fit completely within the era of mass media, 1930 to 1980. In a controlled state, the mass media can be made to support specified goals with considerable power. After becoming chancellor, Hitler developed ways to control German film, newspapers, and radio. In the 1930s, control of the media meant control of the national agenda more than at any other time in history.

Hitler's minister of armaments, Albert Speer (1970), pointed out that the mass media changed the function of political parties. Hitler needed only to state goals through radio, and party members listened like everyone else. The function of party members therefore was less to carry down the word than to make sure instructions were carried out. These two functions require two very different types of people. In the United States, political parties changed as national leaders reached audiences directly through radio and television. In the 1930s, mass media could be used for evil, as by Hitler and Stalin in the Soviet Union, but also for good. In the early depths of the Great Depression, the newly elected Franklin Roosevelt calmed the nation with a series of radio addresses, delivered from beside his fireplace in the White House. A decade later, Winston Churchill rallied his nation with radio addresses that defied Hitler—"We will fight them on the beaches"—and complimented those who were keeping England from falling—"never have so many owed so much to so few" (about English pilots).

National states are organized with leaders and legislative bodies that pass laws to protect and guide the state. These leaders, and all who work for the government, necessarily must work within some kind of consensus. Even dictators are aware of the need to fit their actions to the realities of public opinion. During World War II, Nazis used plain-clothed SS officers to go to bars with the mission of eavesdropping. Every leader works toward consensus. In the age of the mass media, this was easier done than said. In the 1930s and in World War II, President Roosevelt dealt with a few reporters. A few wire services supplied information for the nation's newspapers, magazines, and radio stations. Reporters and columnists often developed close working relationships with leaders—for example, in the 1930s *New York Times* reporter

Arthur Krock would invite the secretary of state to lunch—and had the most direct interest in keeping things the way they were. That relationship is still evident among reporters today. Studies show that most sources are official and at the top. Columnists still write mostly about those at the top of political structures, although the period in which these comments were widely shared and followed is passing into history.

The mass media industry was, and is, well organized for those times when there is national crisis, when millions listen for details or for guidance from leaders. When President John Kennedy was assassinated in 1963, nearly everyone learned of the tragic event within hours, and millions spent the next 4 days in front of a television set watching details of the later murder of suspected assassin Lee Harvey Oswald, the funeral of President Kennedy, and the swearing in of President Lyndon B. Johnson. In 1994, millions watched a televised car chase for professional football star and media personality O. J. Simpson, later acquitted of murdering his wife and another man. At times, the mass media have enormous power to focus on a single event or issue.

THE RISE AND FALL
OF THE MASS MEDIA AUDIENCES

In the 1930s, radio and film were at the top of their power to reach audiences. By the 1950s, television reached millions, causing an erosion of film and prime-time radio audiences, and holding the attention of millions until cable television began to fragment audiences significantly in the 1980s. But the period of 1930 through 1980 was the era of mass media. During that 50-year span—marked at the beginning by the rise of radio and sound film with daily newspapers holding steady, and at the end by the decline of network television—governments and society fit well with the mass media. With a few major mass media, it was easy to contact a few major news sources at the top of governments, businesses, churches, schools, and other organizations. The traditional mass media concentrated on covering a few leaders at the top for the benefit of masses of people at the bottom. During the years between 1930 and 1980, there was not nearly as much competition for audience time as offered by today's faxes, computer electronic mail, videotapes and audiotapes, cable television choices, and mobile phones, or multiple home telephones.

Mass media audiences are influenced by habit and enticed by novelty. In the 1990s, those loyal to the three traditional television networks—NBC, CBS, and ABC—tended to be viewers who had also tuned in earlier in their lives. The same trend was true for daily newspaper readers. Communication scholar Stevenson (1994) concluded that the long-standing hope of newspaper publishers that young people would become readers when they became older and needed solid community information cannot be supported. Instead, audiences continue to use those media that they learned to use and enjoyed in youth and as young adults. Unless older media can find ways to attract audiences they seem doomed to decline to niches with mostly older readers and viewers, with occasional puffs of young interest, depending on the news or programs.

Furthermore, it appears there is a limit on how much entertainment and news and advertising that audiences need or want, just as there is a limit to how much food one can eat in a given day. Charles E. Scripps (1959) of the Scripps-Howard newspaper group concluded in the late 1950s that media audiences and advertisers together account for about 5% of the gross national product (GNP). That figure generally has held steady for about 50 years, as long as it has been measured (McCombs, 1972), in contrast with expenditures for health care, which have exploded during the past two decades from about 5% to around 14% of the GNP. The health care field is expanding and the traditional media are not.

The logical conclusion is that if expenditures for mass media are relatively fixed, whether by economics, habit, or taste, then a new medium takes away from an older medium, as magazines took audiences and advertisers from newspapers, and television took audiences from film and both audiences and advertising from radio. One can argue that technological change causes the mass media to have natural life cycles, from birth and youth through adulthood to declining age. Figure 15.1 sketches one argument for several media. It shows that newspapers achieved their highest point of audience use in the 1920s and 1930s, when each household averaged about 1.5 daily newspapers, as contrasted with less than .5 today. We have seen that film drew the most people in the late 1940s, a period when network radio also gleaned most of the prime-time audience. Commercial television began an audience decline in the early 1980s with competition from cable television. Cable television so far reaches about 60% of U.S. homes and may have stalled unless cable operators can provide a diversity of services that cannot be delivered through small-dish home satellite receivers.

Characteristic of the media in Fig. 15.1 is that each achieved high circulation and that there were relatively few competing media. Even with daily newspapers, the highest number published in the nation, about 2,600 in all languages,

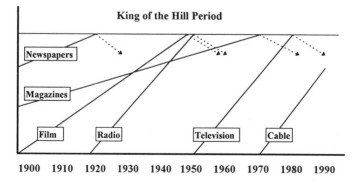

FIG. 15.1. The rise and fall of American mass media.

was before World War I. Now there are about 1,500—the equivalent of about one daily going out of business each month for the past 80 years. Afternoon daily newspapers played an important part in U.S. history and are themselves becoming history. For years NBC, CBS, and ABC dominated television, but their slice of the prime-time audience is less than two thirds of what it was in the 1950s. It is possible for media to disappear (or nearly do so), as have silent films and manual typewriters. Few, if any, use a Linotype machine, and it seems likely that digital imaging processes will replace conventional photographic film. It is difficult to find an device to play 78- or 45-rpm disks, and many early computer programs cannot be read by today's computers. The marketplace for communication technology is very challenging.

THE END OF THE AGE OF JOURNALISTS?

With the decline of U.S. mass media also has come a decline in the stature and function of journalists. For the last third of the 19th century, Edward Lawrence Godkin, editor of both *The Nation* and the *Evening Post*, influenced generations of education, business, and political leaders. Godkin's voice was amplified by the imitation of many journalists. Joseph Pulitzer, once encouraged to be more like Godkin, replied that he wanted to write for the nation, not a select committee. Before Godkin, Horace Greeley was widely read and influential in both the daily and weekly editions of the *New York Tribune*. Abraham Lincoln, still an Illinois lawyer, was a reader of the antislavery weekly edition of the *Tribune*. During the first half of the 19th century, Hezekiah Niles influenced leaders and journalists with his arguments for a strong and diversified industry (and protective tariff), as well as his questioning of slavery. In the 19th century, regional public voices, like those of political leaders Massachusetts' Daniel Webster and South Carolina's Robert Hayne or John C. Calhoun, captured public fancy and respect by being published in the *Register.*

In the 20th century, columnist Walter Lippmann, whose career stretched for about a half-century until his death in 1974, achieved a power similar to Godkin's. Consulted by presidents, read by leaders in all walks of life, widely influential to other journalists, Lippmann stood in the same aloof position as a teacher, philosopher, and perhaps even politician in the sense that he seemed to represent a nation, not just a constituency of that nation. Presidents consulted with Lippmann and sometimes listened. When Lippmann died, newspapers already were in decline—daily newspaper circulation has remained about the same for the past 50 years as the population has grown steadily—and no other journalist has achieved the same stature. Similar public attention is not given to journalists in recent years when mass media audiences are in decline. Without public attention, there is less reason for political or other leaders to pay attention to major columnists, regardless of how excellent they are (and there are excellent columnists, such as William Safire of the *New York Times,* political writer David Broder of the *Washington Post*, and many others). Presidents often meet with journalists today, professionally and socially, but far more to manipulate than to listen.

At the time of his retirement in 1981, Walter Cronkite had achieved something close to the old national power—enough so that President Lyndon Johnson was concerned about Cronkite's views about the Vietnam War. Since then, the traditional networks have steadily declined in audience share, and no television journalist has gained the same level of respect and trust as Cronkite (or earlier network leaders such as the long-running NBC newscasters Chet Huntley and David Brinkley). The decline of the major network share of the prime-time audience continued through 1996.

Lippmann and his predecessors and Cronkite and his predecessors were perceived as something like presidential politicians in the sense that they stood above any political party and spoke for all America. They might be wrong or right. They might at times lean left or right, but they were relatively straight in the long run. Each had major constituencies among the masses or among ruling elites, or both. With the masses divided in their media attention, and with elites making much more use of specialized media and living within specialized communities, fewer people are left to represent the masses in the middle. In short, with the close of the age of mass media, 1930 to 1980, the era of the journalist is also coming to an end, with fewer and fewer people each year paying attention to the important perspectives provided by a special group of people whose mission is to serve as guardian for the whole society. The agenda of these journalists was national in perspective. These agendas have not disappeared, but the large audience for them has, even among some opinion leaders and elites.

FORCE CENTRIFUGAL:
AN AGENDA FRAGMENTATION

Audiences make as much use of the mass media as ever, or even more. The average U.S. television set is on more than 7 hours a day. Nearly 60% of homes have access to cable, and some cable systems offer 70 or more channel choices. That choice, combined with the remote channel selector, allows viewers to cruise choices from their armchairs. Only recently, it was lore in the radio industry that audiences would perhaps listen to two songs they did not like before switching channels, but that reasoning does not apply in an age of easy media choices. For example, the typical car radio allows up to 18 stations to be preprogrammed. Listeners now barely wait two beats—much less two songs—before changing stations.

Today, the power of a few mass media is limited by the alternatives that individuals have to actively gather information from cable outlets that, like cable's CNN, carry information any time someone tunes in. There are many all-news radio stations. There are pseudo-social groups for those who feel isolated from events, such as on talk radio and/or the audience participation shows such as *Oprah*. These alternatives were not often available in the 1930s and 1940s, when national states could control the flow of information by controlling a few spigots. It was possible even in democracies, as the United States showed in controlling and channeling information during World War II.

Communication technologies have eroded the ability of the triangular mass state to control large masses of people. Not only can people tune in to a variety of media, they can gather information through inexpensive, very high quality still and video cameras. In 1992, a citizen videotaped the arrest of Los Angeles motorist Rodney King by chance, and the tape later was widely used to focus attention on the issue of police brutality. Two officers were convicted on charges of violating King's civil rights. Video cameras frequently capture events that once would have passed unnoticed except by those involved. Individual citizens in a sense have the ability to be reporters, and many have done so. Communication technology empowers average people as much as it does reporters.

What is the result of this mix? Audience members can live in groups or communities that might have little or nothing to do with the geographic area in which they live. Although newspapers, local radio, and television focus on specific geographic areas, many in the audience could not care less; they live elsewhere. The mass media target audiences where they live, but audiences may not "live" there. Because many people are able to passively or actively gather information without the mass media, on their own schedule, and to identify passively or actively those who feel, think, and act like themselves, they can isolate themselves from the larger community.

COMMUNICATION AND RESHAPING THE STATE

Communication is changing the way national states are organized by empowering individuals to participate in much wider and responsive—and smaller—social structures. Understanding the phenomenon requires blending what we know from small-group psychology, the history of technology, the organization of mass media, and the structure of the mass state. We know that individuals who value small groups absorb the values of those groups and strongly resist change, or at least change suggested by those outside the group. Early studies with Boy Scouts found that Scouts were strongly resistant to challenges to group solidarity.

Historically, communication technology has demonstrated a pattern of first pulling people together, then dividing them up as a medium becomes less expensive. In the 18th century individuals gathered in inns and coffee houses to share and read the limited newspapers of the community. Those who could not read could listen. Newspapers were absorbed in a social setting and probably never achieved the same power to shape views in later years. When newspapers became inexpensive, individuals read them alone, sometimes in transit on public transportation to their jobs.

At first citizens collected to hear the few radios in bars, and now, with transistors, nearly all can have their own radios, sometimes with earphones to make the communication silent to others. Television pulled people together in groups at first, and then separated them as homes contained a television for all the major living rooms. Film pulled thousands together in some of the larger theaters of the early days for at least some semblance of shared experience, whereas today millions watch videos alone, or perhaps with one or two others. The economics of mass media pull people together and then separate them. The technology first favors a collective and shared agenda and then fragmented and "smaller," less widely shared agendas.

From 1960, after the spread of television sets, to 1980, network television absorbed the major attention of millions at one time. Newspapers and magazines were not able to speak to as many, but they remained powerful voices in the media marketplace. During these years, the newer communication means—cable, faxes, videotapes and audio tapes, computers, satellites—were present but at first did not displace the attention of millions who still faithfully tuned into the relatively few mass media voices. In the sad days after the assassination of President John Kennedy on November 21, 1963, millions turned to the three television commercial networks, eyes glazing over, without being able to turn off the set. By the 1990s, during presidential debates and threatened military actions by U.S. forces, there is always an alternative television choice, which many take. Only the 1994 escape attempt, if it was that, by television and sports personality O. J. Simpson, after his wife and one of her friends were found murdered, could pull millions to one of the many channels that televised the event live. Even then there were many choices.

MANY CHOICES

With the development of recent communication technology has come an erosion of the stability of political, economic, and social triangular structures. This continues the trend in which technology first brings people together because of the expense and novelty of the development, then divides them when unit costs drop and individuals are able to use the development more at their own pace and leisure. In July 1962, the United States launched Telstar, its first successful commercial satellite, a development that, along with the transistor, revolutionized communication transmission. As satellites filled the appropriate spots in the skies, like tiny planets more than 20,000 miles high, the economics of information transfer changed completely. With the telegraph, telephone, and transoceanic cable, it was more difficult and therefore more expensive to send messages long distances. With satellites, distance is all but irrelevant because the cost of sending a telephone message is about the same whether the distance traveled is 6 miles, 600 miles, or 6,000 miles.

Transistors replaced vacuum tubes in radios and televisions and receivers could be made smaller and less expensive. Where family members once huddled around a single television, individuals now watch on their personal receivers. Meanwhile the explosion of FM radio stations provides a wide musical choice, and AM radio offers a range of public service and talk programs. Cable television, through the use of satellites, provides the same enlarging choice on television receivers. Innovator Ted Turner was a pioneer in using cable to provide news (CNN, Headline News) and entertainment programs (TBS, TNT). The direction of communication technology is always toward enlargement of choice.

A newspaper innovator, Al Neuharth of the Gannett Newspaper Group, founded a national newspaper, *USA Today*, in 1982. Using satellites to send ready-to-print pages to printing shops around the nation, *USA Today* soon reached much of the United States (and abroad as well). The latest technological developments showed in the bright pages of *USA Today*, which were imitated by many other newspapers (especially the weather page). Technology could be used to help older media adjust to changes in audience and advertiser tastes.

In the 20th century, the telephone first democratized person-to-person communication with its low cost and, more recently, allowed peoples' telephones to be as mobile as they are, in cars, ships, and even airliners. Small computers became access points to many kinds of information, but far more importantly, to other people of like mind. Since the early 1980s, when the prime-time audience for the traditional television networks (CBS, NBC, and ABC) went into steady decline, the story of communication technology has been the spread of smaller technologies, from audiotapes and videotapes to faxes and electronic mail, down the pyramid structure of society, from those clustered comfortably at the top to those toward the middle and bottom, who are more aware of the pressure of the stone over them.

The cumulative effect of these newer communication technologies has enabled members of the mass media audience:

1. To listen to many sources of information other than those of the mass media, which tend to cover the activities of those in power and official sources.
2. To locate other people like themselves, from those interested in such items as the environment or Star Trek, or those who are Nazi skinheads, to many other types of groups.
3. To gather and send information within a socially reinforcing group without suffering pangs of anxiety from separation from the larger society or pangs of guilt for withdrawing from the common campfire of the larger society.
4. To participate in special groups that try to influence the larger society, such as interest groups with ready fax machines, or to withdraw from the larger society with little sense of social loss or obligation—to live in space, rather than a place.

Of course we continue to live in places, and places are important. Unlike their parents and grandparents, however, millions of people also are living in space, little interested in the spaces where, until recently, so many volunteered for community work and voted in the political process.

PSEUDO-COMMUNITIES

Boorstin (1961) wrote about the pseudo-event in *The Image,* deploring the tendency of the mass media to fill the news hole with stories about events that are contrived, such as a press conference, interview, or other staged event. However, the new technology allows something more significant, the *pseudo-community.* It is possible to shop among, for example, radio talk shows for the content that fits closest to one's own beliefs and vicariously participate in a collective that might have little or nothing to do with the geographic area in which one lives. In fact, few people call in and the same ones tend to call repeatedly. Nevertheless, the content of various programs ratifies how one feels—provides social support—and therefore legitimizes one's point of view regardless of how unconventional the idea might be.

Individuals can share in the pseudo-groups captured by talk shows and therefore decide that voting is not important, or that one political party is unreasonable, or any other view. The difference from earlier periods in history is the availability of immediate social support, regardless of where it is found. For those who do not find a countergroup passively from the widespread media, electronic mail, faxes, telephone, and newsletters of all types are available to find social support. People are no longer isolated, and no longer have to listen for the sounds of messages coming down, although such messages remain important. Followers can listen from anywhere. The fragmentation that results from media downsizing challenges the power of the larger society, as the tide nibbles away at the sandcastle on the shore.

U.S. communication scholar Bradley Greenberg (1972) in one study found that viewers tend to use "real" events to make judgments about others (about Blacks in his study), but when there is no actual experience, television reality is substituted. Television viewers make judgments about occupations (such as detectives) from television watching, and sometimes they feel fearful because they view a large number of crime stories, although they might not actually live in a dangerous area. The weight of the evidence is that television does, over time, lead certain types of viewers to engage in more violent or disruptive behavior.

Since the early radio "soap" operas—named for the sponsors of these ongoing dramatic shows—some members of the audience have related to media characters as if they were real. In 1938, Orson Welles' dramatized show about an invasion from Mars reached about 6 million people, disturbing about a million of them, a few seriously enough that they attempted to escape what appeared to be annihilation. Radio brought the human voice to listeners and television added a picture. Both media showed the power of technology to change perceptions.

Individuals can find others like themselves through new communication technology, especially by electronic computer mail. People can find communities by any reasonable category. Today there are informal groups that share information about old television shows, films, scientific topics of all kinds, travel, the environment—the list is as wide as the imagination. One recent book, *The Virtual Community* (Rheingold, 1993), describes how some people, in effect, have traded the place in which they actually live for a distant, electronically connected virtual community. Some people who first met electronically have married. Some feelings of kinship are so strong that people attend funerals of those whom they knew only as electronic responders.

REVOLT OF THE MASSES?

Ortega y Gasset in the 1930s wrote about the revolt of the masses. In his argument, the masses that had largely been docile or easily controllable throughout most of history had, by the end of the 19th and early 20th centuries, become more restive and articulate, if conventional or undifferentiated. The 1930s provided a vivid demonstration of how the mass media, combined with powerful armed forces, could keep masses in line in Germany and in the former Soviet Union, in a period in which the mass media were far more important than smaller media. (Even telephones were not that widely distributed in the 1930s.) Hitler crushed the labor unions, for example, and Stalin crushed the kulaks.

In the years from 1930 to 1980, the mass media remained dominant, even as satellites, transistors, and mobile communication means transferred power from the sender to the receiver. By the 1980s and beyond, the masses are again able to revolt, but they no longer need to do so as a mass. Instead, groups of individuals have gathered to nourish and reinforce each other's views. They collect around individualized media, from small magazines to large electronic mail groups. Many individuals, alone or in collectives, no longer read newspapers, general circulation magazines, or listen to radio or watch network television—all media that many see as too liberal or too conservative. Instead, these individuals and groups have gathered to challenge the core.

HORIZONTAL COMMUNICATION, HORIZONTAL POWER

New communication methods have empowered average, ordinary people throughout social systems. Social organizations that are structured for efficient functioning have long been accustomed to the selection of leaders who send orders down to where members both relay the word and make sure that action is taken. People at the bottom send reports back up. This remains the structure of the military, government, schools, and most large business and civic organizations. Today the availability of easily accessible points of view different from those of leaders makes it easy for those at any level of social triangles to opt out of listening or believing (even if they keep their jobs).

Communication technologies have enabled human communication to expand exponentially, if horizontal communication is included. Communication from the top down is still very important, but this communication must compete with information that is gathered, distributed, and discussed at every level. This reinforces the view that individuals are not atoms, but very much involved with social settings. In the 1940s and 1950s, scholars showed that individuals were not passive receivers of mass media information but very often asked opinions of others before making major decisions. They often passed along information from the mass media.

We are suggesting an additional step. Today, individuals may not hear some information because they are not attending to it, so busy are they with gathering and sending their own information. And, in contrast to earlier periods, individuals are no longer limited to finding social support in their immediate families or local communities, with the implication that they will be isolated without that support. Instead, today individuals can listen to radio talk shows of all persuasions and become part of a passive, if pseudo, community. They can actively connect with a larger community through computers, faxes, or other means. They can obtain a magazine close to their own interests, or they can even create their own magazines. Audience members are no longer the potentially isolated individuals that shrink back if they see their views are not mirrored in the major mass media. If their views are not there, they can find them in someone, somewhere, if they make the effort. People do not have to accept the general mass media agenda. They can shop for agendas that fit as comfortably as a new (or old) suit.

A BALANCE OF AGENDAS IN THE 21ST CENTURY

We confront a potential crisis. As people abandon or at least deemphasize the agendas of the larger community, they weaken the core values of sharing and compromise. They also are leaving the mass media, which come closest to reflecting these core values for the larger community. The decline of the mass media audience means there has been a drop in common focus, as audience members scurry to their own information sources. We share less, and there has been a disruption of social union.

One can argue that audiences are more informed than ever, and determined to influence the larger society. In this view, newer technologies empower individuals at all levels of the social structure. Hence the newer technologies have empowered minorities and special public interest groups to get in touch with each other and to plan coordinated programs to influence legislation and other public actions. The result has been an extension of social rights for minorities, the handicapped, the environment, and the economically deprived.

In a darker view, one can argue that the political revolution of 1994, when the Republicans took control of both the U.S. House of Representatives and U.S. Senate, after those houses had been controlled mostly by Democrats for decades, is little more than the angry public expression of a subgroup of the larger society—some argue mainly White men. This segment, as any other, is as likely to vote for the other party, or a new party, or no party at all in the future. It seems likely that small communication means will enable a variety of smaller political parties to emerge and that the Republican and Democratic parties both may, in the end, seem to be mass media elephants in the midst of political mice.

Communication technologies have directly affected our ability to listen and speak widely and instantaneously and, comparatively speaking, inexpensively. Indirectly, these technologies have undermined our political organizations based on place and left us wondering how well our place organizations—national armies and governments, for example—are equipped for service in the new century, where communities are organized in space as importantly as in place.

As the mass media decline in audience community, they also decline in power. The ability of the mass media to stand up for civil liberties, such as civil rights in the 1950s and 1960s and women's rights in the 1970s and 1980s, has declined as an artifact of audience inattention, and therefore government inattention. The mice cannot do what the elephants still barely can. Small media are centrifugal in force and are winning sufficient audiences to weaken the power of the established media.

CHANGES IN COMMUNICATION APPROACHES

Changes in the evolution of the public media result in social changes that cannot be anticipated. One change is that audience members do not live in a world of isolation if they hold views at variance with those evidenced in the mass media. German scholar Noelle-Neumann (1984) argued that isolated individuals, perceiving their views to be out of agreement with the larger group, fall more and more silent, giving way to a spiral of silence in which it appears there is one predominant point of view. Her study, however, and studies by U.S. scholars have discovered a definite, if small, number of citizens who bravely speak out or think differently from the supposed majority.

That group in the 1930s, of course, was soon isolated by the Nazis. Today individuals who hold views at variance with the perceived majority need not suffer in silence. They may find radio talk shows or other smaller media that fit their views or they may actively use the communication means at hand to find other people like themselves, perhaps establishing their own protective group. One can visualize the mass state as a body in which the body can, on occasion, reverse flow from the mass media arteries back through the capillaries to smaller sites.

The power of a large community, therefore, can be attenuated by the natural creation of many smaller groups that are intellectually self supporting because individuals can gather and spread information to others of like mind, regardless of the direction of the larger community, as represented by the mass media. In a sense, it is becoming within the power of all individuals to be something like a Boy Scout or Girl Scout, secure in the loyalty of your group and suspicious of those who would threaten its values. The emerging power of politically conservative and liberal groups in the United States provides one example of such groups whose members seem resistant to all moderating messages from the established mass media. "Forget, hell," says one bumper sticker about the outcome of the U.S. Civil War. Sore losers can today easily find consolation from others like them, perhaps as closely as on a talk radio program as they drive to work. Why compromise?

For leaders this means that the collective interest in general public institutions, such as schools, hospitals, and local government, has been substantially eroded, or always is in danger of being so, except by those often tightly knit groups for which that institution is the center of their interest agenda. This public interest is not always balanced with a willingness to compromise, as required if collective democracy is to survive in the long run. Leaders therefore must embrace the new technologies themselves to reach audiences and, more than ever, need to sell programs to their followers, not just to announce policies as if those lower in the organization simply await orders. The spread of communication technology provides leaders with new opportunities, just as it provides the same opportunities to followers. Social organizations can be strengthened, or they can as easily be shattered. As with schools, governments, and churches, the old mass media—daily newspapers, mass magazines, network television, radio, and films—no longer have the same power to hold social structures together. That power is passing into the hands of ordinary men and women.

There seems little way anymore for leaders monolithically to control communication. Satellite-receiving antennas have sprouted across rooftops in Beijing, although these antennas are illegal. Home computer workstations enable individuals to produce publications—called *zines*—that reach small, like-minded audiences, as they did in the 18th century. The success of the Iranian cleric Ayatollah Khomeini came partly from the successful circulation of audiotapes sent from Khomeini's home in Paris while he was in exile. Citizens are not passive in gathering news information. Videotapes are so common that they have become the basis of a popular television show, *America's Funniest Home Videos*. Cameras can develop pictures instantly, and these pictures can be sent by reproduction machines.

Communication has made history a poor predictor of the future. Once one could stand on the (now-gone) caboose of a train and predict the direction of the train by looking at the rails behind. If the route was straight, one would predict a smooth straight route, and if curving, one would predict some curves ahead. One could sense the future by looking behind. One could make predictions based on the solid ground of history. That was the era of analog thinking.

Today it is more like looking at the wisps of vapor left behind the engines of a 747 jumbo jet. One can see those without knowing for sure which way the jet is going: straight, curved, up, or down. The wisps also soon drift in the wind. One cannot know for sure which way he or she is headed from the past. The future is a guess based on rearranging bits and pieces. This is the era of digital thinking.

A PERIOD OF HOPE

Although the mass media seem to be constantly displaced by smaller media, size is not always a disadvantage. Wal-Mart is a merchandising wonder of our times, and the opening of a Wal-Mart often means that the days of the smaller, more localized merchants are doomed—as if *USA Today* were going to displace all the local dailies. That has not happened. How has Wal-Mart (among others) countered the trend of large to small downsizing that permeates world manufacturing and business? One would guess that there are two reasons. The first is low prices, always an attraction. However, second is the effort that Wal-Mart makes to make it appear that the giant merchandiser has your interests at heart, from the greeter at the front door, to the sales associates who are trained to focus on you; the giant makes itself into a friendly dwarf.

By contrast, unfortunately, many large newspapers have gone in the opposite direction, making themselves into relatively distant giants. Where the average person once could expect to be in the newspaper three times without charge—at birth, marriage, and death—now that person often must pay for these notices, including his or her own death. Most people cannot enter a newspaper or television office without passing through extensive security. It would be as if Wal-Mart took away its greeters and depended on price alone and, if one needed help, one could dial an 800 number. The mass media, once a public meeting place, now charge access fees for those passing through, and it can be little wonder that there is a disconnection between mass media and audience.

Still, creative leaders of the media can find ways to reach audiences and invite them in, perhaps using the new media themselves. Opportunities for individuals are also opportunities for leaders. But indeed, leaders cannot do it alone. Audiences themselves need to be aware of the limitations of information. Information alone does not make for an improved and more cohesive and tolerant society; human values do. The mass media need to treat the audience like communities of common interests and not a collection of special interests.

Diverse points of view need to be illuminated within mass media. Public journalism offers a new opportunity to focus on community.

With the disruption of social union comes the opportunity to use the newer technologies in creative ways to pull us together in more equitable societies, regardless of the country in which we live. Leaders in Northern Ireland seemed on the edge of finding a peaceful solution to that nation's wrenching differences between Catholics and Protestants in 1996, and it seems possible there will be peace in the Middle East between Israel and its neighbors. With the informational empowerment that comes with small communication comes a need to renew our commitment to the core of our social union, that union served by the mass media. Our own past gives us a chance to apply digital thinking. One can assemble hopeful signs as easily as discouraging ones. In the late 1980s and early 1990s, the wall that divided Berlin came down and East and West Germany were reunited, even as Yugoslavia and Bosnia underwent an agonizing fragmentation in the same region.

Communication empowers people at all levels of society, and it may be that tolerance for each other will surface in individuals and the groups in which they decide to become linked so that governments will be forced to take account of the views of many citizens. There needs to be tolerance for competing agendas. If so, communication will not divide us but will enable us to build just and equitable societies, capable of listening and communicating with each other. That always was the promise that undergirded Milton's argument for many voices. At last, we have at least the potential to try the experiment.

THE POST MASS MEDIA AGE

In the post 1930 to 1980 mass media era, it will be more challenging to govern large mass states, whether by dictatorships or democracy. Leaders can no longer be assured of the attention of large, accepting audiences. Never have so many ordinary citizens had access to so many communication opportunities for other points of view. Technologies such as electronic mail allow birds of a feather to flock together around interests that range from the environment to pornography.

The spread of communication technology provides leaders with new opportunities to listen, just as it provides new opportunities for citizens to speak. Social organizations can be strengthened, or they as easily can be shattered. As with other established institutions such as schools, governments and churches, the "old" mass media—daily newspapers, mass magazines, network television, radio, and films—no longer have the power alone to bind structures as social glue. That power is passing partly into the hands of ordinary men and women. Today the agenda-setting power of the mass media, although still great, is being widely diffused, along with the power of the journalists and national leaders who once could direct public attention. Leaders at all levels, including those who direct the older mass media, must learn to listen to those who live at all levels of the social pyramid, and the new communication does make that easier. Leaders must devise ways for individuals at each level of society to see the relationship between their lives and the lives of others. That is also a challenge for the leaders of the mass media, if the media are to work for a just and equitable society for all people in a dynamic and collective democracy. The agenda-setting power of the press remains the power to help build what Lippmann called a good society. All the early U.S. presidents from Washington to Lincoln reminded citizens that the United States is an experiment. It remains an exciting one.

ACKNOWLEDGMENTS

This chapter is a revision of a lecture given by Shaw at the University of Texas on November 4, 1994. This work resulted from the 1992–1993 year that Shaw spent as senior fellow at The Freedom Forum Media Studies Center in New York. Hamm, a former journalist, teaches at Elon College. The authors would like to thank Shaw's assistant Randall Patnode for his help in preparing this chapter.

References

Adoni, H., Cohen, A., & Mane, S. (1984). Social reality and television news: Perceptual dimension of social conflicts in selected life areas. *Journal of Broadcasting, 28*, 33–49.

Adoni, H., & Mane, S. (1984). Media and the social construction of reality: Toward an integration of theory and research. *Communication Research, 11*, 324–340.

Albrecht, J. E., & O'Brien, E. J. (1990). Effects of centrality on retrieval of text- based concepts. *Journal of Experimental Psychology: Learning, Memory, and Cognition, 17*, 932–939.

Allport, F. H. & Lepkin, M. (1943). Building war morale with news headlines. *Public Opinion Quarterly, 7*, 211–221.

Almond, G. (1990). *A discipline divided: Schools and sects in political science.* Newbury Park, CA: Sage.

Almond, G. & Verba, S. (1963). *The civic culture: Political attitudes and democracy in five nations.* Princeton, NJ: Princeton University Press.

Almond, G. & Verba, S. (1980). *The civic culture revisited.* Boston: Little, Brown.

Althaus, S., Edy, J., Entman, R., & Phalen, P. (1995, May). *Revising the indexing hypotheses: Officials, media, and the Libya crisis.* Paper presented at the meeting of the International Communication Association, Albuquerque, NM.

Altheide, D. L., & Johnson, J. M. (Eds.). (1980). *Bureaucratic propaganda.* Boston: Allyn & Bacon.

Altschull, J. H. (1984). *Agents of power: The role of the news media in human affairs.* New York: Longman.

American Institute for Political Communication. (1970). *Anatomy of a crucial election.* Washington, DC: Author.

Anderson, J. R., & Bower, G. H. (1973). *Human associative memory.* Washington, DC: Winston.

Andeweg, R. B., & Galen, A. I. (1993, September). *Dutch government and politics.* Paper presented at the meeting of the American Political Science Association, San Francisco, CA.

Aoki, I. (1995). Entropy production in living systems: From organisms to ecosystems. *Thermochimica Acta, 250*, 359–370.

Atkin, C. K., Bowen, L., Nayman, O. B., & Sheinkopf, K. G. (1973). Quantity versus quality in televised political ads. *Public Opinion Quarterly, 37*, 209–224.

Atkin, C. K., & Heald, G. (1976). Effects of political advertising. *Public Opinion Quarterly, 40*, 216–228.

Atwater, T., Salwen, M. B., & Anderson, R.B. (1985). Media agenda-setting with environmental issues. *Journalism Quarterly, 62*, 393–397.

Atwood, L. E., Sohn, A., & Sohn, H. (1978). Daily newspaper contributions to community discussion. *Journalism Quarterly, 55*, 570–576.

Ball-Rokeach, S. J. (1985). The origins of individual media system dependency. *Communication Research, 12*, 485–510.

Ball-Rokeach, S. J., & DeFleur, M. (1976). Dependency theory and mass media effects. *Communication Research, 3*, 3–21.

Ball-Rokeach, S. J., Power, G. J., Guthrie, K. K., & Waring, H. R. (1990). Value-framing abortion in the United States: An application of media system dependency theory. *International Journal of Public Opinion Research, 2*, 249–273.

Bancroft, G. (1834–1875). *A history of the United States*. Boston: Little, Brown.

Baran, S. J., & Davis, D. (1995). *Mass communication theory: Foundation, ferment and future*. Belmont, CA: Wadsworth.

Bargh, J. A., Bond, R. N., Lombardi, W. J., & Tota, M. E. (1986). The additive nature of chronic and temporary sources of construct accessibility. *Journal of Personality and Social Psychology, 50*, 869–878.

Bargh, J. A., & Pietromonaco, P. (1982). Automatic information processing and social perception: The influence of trait information presented outside of conscious awareness on impression formation. *Journal of Personality and Social Psychology, 43*, 437–449.

Bargh, J. A., & Prato, F. (1986). Individual construct accessibility and perceptual selection. *Journal of Experimental Social Psychology, 22*, 293–311.

Bargh, J. A., & Thein, R. D. (1985). Individual construct accessibility, person memory, and the recall-judgment link: The case of information overload. *Journal of Personality and Social Psychology, 49*, 1129–1146.

Barkin, S. (1984). The journalist as storyteller: An interdisciplinary perspective. *American Journalism: The publication of the American Journalism Historians Association, 1*(2), 27–33.

Barnes, B. E., & Thomson, L. M. (1994). Power to the people (meter): Audience measurment technology and media specialization. In J. S. Ettema & D. C. Whitney (Eds.), *Audiencemaking: How the media create the audience* (pp. 78–94). Thousand Oaks, CA: Sage.

Barrat, D. (1986). *Media sociology*. London: Tavistock.

Bateson, G. (1955). A theory of play and fantasy. *A.P.A. Psychiatric Research Reports, 2*, 39–51.

Bateson, G. (1972). *Steps to an ecology of mind: A revolutionary approach to man's understanding of himself*. New York: Ballantine Books.

Baumgartner, F., & Jones, B. (1993). *Agendas and instability in American politics*. Chicago: University of Chicago Press.

Becker, L., & McCombs, M. (1978). The role of the press in determining voter reactions to presidential primaries. *Human Communication Research, 4*, 301–307.

Behr, R. L., & Iyengar, S. (1985). Television news, real-world cues, and changes in the public agenda. *Public Opinion Quarterly, 49*, 38–57.

Beniger, J. R. (1978). Media content as social indicators: The Greenfield index of agenda-setting. *Communication Research, 5*, 437–451.

Bennett, W. (1990). Toward a theory of press-state relations in the United States. *Journal of Communication, 40*, 103–125.

Bennett, W., & Edelman, M. (1985). Toward a new political narrative. *Journal of Communication, 35*, 156–171.

Benson, L. (1967). An approach to the study of past public opinion. *Public Opinion Quarterly,* *31*, 522–567.

Benton, M., & Frazier, P. (1976). The agenda setting function of the mass media at three levels of "information holding." *Communication Research, 3*, 261–274.

Benziman, O., & Manzur, A. (1992). *Sub-tenants*. Jerusalem: Keter.

Berelson, B. R., Lazarsfeld, P. F., & McPhee, W. N. (1954). *Voting: A study of opinion formation in a presidential campaign*. Chicago: University of Chicago Press.

Berger, P. L. & Luckmann, T. (1967). *The social construction of reality*. New York: Anchor.

Berkowitz, L., & Heimer, K. (1989). On the construction of the anger experience: Aversive events and negative priming. *Advances in Experimental Social Psychology, 22*, 1–37.

Berkowitz, L., & Rogers, K. H. (1986). A priming effect analysis of media influences. In J. Bryant & D. Zillmann (Eds.), *Perspectives on media effects* (pp. 57–81). Hillsdale, NJ: Lawrence Erlbaum Associates.

Biocca, F. (1991). Viewers' mental models of political messages: Toward a theory of the semantic processing of television. In F. Biocca (Ed.), *Television and political advertising: Vol. 1. Psychological processes* (pp. 27–89). Hillsdale, NJ: Lawrence Erlbaum Associates.

Bleske, G. (1995a, May). *Headlines and their effects on the processing of a newspaper story*. Paper presented to the International Communication Association, Albuquerque, NM.

Bleske, G. (1995b, August). *Schematic frames and reader learning: The effect of headlines*. Paper presented to the Association for Education in Journalism and Mass Communication, Washington, DC.

Blood, D. (1996). *Economic headline news, consumer sentiment, presidential popularity and the state of the economy: A study of their dynamic relationship, 1980–1993*. Unpublished doctoral dissertation, University of Connecticut, Storrs.

Blood, D., & Phillips, P. C. B. (1995). Recession headlines, consumer sentiment, the state of the economy and presidential popularity: A time series analysis, 1989–1993. *International Journal of Public Opinion Research, 7*(1), 2–22.

Blood, R. W. (1981). *Unobtrusive issues in the agenda-setting role of the press*. Unpublished doctoral dissertation, Syracuse University, Syracuse, NY.

Blumler, J. G., Brynin, M., & Nossiter, T. J. (1986). Broadcasting finance in transition. *European Journal of Communication, 1*(3), 343–364.

Blumler, J. G. & Gurevitch, M. (1995). *The crisis of public communication*. London: Routledge.

Blumler, J. G. & Nossiter, T. J. (1991). *Broadcasting finance in transition*. Oxford, UK: Oxford University Press.

Blumler, J. G., McLeod, J., & Rosengren, K. E. (1992). *Comparatively speaking*. Newbury Park, CA: Sage.

Boorstin, D. J. (1961). *The image: A guide to pseudo-events in America*. New York: Atheneum.

Bowers, T. A. (1973). Newspaper political advertising and the agenda-setting function. *Journalism Quarterly, 50*, 552–556.

Bowers, T. A. (1977). Candidate advertising: The agenda is the message. In D. L. Shaw & M. McCombs (Eds.), *The emergence of American political issues: The agenda-setting function of the press* (pp. 53–67). St. Paul, MN: West.

Bowes, J. E., & Strentz, H. (1978). Candidate images: Stereotyping and the 1976 debates. In B. Ruben (Ed.), *Communication yearbook 2* (pp. 1–406). New Brunswick, NJ: Transaction.

Box, G. E., & Jenkins, G. M. (1976). *Time series analysis: Forecasting and control* (rev. ed.). San Francisco: Holden-Day.

Boyce, D. G. (1978). Public opinion and historians. *History, 63*, 214–226.

Brants, K., & Siune, K. (1992). Public broadcasting in a state of flux. In K. Siune & W. Truetzschler (Eds.), *Dynamics of media politics: Broadcasting and electronic media in western Europe* (pp. 101–115). Beverly Hills, CA: Sage.

Brosius, H., Donsbach, W., & Birk, M. (1995, May), *How do text–picture relations affect the informational effectiveness of television newscasts.* Paper presented at the International Communication Association, Albuquerque, NM.

Brosius, H., & Eps, P. (1994, May). *The role of key events in news selection: Framing in the coverage of attacks against foreigners and asylum seekers in Germany.* Paper presented at the International Communication Association, Sydney, Australia.

Brosius, H., & Kepplinger, H. M. (1990a). The agenda-setting function of television news: Static and dynamic views. *Communication Research, 17*, 183–211.

Brosius, H., & Kepplinger, H. M. (1990b, May). *Linear and nonlinear models of agenda-setting in television.* Paper presented at the International Communication Association, Dublin, Ireland.

Brosius, H., & Kepplinger, H. M. (1992). Linear and nonlinear models of agenda setting in television. *Journal of Broadcasting & Electronic Media, 36*, 5–23.

Brown, C. (1991). *Ballots of tumult: A portrait of volatility in American voting.* Ann Arbor: University of Michigan Press.

Brown, L. (1971). *Television.* New York: Harcourt Brace Jovanovich.

Bryan, K. M. (1987). *Content analysis of televised political advertising in low involvement political races.* Unpublished master's thesis, University of Texas, Austin.

Buchanan, B. (1991). *Electing a president: The Markle commission research on campaign '88.* Austin: University of Texas Press.

Carmines, E. G., & Stimson, J. A. (1989). *Issue evolution.* Princeton, NJ: Princeton University Press.

Casti, J. L. (1989). *Paradigms lost.* New York: William Morrow.

Chaffee, S. H. (1972, August). *Longitudinal designs for communication research: Cross-lagged correlations.* Paper presented at the Association for Education in Journalism and Mass Communication, Carbondale, IL.

Chaffee, S. (Ed.). (1975). *Political communication: Issues and strategies for research.* Beverly Hills, CA: Sage.

Chaffee, S. H. (1980). Comments on the Weaver–Gray paper. In G. C. Wilhoit & H. de Bock (Eds.), *Mass communication review yearbook 1* (pp. 156–160). Beverly Hills, CA: Sage.

Chaffee, S. H., & Hochheimer, J. L. (1985). The beginnings of political communication research in the United States: Origins of the 'limited effects' model. In E. M. Rogers & F. Balle (Eds.), *The media revolution in America and in Western Europe* (pp. 267–296). Norwood, NJ: Ablex.

Chaffee, S. H., & Yang, S. (1990). The bridging role of television in immigration political socialization. *Human Communication Research, 17*, 266–288.

Chen, S. M. (1992). Political candidate images and voters' voting behaviors. *Mass Communication Research, 46*, 149–168.

Chen, Y. Y. (1986). The retrospect and prospect of the research of Taiwan's voting behavior. *Think and Talk, 23*, 6.

Chen, Y. Y. (1993). *Voting behaviors and democratization in Taiwan: Examining the 1992 legislative election* (Rep. No. NSC 82–0301-H004-034-B2). Taipei: National Science Council.

Cheng, S. F. (1994). The correlations between political candidate images and voting behavior. In Y. Y. Chen (Ed.), *Voting behaviors and democratization in Taiwan: Examining the 1992 legislative election* (Rep. No. NSC 82-0301-H004-034-B2, pp. 62–81). Taipei: National Science Council.

Choi, H. C., & Becker, S. L. (1987). Media use, issue/image discriminations and voting. *Communication Research, 14*(3), 267–291.

Cobb, R. W., & Elder, C. D. (1972). *Participation in American politics: The dynamics of agenda-building.* Baltimore: Johns Hopkins University Press.

Cobb, R., Ross, J., & Ross, M. H. (1976). Agenda building as a comparative political process. *American Political Science Review, 70*, 126–138.

Cohen, A. A., Adoni, H., & Bantz, C. (1990). *Social conflicts and television news: A cross-national study of presentation and perception*. London: Sage.

Cohen, A. A., & Wolfsfeld, G. (1995). Overcoming adversity and diversity: The utility of television political advertising in Israel. In L. L. Kaid & C. Holz-Bacha (Eds.), *Political advertising in western democracies*. (pp. 109–123). Beverly Hills, CA: Sage.

Cohen, B. (1963). *The press and foreign policy*. Princeton, NJ: Princeton University Press.

Cohen, D. (1975, August). *A report on a non-election agenda-setting study*. Paper presented at the Association for Education in Journalism, Ottawa, Canada.

Cohen, J., & Stewart, I. (1994). *The collapse of chaos*. New York: Viking.

Cohen, M. R., & Nagel, E. (1934). *An introduction to logic and the scientific method*. New York: Harcourt, Brace.

Cohen, S. (Ed.). (1981). *The manufacture of news: Deviance, social problems and the mass media* (rev. ed.). London: Constable.

Cohen, S., & Young, J. (Eds.). (1973). *The manufacture of news: Deviance, social problems and the mass media*. London: Constable.

Coleman, S. (1993). Cycles and chaos in political party voting. *Journal of Mathematical Sociology, 18*(1), 47–64.

Collins, A. M., & Loftus, E. F. (1975). A spreading activation theory of semantic processing. *Psychological Review, 82*, 407–428.

Comfort, L. K. (1994). Self-organization in complex systems. *Journal of Public Administration Research and Theory, 4*(3), 393–411.

Commission on Freedom of the Press. (1947). *A free and responsible press: A general report on mass communication: Newspapers, radio, motion pictures, magazines and books*. Chicago: University of Chicago Press.

Conover, P. J., & Feldman, S. (1986). The role of inference in the perception of political candidates. In R. R. Lau & D. O. Sears (Eds.), *Political cognition* (pp. 127–158). Hillsdale, NJ: Lawrence Erlbaum Associates.

Converse, P. E. (1972). Change in the American electorate. In A. Campbell & P. E. Converse (Eds.), *The human meaning of social change* (pp. 263–338). New York: Russell Sage.

Corbett, M. (1991). *American public opinion: Trends, processes, and patterns*. New York: Longman.

Cornelius, W. A. (1992). From sojourners to settlers: The changing profile of Mexican immigration to the United States. In J. A. Bestamante, C. W. Reynolds, & R. A. Hinojosa (Eds.), *U.S.–Mexico relations: Labor market interdependence* (pp. 143–162). Stanford, CA: Stanford University Press.

Cort, D. (1966, May 1). "Any number can play." *New York Times*, pp. 6, 26.

Covington, C. R., Kroeger, K., Richardson, G., & Woodard, J. D. (1993). Shaping a candidate's image in the press: Ronald Reagan and the 1980 presidential election. *Political Research Quarterly, 46*, 783–798.

Crouse, T. (1973). *The boys on the bus*. New York: Random House.

Cuddington, J. T. (1980). Simultaneous-equations test of the natural rate and other classical hypotheses. *Journal of Political Economy, 88*, 539–549.

Culbertson, H. (1974). Words vs. pictures: Perceived impact and connotative meaning. *Journalism Quarterly, 51*, 226–237.

Curtice, J., & Semetko, H. A. (1994). Does it matter what the papers say? In A. Heath, R. Jowell, & J. Curtice (Eds.), *Labour's last chance?* (pp. 43–64). Aldershot, UK: Dartmouth.

Dalton, R. (1988). *Citizen politics in western democracies*. Chatham, NJ: Chatham House.

Dalton, R. (1996). *Citizen politics in western democracies* (2nd ed.). Chatham, NJ: Chatham House.

Danielian, L. H., & Reese, S. D. (1989). A closer look at intermedia influences on agenda setting: The cocaine issue of 1986. In P. J. Shoemaker (Ed.), *Communication campaigns about drugs: Government, media and the public* (pp. 47–66). Hillsdale, NJ: Lawrence Erlbaum Associates.

Davis, D. F. (1981). Issue information and connotation in candidate imagery: Evidence from a laboratory experiment. *International Political Science Review, 2*, 461–479.

Davis, D. K. (1990). News and politics. In D. L. Swanson & D. Nimmo (Eds.), *New directions in political communication: A resource book* (pp. 147–184). Newbury Park, CA: Sage.

Davis, J. A. (1996). Review essay on value change. *Public Opinion Quarterly, 60*, 322–331.

Dearing, J. W. (1989). Setting the polling agenda for the issue of AIDS. *Public Opinion Quarterly, 53*, 309–329.

Dearing, J. W., & Rogers, E. M. (1996). *Agenda-setting.* Thousand Oaks, CA: Sage.

DeFleur, M. L., & Ball-Rokeach, S. J. (1989). *Theories of mass communication.* New York: Longman.

de la Garza, R. (1992). *Latino voices: Mexican, Puerto Rican and Cuban perspectives on American politics.* Hartford, CT: Westview Press.

de Lima, V. (1993). Brazilian television in the 1989 presidential campaign: Constructing a president. In T. Skidmore (Ed.), *Television, politics and the transition to democracy in Latin America.* Baltimore: Johns Hopkins University Press.

Dennis, J., Chaffee, S. H., & Choe, S. V. (1979). Impact on partisan, image and issue voting. In S. Kraus (Ed), *The great debates: Carter vs. Ford, 1976* (pp. 314–330). Bloomington: Indiana University Press.

Diez-Nicolas, J. & Semetko, H. A. (1995). La television ye las elecciones de 1993 [Television and the elections of 1993]. In A. Munoz-Alonson & J. Ignacio Rospir (Eds.), *Comunicacion politica* (pp. 221–242). Madrid: Editorial Universitas.

Donohew, L. (1983). Newswriting styles: What arouses the reader? *Newspaper Research Journal, 3*, 3–6.

Downs, A. (1972). Up and down with ecology—The "issue-attention cycle." *Public Interest, 28*, 28–50.

Eckstein, H. (1988). A culturalist theory of political change. *American Political Science Review, 82*, 789–804.

Edelman, M. (1964). *The symbolic use of politics.* Urbana: University of Illinois Press.

Edelstein, A. (1993). Thinking about the criterion variable in agenda-setting research. *Journal of Communication, 43*, 85–99.

Edelstein, A., Ito, Y., & Kepplinger, H. (1989). *Communication & culture: A comparative approach.* New York: Longman.

Ellegard, A. (1958). *Darwin and the general reader.* Chicago: University of Chicago Press.

Elliott, D. (1988). Family ties: A case study of coverage of families and friends during the hijacking of TWA flight 847. *Political Communication and Persuasion, 5*, 67–75.

Elster, J. (1990). When rationality fails. In K. S. Cook & M. Levi (Eds.), *The limits of rationality* (pp. 19–51). Chicago: The University of Chicago Press.

Emig, E. (1928). The connotation of newspaper headlines. *Journalism Quarterly, 4*, 53–59.

Engle, R. F., & Granger, C. W. J. (1987). Cointegration and error-correction: Representation, estimation and testing. *Econometrica, 55*, 251–276.

Entman, R. (1989). *Democracy without citizens: Media and the decay of American politics.* New York: Oxford University Press.

Entman, R. (1993). Framing: Toward clarification of a fractured paradigm. *Journal of Communication, 43*, 51–58.

Erbring, L., Goldenberg, E., & Miller, A. (1980). Front-page news and real-world cues: A new look at agenda-setting by the media. *American Journal of Political Science, 24*, 16–49.

European Journal of Communication [Special Issue]. (1992). Media and the law: The changing landscape of western Europe, 7(2).

Eyal, C. H. (1979). *Time-frame in agenda-setting research: A study of the conceptual and methodological factors affecting the time frame context of the agenda-setting process.* Unpublished doctoral dissertation, Syracuse University, Syracuse, NY.

Faber, R. J., Tims, A., & Schmitt, K. (1990). Accentuate the negative? The impact of negative political appeals on voting intent. In P. A. Stout (Ed.), *Proceedings of the 1990 conference of the American Academy of Advertising* (pp. 10–16). Austin, TX: American Academy of Advertising.

Fan, D. P. (1988). *Predictions of public opinion from the mass media: Computer content analysis and mathematical modeling.* New York: Greenwood Press.

Fan, D. P. (1993, May). *Predictions of consumer confidence/sentiment from the press.* Paper presented at the American Association for Public Opinion Research.

Fan, D. P., & Elketroussi, M. (1989). Mathematical model for addiction: Application to multiple risk factor intervention trial data for smoking. *Journal of Consulting and Clinical Psychology, 57*(3), 456–460.

Fan, D. P., & McAvoy, G. (1989). Predictions of public opinion on the spread of AIDS: Introduction of new computer methodologies. *Journal of Sex Research, 26*(2), 159–188.

Fine, T. (1992). The impact of issue framing on public opinion toward affirmative action programs. *Social Science Journal, 29,* 323–334.

Finkelstein, S. (1968). *Sense and nonsense of McLuhan.* New York: International Publishers.

Fischer, D. H. (1970). *Historians' fallacies: Toward a logic of historical thought.* New York: Harper & Row.

Fishbein, M., & Ajzen, I. (1975). *Belief, attitude, intention and behavior: An introduction to theory and research.* Reading, MA: Addison-Wesley.

Fishman, J. (1989). *Language and ethnicity in minority sociolinguistic perspective.* Claredon, UK: Multilingual Matters.

Fishman, M. (1980). *Manufacturing the news.* Austin: University of Texas Press.

Fiske, S., & Linville, P. (1980). What does the schema concept buy us? *Personality and Social Psychology, 6,* 543–557.

Fiske, S., & Taylor, S. (1991). *Social cognition.* New York: McGraw-Hill.

Fowler, G., & Crawford, B. (1987). *Border radio: Quacks, yodelers, pitchmen, psychics, and other amazing broadcasters of the American airwaves.* Austin: University of Texas Press.

Fowler, R. (1991). *Language in the news: Discourse and ideology in the British press.* New York: Routledge.

Friedman, A. (1979). Frame theory, comprehension, and picture memory. *Journal of Experimental Psychology: General, 108,* 316–355.

Fujitake, A. (1968). *Gendai-masu-komyunikeishon no riron* [Theory of contemporary mass communication]. Tokyo: NHK Press.

Funkhouser, G. R. (1973). The issues of the sixties: An exploratory study of the dynamics of public opinion. *Public Opinion Quarterly, 37,* 62–75.

Gamson, W. (1988). Political discourse and collective action. In B. Klandermans, H. Friesi, & S. Tarrow (Eds.), *International social movement research: A research annual. From structure to action: Comparing social movement research across cultures* (pp. 219–244). Greenwich: JAI.

Gamson, W. (1989). News as framing. *American Behavioral Scientist, 33,* 157–161.

Gamson, W. (1992). *Talking politics.* New York: Cambridge University Press.

Gamson, W. A., & Modigliani, A. (1989). Media discourse and public opinion on nuclear power: A constructionist approach. *American Journal of Sociology, 95,* 1–37.

Gandy, O. H. (1982). *Beyond agenda setting: Information subsidies and public policy.* Norwood, NJ: Ablex.

Gans, H. (1979). *Deciding what's news: A study of CBS Evening News, NBC Nightly News, Newsweek and Time.* New York: Random House.

Garramone, G. M. (1983). Issue versus image: Orientation and effects of political advertising. *Communication Research, 10* (1), 59–76.

Gerbner, G., Gross, L., Morgan, M., & Signorielli, N. (1994). Growing up with television: The cultivation perspective. In J. Bryant & D. Zillmann (Eds.), *Media effects: Advances in theory and research* (pp. 17–41). Hillsdale, NJ: Lawrence Erlbaum Associates.

Ghanem, S. (1996). *Media coverage of crime and public opinion: An exploration of the second level of agenda setting.* Unpublished doctoral dissertation. University of Texas, Austin.

Ghorpade, S. (1986). Agenda setting: A test of advertising's neglected function. *Journal of Advertising Research, 25,* 23–27.

Gitlin, T. (1978). Media sociology: The dominant paradigm. *Theory and Society, 6,* 205–253.

Gitlin, T. (1980). *The whole world is watching: Mass media in the making and unmaking of the new left.* Berkeley: University of California Press.

Glassman, J. K. (1993, November 19). TV has a lot to do with fear and loathing of NAFTA. *Washington Post,* p. 61.

Goffman, E. (1959). *The presentation of self in everyday life.* New York: Doubleday.

Goffman, E. (1974). *Frame analysis: An essay on the organization of experience.* Cambridge, MA: Harvard University Press.

Gonzenbach, W. J. (1992). A time-series analysis of the drug issue, 1985–1990: The press, the president and public opinion. *International Journal of Public Opinion Research, 4,* 126–147.

Gonzenbach, W. J. (1995). *The media, the president, and public opinion: A longitudinal analysis of the drug issue, 1984–1991.* Mahwah, NJ: Lawrence Erlbaum Associates.

Gottschalk, L. (1963). *Generalization in the writing of history.* Chicago: University of Chicago Press.

Graber, D. (1972). Personal qualities in presidential images: The contribution of the press. *Midwest Journal of Political Science, 16,* 46–76.

Graber, D. (1988). *Processing the news: How people tame the information tide* (2nd ed.). New York: Longman.

Graber, D. (1993). *Mass media and American politics* (4th ed.). Washington, DC: Congressional Quarterly Press.

Granger, C. W. J. (1969). Investigating causal relations by econometric models and cross-spectral methods. *Econometrica, 37,* 424–438.

Granger, C. W. J. (1980). Testing for causality: A personal viewpoint. *Journal of Economic Dynamics and Control, 2,* 329–352.

Greenberg, B. (1972). Children's reactions to TV blacks. *Journalism Quarterly, 45,* 5–14.

Guastello, S. J. (1995). *Chaos, catastrophe, and human affairs: Applications of nonlinear dynamics to work, organizations, and social evolution.* Hillsdale, NJ: Lawrence Erlbaum Associates.

Gutiérrez, F. (1977). Spanish language media in America: Background, resources, history. *Journalism History, 4*(2), 1–6.

Gutiérrez, F., & Schement, J. (1979). *Spanish language radio in the southwestern United States.* Austin, TX: Center for Mexican-American Studies.

Hackett, R. (1984). Decline of a paradigm? Bias and objectivity in news media studies. In M. Gurevitch & M. R. Levy (Eds.), *Mass communication review yearbook,* (Vol. 5, pp. 251–274). Beverly Hills, CA: Sage.

Hage, J. (1972). *Techniques and problems of theory construction in sociology.* New York: Wiley.

Hagen, L. (1995, May). *How to compare the relevance of news: A method of content analysis and its application to the news coverage of wire services.* Paper presented at the International Communication Association, Albuquerque, NM.

Hahn, D. F., & Gonchar, R. M. (1972). Political myth: The image and the issue. *Today's Speech, 20*, 57–65.

Haken, H. (1988). *Information and self-organization: A macroscopic approach to complex systems*. Berlin: Springer-Verlag.

Hall, S. (1981). A world at one with itself. In S. Cohen & J. Young (Eds.), *The manufacture of news: Social problems, deviance and the mass media*. (pp. 147–156). Newbury, CA: Sage.

Halloran, J. D., Elliott, P., & Murdock, G. (1970). *Demonstrations and communication: A case study*. Harmondsworth, UK: Penguin.

Hamilton, J. (1994). *Time series analysis*. Princeton, NJ: Princeton University Press.

Handlin, O. (1979). *Boston's immigrants: A study in acculturation*. Cambridge, MA: Bellknap Press of Harvard University Press. (Original work published 1941)

Harding, D. W. (1937). General conceptions in the study of the press and public opinion. *Sociological Review, 29*, 370–390.

Hareven, A. (1989). *Wars and peace*. Jerusalem: Zemurra-Beitan.

Hastie, R., & Park, B. (1986). The relationship between memory and judgment depends on whether the judgment task is memory-based or on-line. *Psychological Review, 93*, 258–268.

Hayes, J. (1993). Early Mexican radio broadcasting: Media imperialism, state paternalism or Mexican nationalism? *Studies in Latin American Popular Culture, 12*, 31–55.

Hellweg, S. A., Dionisopoulos, G. N. & Kugler, D. B. (1989). Political candidate image: A state-of-the-art review in progress. In B. Dervin & M. J. Voigt (Eds.), *Progress in communication sciences IX* (pp. 43–78). Norwood, NJ: Ablex.

Hendrickson, L. (1995, May). *Effects of framing uniformity on the perception of child neglect as a "family problem."* Paper presented at the International Communication Association, Albuquerque, NM.

Herr, P. M., Sherman, S. J., & Fazio, R. H. (1983). On the consequences of priming: Assimilation and contrast effects. *Journal of Experimental Social Psychology, 19*, 323–340.

Hibbs, D. A., Jr. (1974). Problems of statistical estimation and causal inference in time-series regression models. In H. L. Costner (Ed.), *Sociological methodology 1973–1974* (pp. 252–308). San Francisco: Jossey-Bass.

Higgins, E. T., Bargh, J. A., & Lombardi, W. (1985). The nature of priming effects on categorization. *Journal of Experimental Psychology: Learning, Memory and Cognition, 11*, 59–69.

Higgins, E. T., & King, G. A. (1981). Accessibility of social constructs: Information-processing consequences of individual and contextual variability. In N. Cantor & J. F. Kihlstrom (Eds.), *Personality, cognition, and social interaction* (pp. 69–121). Hillsdale, NJ: Lawrence Erlbaum Associates.

Higgins, E. T., Rholes, W. S., & Jones, C. R. (1977). Category accessibility and impression formation. *Journal of Experimental Social Psychology, 13*, 141–154.

Higham, J. (1988). *Strangers in the land: Patterns of American nativism, 1860–1925*. New Brunswick, NJ: Rutgers University Press. (Original work published 1955)

Hildreth, R. (1969). *Theory of politics: An inquiry into the foundations of governments and the causes and progress of political revolutions*. New York: A. M. Kelley.

Hill, D. B. (1985). Viewer characteristics and agenda setting by television news. *Public Opinion Quarterly, 49*, 340–350.

Hilliard, R. D. (1991). Nut grafs: A powerful tool for attracting, holding readers. *Newspaper Research Journal, 12*(3), 76–90.

Hirsch, P. M. (1977). Occupational, organizational, and institutional models in mass media research: Toward an integrated framework. In P. M. Hirsch, P. V. Miller, & F. G. Kline (Eds.), *Strategies for communication research* (pp. 13–42). Beverly Hills, CA: Sage.

Hofstadter, D. R. (1985). Mathematical chaos and strange attractors. In D. R. Hofstadter (Ed.), *Metamagical themas* (pp. 364–395). New York: Basic Books.

Hofstadter, R. (1957). *The American political tradition and the men who made it.* New York: Vintage.

Hofstetter, C. R., Zukin, C., & Buss, T. F. (1978). Political imagery and information in an age of television. *Journalism Quarterly 55*, 562–569.

Holloway, S., Tucker, L., & Hornstein, H. (1977). The effects of social and nonsocial information on interpersonal behavior of males: The news makes news. *Journal of Personality and Social Psychology, 35*, 514–522.

Hornstein, H., LaKind, E., Frankel, G., & Manne, S. (1975). The effects of knowledge about remote social events on prosocial behavior, social perception, and mood. *Journal of Personality and Social Psychology, 32*, 1038–1046.

Hovland, C. I. (1959). Reconciling conflicting results derived from experimental and survey studies of attitude change. *American Psychologist, 14*, 8–17.

Howard, J. (1966, February 28), Oracle of the electric age. *Life*, pp. 91–99.

Hu, S. Y. (1987). The images of political figures shaped by the mass media: The case studies of Yun-shun Sun, Yun-gung Ling and Teng-huei Lee. Unpublished master's thesis, Chinese Culture University, Taipei.

Husson,W., Stephen, T., Harrison, T. M., & Fehr, B. J. (1988). An interpersonal communication perspective on images of political candidates. *Human Communication Research, 14*(3), 397–421.

Inglehart, R. (1977). *The silent revolution: Changing values and political styles among the western publics.* Princeton, NJ: Princeton University Press.

Inglehart, R. (1990). *Culture shift in advanced industrial societies.* Princeton, NJ: Princeton University Press.

Innis, H. A. (1950). *Empire and communications.* Oxford, UK: Clarendon Press.

Institute for Applied Economics. (1984). *Network television coverage of economic news* (Mimeograph). New York: Author.

Ito, Y. (1987). Mass communication research in Japan: History and present state. In M. McLaughlin (Ed.), *Communication yearbook 10* (pp. 49–85). Newbury Park, CA: Sage.

Iyengar, S. (1979). Television news and issue salience: A reexamination of the agenda-setting hypothesis. *American Politics Quarterly, 7*, 395–416.

Iyengar, S. (1988). New directions of agenda-setting research. In J. A. Anderson (Ed.), *Communication yearbook 11* (pp. 595–602). Newbury Park, CA: Sage.

Iyengar, S. (1990a). The accessibility bias in politics: Television news and public opinion. *International Journal of Public Opinion Research, 10*, 257–268.

Iyengar, S. (1990b). Shortcuts to political knowledge: The role of selective attention and accessibility. In J. F. Ferejohn & J. H. Kuklinski (Eds.), *Information and democratic processes* (pp. 160–185). Urbana: University of Illinois Press.

Iyengar, S. (1991). *Is anyone responsible? How television frames political issues.* Chicago: University of Chicago Press.

Iyengar, S., & Kinder, D. R. (1984). The evening news and presidential evaluations. *Journal of Personality and Social Psychology, 46*, 778–787.

Iyengar, S., & Kinder, D. R. (1985). Psychological accounts of agenda setting. In S. Kraus & R. Perloff (Eds.), *Mass media and political thought: An information processing approach* (pp. 117–140). Newbury Park, CA: Sage.

Iyengar, S., & Kinder, D. (1987). *News that matters: Television and American opinion.* Chicago: University of Chicago Press.

Iyengar, S., & Ottati, V. (1994). Cognitive perspective in political psychology. In R. S. Wyer & T. K. Srull (Eds.), *Handbook of social cognition* (Vol.2, pp. 143–187). Hillsdale, NJ: Lawrence Erlbaum Associates.

Iyengar, S., Peters, M. D., & Kinder, D. R. (1982). Experimental demonstrations of the not-so-minimal political consequences of mass media. *American Political Science Review, 46,* 848–858.

Iyengar, S., Peters, M. D., Kinder, D. R., & Krosnick, J. A. (1984). The evening news and presidential evaluations. *Journal of Personality and Social Psychology, 4,* 778–787.

Iyengar, S., & Simon, A. (1993). News coverage of the Gulf crisis and public opinion. A study of agenda-setting, priming, and framing. *Communication Research, 20,* 365–383.

Jacobs, L. R., & Shapiro, R. Y. (1994). Issues, candidate image, and priming: The use of private polls in Kennedy's 1960 presidential campaign. *American Political Science Review, 88*(3), 527–540.

Jamieson, K. H. (1992). *Dirty politics: Deception, distraction, and democracy.* New York: Oxford University Press.

Johansen, S. (1988). Statistical analysis of cointegration vectors. *Journal of Economic Dynamics and Control, 12,* 231–254.

Johnson, T. L., & Dooley, K. J. (1995). *Looking for chaos in time series data.* [On line]. Available FTP: Hostname: ftp.tmn.com Directory: Chaos-Complexity File: Dooley-tschaos.txt.

Kahneman, D., & Tversky, A. (1984). Choices, values, and frames. *American Psychologist, 39,* 341–350.

Kaid, L., & Holz-Bacha, C. (Eds.). (1995). *Political advertising in western democracies.* Beverly Hills, CA: Sage.

Kaid, L. L. (1976). Measures of political advertising. *Journal of Advertising Research, 16,* 49–53.

Katz, E., & Lazarsfeld, P. F. (1955). *Personal influence: The part played by people in the flow of mass communications.* Glencoe, IL: The Free Press.

Katz, J. (1987). What makes crime "news"? *Media, Culture and Society, 9,* 47–75.

Kendall, K. E., & Yum, J. O. (1984). Persuading the blue-collar voter: Issues, images and homophily. In R. N. Bostrom (Ed.), *Communication Yearbook, 8* (pp. 707–722). Beverly Hills: Sage.

Kepplinger, H. M., Donsbach, W., Brosius, H.-B., & Staab, J. F. (1989). Media tone and public opinion: A longitudinal study of media coverage and public opinion on Chancellor Kohl. *International Journal of Public Opinion Research, 1,* 326–342.

Kern, M. (1989). *30-second politics: Political advertising in the eighties.* New York: Praeger.

Kessler, R. C., & Greenberg, D. F. (1981). *Linear panel analysis: Models of quantitative change.* New York: Academic Press.

Kinder, D., & Sears, D. (1985). Public opinion and political action. In G. Lindzey & E. Aronson (Eds.), *The handbook of social psychology* (3rd ed., pp. 659–742). New York: Random House.

King, P. T. (1994). *Issue agendas in the 1992 legislative election.* Unpublished doctoral dissertation, University of Texas, Austin.

Klandermans, H., & Sidney, T. (1988). *International social movement research: A research annual. From structure to action: comparing social movement research across cultures.* Greenwich, CT: JAI.

Klapper, J. T. (1960). *The effects of mass communication.* New York: The Free Press.

Kleinnijenhuis, J., Oegema, J. D., & de Ridder, J. A. (1995). *De democratie op drift* [The drifting democracy]. Amsterdam: VU-uitgeverij.

Knight, O. (1960). *Following the Indian wars: The story of the newspaper correspondents among the Indian campaigners.* Stillwater: University of Oklahoma Press.

Kocak, H. (1989). *Differential and difference equations through computer experiments: With a supplementary diskette containing Phaser: An animator/simulator for IBM personal computers.* New York: Springer-Verlag.

Koch, T. (1990). *The news as myth: Fact and context in journalism.* New York: Greenwood Press.

Kohn, M. (1989) Cross-national research as an analytic strategy. In M. L. Kohn (Ed.), *Cross-national research in sociology* (pp. 77–103). Newbury Park, CA: Sage.

Kosicki, G. (1993). Problems and opportunities in agenda setting research. *Journal of Communication, 43*(2), 100–127.

Kriesberg, L. (1973). *The sociology of social conflicts.* Englewood Cliffs, NJ: Prentice-Hall.

Krippendorff, K. (1980). *Content analysis: An introduction to its methodology.* Beverly Hills, CA: Sage.

Krosnick, J. A., & Brannon, L. A. (1993). The impact of war on the ingredients of presidential evaluations: Multidimensional effects on political involvement. *American Political Science Review, 87,* 963–975.

Krosnick, J., & Kinder, D. R. (1990). Altering the foundations of support for the president through priming. *American Political Science Review, 84,* 497–512.

Krugman, H. E. (1965). The impact of television advertising: Learning without involvement. *Public Opinion Quarterly, 29,* 349–356.

Krugman, H. E. (1966). The measurement of advertising involvement. *Public Opinion Quarterly, 30,* 583–596.

Krugman, H. E., & Hartley, E. L. (1970). Passive learning from television. *Public Opinion Quarterly, 34,* 184–190.

Kuhn, T. (1970). *The structure of scientific revolutions* (2nd ed.). Chicago: University of Chicago Press.

Kuklinski, J. H., Riggle, E., Ottati, V., & Wyer, R. S. (1991). The basis of political tolerance judgments: Cognition or emotion? *American Journal of Political Science, 35,* 1–27.

Kurtz, H. (1990, October 28). Is the economy suffering from media malady? *Washington Post,* p. H1.

Lai, F. L. (1992). Electoral systems and voting behaviors in Taiwan. In K. Y. Chang (Ed.), *The democratization of the Republic of China: Its process, systems and impacts* (pp. 225–242). Taipei: Institute of International Relations of the National Chengchi University.

Lang, G. E., & Lang, K. (1955). The inferential structure of political communications: A study in unwitting bias. *Public Opinion Quarterly, 19,* 168–183.

Lang, G. E., & Lang, K. (1984). *Politics and television re-viewed.* Beverly Hills, CA: Sage.

Lang, K., & Lang, G. E. (1953). The unique perspective of television and its effects: A pilot study. *American Sociological Review, 18,* 3–12.

La Palombara, J. G. (1987). *Democracy, Italian style.* New Haven, CT: Yale University Press.

Lasorsa, D. L., & Reese, S. D. (1990). News source use in the crash of 1987: A study of four national media. *Journalism Quarterly, 67,* 60–71.

Lasorsa, D. L., & Wanta, W. (1990). Effects of personal, interpersonal and media experiences on issue saliences. *Journalism Quarterly, 67,* 804–813.

Lasswell, H. (1948). The structure and function of communication in society. In L. Bryson (Ed.), *The communication of ideas* (pp. 37–51). New York: Institute for Religious and Social Studies.

Lau, R. R. (1995). Information search during an election campaign: Introducing a processing-tracing methodology for political scientists. In M. Lodge & K. M. McGraw (Eds.), *Political judgment: Structure and process* (pp. 179–205). Ann Arbor: University of Michigan Press.

Lazarsfeld, P. F., Berelson, B. R., & Gaudet, H. (1948). *The people's choice.* New York: Columbia University Press.

Lemert, J. B. (1981). *Does mass communication change public opinion after all? A new approach to effects analysis.* Chicago: Nelson-Hall.

Lester, P. (1995). *Visual communication: Images with messages.* Belmont, CA: Wadsworth.

Lichtenstein, M., & Srull, T. K. (1987). Processing objectives as a determinant of the relationship between recall and judgment. *Journal of Experimental Social Psychology, 23,* 93–118.

Liebes, T., & Ribak, R. (1992). The contribution of family culture to political participation, political outlook, and its reproduction. *Communication Research, 19*(5), 618–641.

Linden, F. (1982). The consumer as forecaster. *Public Opinion Quarterly, 46*, 353–360.

Lippmann, W. (1922). *Public opinion.* New York: Macmillan.

Lissak, M. (1990). The intifada and the society. In R. Gal (Ed.), *The seventh war* (pp. 17–34). Tel Aviv: Hakibutz Hameuchad.

Lodge, M., McGraw, K., & Stroh, P. (1989). An impression-driven model of candidate evaluation. *American Political Science Review, 83*, 399–420.

Lodge, M., Steenbergen, M. R., & Brau, S. (1995). The responsive voter: Campaign information and the dynamics of candidate evaluation. *American Political Science Review, 89*, 309–326.

Lopez-Escobar, E. (1992). Spanish media law: Changes in the landscape. *European Journal of Communication 7*(2), 241–260.

Lopez-Escobar, E., & Faus-Belau, A. (1985). Broadcasting in Spain: A history of heavy-handed state control. In R. Kuhn (Ed.), *Broadcasting and politics in western Europe* (pp. 122–136). London: Frank Cass.

Lorenz, B. N. (1963a). Deterministic nonperiodic flow. *Journal of Atmospheric Science, 20*, 130–141.

Lorenz, B. N. (1963b). The mechanics of vacillation. *Journal of Atmospheric Science, 20*, 448–464.

Lorenz, B. N. (1964). The problem of deducing the climate from governing equations. *Tellus, 16*, 1–11.

Lotz, R. (1991). *Crime and the American press.* New York: Praeger.

Lowery, S. A., & DeFleur, M. (1988). *Milestones in mass communication research* (2nd ed.). New York: Longman.

Lutkepohl, H. (1993). *Introduction to multiple time series analysis.* New York: Springer Verlag.

Machiavelli, N. (1995). *The prince.* D. Wootton (Ed. and Trans.). Indianapolis, IN: Hackett. (Original work published 1532)

Machina, M. (1990). Choice under uncertainty: Problems solved and unsolved. In K. S. Cook & M. Levi (Eds.), *The limits of rationality* (pp. 90–132). Chicago: University of Chicago Press.

Mackie, T., Mannheimer, R., & Sami, G. (1992). Italy. In M. Franklin (Ed.), *Electoral change.* Cambridge, UK: Cambridge University Press.

MacKuen, M. (1981). Social communication and the mass policy agenda. In M. MacKuen & S. Coombs (Eds.), *More than news: Media power in public affairs* (pp. 19–144). Beverly Hills, CA: Sage.

MacKuen, M., Erikson, R., & Stimson, J. (1992). Peasants or bankers? The American electorate and the U.S. economy. *American Political Science Review, 86*(3), 597–611.

Maher, M. (1995). *Media framing and salience of the population issue: A multi-method approach.* Unpublished doctoral dissertation, University of Texas, Austin.

Mandelli, A. (1997). *The agenda-setting of public sentiments: Studying the Italian case of Tangentopoli.* Unpublished manuscript, Indiana University, Bloomington.

Manheim, J. B. (1987). A model of agenda dynamics. In M. McLaughin (Ed.), *Communication yearbook 10* (pp. 499–516). Newbury Park, CA: Sage.

Markus, G. B. (1979). *Analyzing panel data.* Beverly Hills, CA: Sage.

Martingale, C. (1995, August). *Only in glimpses: Portrayal of America's largest minority groups by the New York Times, 1934–1994.* Paper presented at the Association for Education in Journalism and Mass Communication, Washington, DC.

Mayer, W. G. (1992). *The changing American mind: How and why American public opinion changed between 1960 and 1988.* Ann Arbor: University of Michigan Press.

McCain, L. J., & McCleary, R. (1979). The statistical analysis of the simple interrupted time-series quasi-experiment. In T. D. Cook & D. T. Campbell (Eds.), *Quasi-experimentation: Design & analysis issues for field settings* (pp. 233–294). Boston: Houghton Mifflin.

McCleary, R., & Hay, R. A. (1980). *Applied times series analysis for the social sciences*. Beverly Hills, CA: Sage.

McClure, R. D., & Patterson, T. E. (1976). Print vs. network news. *Journal of Communication, 26*, 23–28.

McCombs, M. E. (1972). Mass media in the marketplace. *Journalism Monographs, 24*.

McCombs, M. (1977a, October). *Expanding the domain of agenda-setting research: Strategies for theoretical development*. Invited paper for the Speech Communication Association, Washington, DC.

McCombs, M. E. (1977b). Newspaper versus television: Mass communication effects across time In D. L. Shaw & M. E. McCombs (Eds.), *The emergence of American political issues: The agenda-setting function of the press* (pp. 89–106). St. Paul, MN: West.

McCombs, M. E. (1987). Effect of monopoly in Cleveland on diversity of newspaper content. *Journalism Quarterly, 64*, 740–744, 792.

McCombs, M. (1992). Explorers and surveyors: Expanding strategies for agenda setting research. *Journalism Quarterly, 69*, 813–824.

McCombs, M. (1994). The future agenda for agenda setting research. *Masu-Komyunikeishon Kenkyu* [Journal of Mass Communication Studies], *45*, 171–181.

McCombs, M. (1995, September). *The media outside and the pictures in our heads: Surveying the second dimension of agenda-setting*. Paper presented at "New trends in communication," A conference of the Universita Degli Studi di Roma La Sapienza, Rome, Italy.

McCombs, M. (1996, April). *The pictures of politics in our heads*. Keynote address presented at National Chengchi University, Taipei, Taiwan.

McCombs, M. E., Einsiedel, E., & Weaver, D. H. (1991). *Contemporary public opinion: Issues and the news*. Hillsdale, NJ: Lawrence Erlbaum Associates.

McCombs, M., & Evatt, D. (1995). Issues and attributes: Exploring a new dimension in agenda setting. *Comunicacion y Sociedad 8*(1), 7–32.

McCombs, M. E., & Shaw, D. L. (1972). The agenda-setting function of mass media. *Public Opinion Quarterly, 36*, 176–187.

McCombs, M. E., & Shaw, D. L. (1976). Structuring the "unseen environment." *Journal of Communication, 26*(2), 18–22.

McCombs, M. E., & Shaw, D. L. (1993). The evolution of agenda-setting research: Twenty-five years in the marketplace of ideas. *Journal of Communication, 43*, 58–67.

McCombs, M., & Zhu, J. (1995). Capacity, diversity and volatility of the public agenda: Trends from 1939 to 1994. *Public Opinion Quarterly, 59*, 495–525.

McGavin, L. H. (1996). *Information in chaos: A nonlinear approach to the methods of information and entropy in communication research*. Unpublished doctoral dissertion, University of Alabama, Tuscaloosa.

McGee, M. C. (1978). Not men but measures: The origins and support of an ideological principle. *Quarterly Journal of Speech, 64*, 141–156.

McGrath, J. E., & McGrath, M. F. (1962). Effects of partisanship on perceptions of political figures. *Public Opinion Quarterly, 26*, 236–248.

McGraw, K., & Pinney, N. (1990). The effects of general and domain-specific expertise on political memory and judgment. *Social Cognition, 8*, 9–30.

McLeod, J. M., Becker L. B., & Byrnes, J. E. (1974). Another look at the agenda-setting function of the press. *Communication Research, 1*, 131–166.

McLeod, J., Sun, S., Chi, H., & Pan, Z. (1990, August). *Metaphor and the media: What shapes public understanding of the "war" against drugs.* Paper presented at the Association for Education in Journalism and Mass Communication, Minneapolis, MN.

McLuhan, M. (1964). *Understanding media: The extensions of man.* New York: McGraw-Hill.

McLuhan, M., & Fiore, Q. (1967). *The medium is the message.* New York: Random House

McQuail, D. (1994). *Media performance.* Newbury Park, CA: Sage.

Meadowcroft, J. M., & Olson B. (1995, August). *Television viewing vs. reading: Testing information processing assumptions.* Paper presented at the Association for Education in Journalism and Mass Communication, Washington, DC.

Mendelsohn, M. (1993). Television's frames in the 1988 Canadian election. *Canadian Journal of Communication, 18,* 149–171.

Mendelsohn, M. (1994). The media's persuasive effects: The priming of leadership in the 1988 Canadian election. *Canadian Journal of Political Science, 27,* 81–97.

Merritt, R. L. (1965). The emergence of American nationalism: A quantitative approach. *American Quarterly, 17*(2), 319–334.

Merritt, R. L. (1966). *Symbols of American community, 1735–1775.* New Haven, CT: Yale University Press.

Merton, R. K. (1957). *Social theory and social structure* (rev. ed.). Glencoe, IL: The Free Press.

Meyer, C. B., & Schvaneveldt, R. W. (1976). Meaning, memory structure, and mental processes. *Science, 192,* 27–33.

Mikami, S., Takeshita, T., Nakada, M., & Kawabata, M. (1995). The media coverage and public awareness of environmental issues in Japan. *Gazette, 54,* 209–226.

Millar, M. G., & Tesser, A. (1989). The effects of affective-cognitive consistency and thought on the attitude-behavior relation. *Journal of Experimental Social Psychology, 25,* 189–202.

Miller, A. H., Wattenberg, M. P., & Malanchuk, O. (1986). Schematic assessments of presidential candidates. *American Political Science Review, 80,* 521–540.

Miller, G. A. (1956). The magical number seven, plus or minus two: Some limits on our capacity for processing information. *Psychological Review, 63,* 81–97.

Miller, W. L., Clarke, H. D., Harrop, M., LeDuc, L., & Whiteley, P. (1990). *How voters change: The 1987 British election campaign in perspective.* Oxford, UK: Clarendon Press.

Minsky, M. (1975). A framework for representing knowledge. In P. H. Winston (Ed.), *The psychology of computer vision* (pp. 211–277). New York: McGraw-Hill.

Myerson, A. (1995, October 16). Newspapers cut Spanish language publications. *New York Times,* p. C7.

Namba, K. (1993). Situational perspectives in studies of advertising. *Masu-Komyuikeishon Kenkyu* [Journal of Mass Communication Studies], *42,* 179–193.

Natchez, P. B., & Bupp, I. C. (1968). Candidates, issues, and voters. *Public Policy, 17,* 409–437.

Nelson, C., & Tienda M. (1985). The structuring of Hispanic ethnicity: Historical and contemporary perspectives. *Ethnic and Racial Studies, 8*(1), 49–74.

Neuman, W. R. (1990). The threshold of public attention. *Public Opinion Quarterly, 54,* 159–176.

Neuman, W. R., Just, M. R., & Crigler, A. N. (1992). *Common knowledge: News and the construction of political meaning.* Chicago: University of Chicago Press.

Nickerson, R. S. (1968). A note on long-term recognition memory for pictorial material. *Psychonomic Science, 11,* 58.

Nie, N. H., Verba, S., & Petrocik, J. R. (1976). *The changing American voter.* Cambridge, MA: Harvard University Press.

Nimmo, D., & Savage, R. L. (1976). *Candidates and their images: Concepts, methods, and findings.* Santa Monica, CA: Goodyear.

Noelle-Neumann, E. (1984). *The spiral of silence: Public opinion, our social skin.* Chicago: University of Chicago Press.

Noelle-Neumann, E. & Mathes, R. (1987). The "event as event" and the "event as news": The significance of "consonance" for media effects research. *European Journal of Communication, 2*, 391–414.

Nord, D. (1981). The politics of agenda setting in late 19th century cities. *Journalism Quarterly, 58*, 565–574, 612.

Nord, D. (1982). What we can do for them: Journalism history and the history profession. *Journalism History, 9*(2), 56–60.

Nordlinger, E. A. (1972). *Conflict regulation in divided societies.* Cambridge, MA: Center for International Affairs, Harvard University.

Nossiter, T. J., Scammell, M., & Semetko, H. A. (1995). Old values versus news values. In I. Crewe & B. Gosschalk (Eds.), *Political communications: The British 1992 general election campaign.* Cambridge, UK: Cambridge University Press.

Notes from underground. (1995, June). *U.S. News and World Report,* p. 25.

Ortega y Gasset, J. (1932). *The revolt of the masses* (authorized, anonymous translation from Spanish). New York: Norton.

Ostrom, C. W. (1990). *Time series analysis: Regression techniques* (2nd ed.). Beverly Hills, CA: Sage.

Ottati, V., Riggle, E., Wyer, R. S., Schwarz, N., & Kuklinski, J. (1989). The cognitive and affective bases of opinion survey responses. *Journal of Personality and Social Psychology, 545*, 404–415.

Ottati, V., & Wyer, R. S. (1991). The cognitive mediators of political choice: Toward a comprehensive model of political information processing. In J. Ferejohn & J. H. Kuklinski (Eds.), *Information and the democratic process* (pp. 186–216). Champaign: University of Illinois Press.

Ouliaris, S., & Phillips, P. C. B. (1994). *COINT 2.0: GAUSS procedures for cointegrated regressions.* Maple Valley, WA: APTECH Systems, Inc.

Palmgreen, P., & Clarke, P. (1977). Agenda-setting with local and national issues. *Communication Research, 4*, 435–452.

Pan, Z., & Kosicki, G. M. (1993). Framing analysis: An approach to news discourse. *Political Communication, 10*, 55–75.

Park, R. (1922). *The immigrant press and its control.* New York: Harper & Brothers.

Pasternack, S. (1987). Headlines and libel: Is the "unit" approach the most effective? *Newspaper Research Journal, 8*(2), 33–41.

Patterson, T. (1993a). For the negative: Fourth branch or fourth rate? The press's failure to live up to the founders' expectations. *Political Communication, 10*, 8–15.

Patterson, T. (1993b). *Out of order.* New York: Knopf.

Patterson, T. E. (1989). The press and candidate images. *International Journal of Public Opinion Research 1*(2), 123–135.

Perfetti, C. A., Beverly, S., Bell, L., Rodgers, K., & Faux, R. (1987). Comprehending newspaper headlines. *Journal of Memory and Language, 26*, 692–713.

Phillips, P. C. B., & Hansen, B. (1990). Statistical inference in instrumental variables regression with I(1) processes. *Review of Economic Studies, 57*, 99–125.

Phillips, P. C. B., & Ouliaris, S. (1990). Asymptotic properties of residual based tests for cointegration. *Econometrica, 58*, 165–194.

Pike, G. R. (1985, May). *Toward a transactional model of political images: Collective images of the candidates in the 1984 election.* Paper presented at the International Communication Association, Honolulu, HI.

Portes, A., & Truelove, C. (1987). Making sense of diversity: Recent research on Hispanic minorities in the United States. *Annual Review of Sociology, 13*, 359–385.

Prezworski, A., & Teune, H. (1970). *The logic of comparative social inquiry.* New York: Wiley.

Price, V., & Tewksbury, D. (1995). News values and public opinion: A process: How political advertising and TV news prime viewers to think about issues and candidates. In F. Biocca (Ed.), *Television and political advertising* (pp. 265–309). Hillsdale, NJ: Lawrence Erlbaum Associates.

Protess, D., & McCombs, M. E. (Eds.). (1991). *Agenda setting: Readings on media, policymaking, and public opinion.* Hillsdale, NJ: Lawrence Erlbaum Associates.

Putnam, R. D. (1993). *L'lutime parlamento: sulla fine della prima repubblica.* Rome: La Nuova Italia.

Rahn, W., Aldrich, J. H., Borgida, E., & Sullivan, J. L. (1990). A social-cognitive model of candidate appraisal. In J. Ferejohn & J. H. Kuklinski (Eds.), *Information and democratic processes* (pp. 136–159). Champaign: University of Illinois Press.

Rarick, D. L., Duncan, M. B., Lee, D. G., & Porter, L. W. (1977). The Carter persona: An empirical analysis of the rhetorical visions of campaign '76. *Quarterly Journal of Speech, 63,* 258–273.

Reese, S. D., & Danielian, L. H. (1989). Intermedia influence and the drug issue: Converging on cocaine. In P. J. Shoemaker (Ed.), *Communication campaigns about drugs: Government, media, and the public* (pp. 29–45). Hillsdale, NJ: Lawrence Erlbaum Associates.

Reiter, Y., & Aharoni., R. (1992). *The political world of the Israeli-Arabs.* Beit Berl, Israel: The Arab Society Research Center.

Rheingold, H. (1993). *The virtual community: Homesteading on the electronic frontier.* Reading, MA: Addison-Wesley.

Riffe, D., Aust, C. F., & Lacy, S. R. (1993). The effectiveness of random, consecutive day and constructed week sampling in newspaper content analysis. *Journalism Quarterly, 70,* 133–139.

Riggins, S. (Ed.). (1992). *Ethnic minority media: An international perspective.* Thousand Oaks, CA: Sage.

Roberts, M., Anderson, R., & McCombs, M. (1994). 1990 Texas gubernatorial campaign: Influence of issues and images. *Mass Comm Review, 21* (1–2), 20–35.

Roberts, M., & McCombs, M. (1994). Agenda setting and political advertising: Origins of the news agenda. *Political Communication, 11,* 249–262.

Roberts, M. S. (1991). *The agenda-setting power of political advertising.* Unpublished doctoral dissertation, University of Texas, Austin.

Roberts, M. S. (1992). Predicting voting behavior via the agenda-setting tradition. *Journalism Quarterly, 69,* 878–892.

Robinson, M. J., & Sheehan, M. A. (1983). *Over the wire and on TV: CBS and UPI in campaign '80.* New York: Russell Sage Foundation.

Rodriguez, A. (1993). *Made in the USA: The constructions of the Noticiero Univision.* Unpublished doctoral dissertation, University of California, San Diego.

Rodriguez, A. (1995). Objectivity and ethnicity in the production of the Noticiero Univision. *Critical Studies in Mass Communication, 13,* 59–81.

Rodriguez, A. (in press). Creating an audience and remapping a nation: A brief history of U.S. Spanish language braodcasting, 1930–1980. *Quarterly Review of Film and Video.*

Rogers, E. M., & Dearing, J. W. (1988). Agenda-setting research: Where it has been, where is it going? In J. A. Anderson (Ed.), *Communication yearbook 11* (pp. 555–594). Newbury Park, CA: Sage.

Rogers, E., Dearing, J., & Bregman, D. (1993). The anatomy of agenda-setting research. *Journal of Communication, 43,* 68–84.

Rogers, E. M., Dearing, J. W., & Chang, S. (1991). AIDS in the 1980s: The agenda-setting process of a public issue. *Journalism Monographs, 126.*

Rosenberg, S. W., Kahn, S., & Tran, T. (1991). Creating a political image: Shaping appearance and manipulating the vote. *Political Behavior, 13*(4), 345–367.

Rosenberg, S. W., & McCafferty, P. (1987). The image and the vote: Manipulating voters' preferences. *Public Opinion Quarterly, 51*, 31–47.

Rosengren, K. E., & Windahl, S. (1989). *Media matter: TV use in childhood and adolescence.* Norwood, NJ: Ablex.

Rosenthal, R. (1991). *Meta-analytic procedure for social research* (rev. ed.). Newbury, CA: Sage.

Rucinski, D. (1992). Personalized bias in news: The potency of the particular. *Communication Research, 19*, 91–108.

Salomon, G. (1979). *Interaction of media, cognition and learning.* San Francisco: Jossey-Bass.

Salwen, M. B. (1988), Effect of accumulation of coverage on issue salience in agenda setting. *Journalism Quarterly, 65*, 100–106, 130.

Sanchez, G. (1933). *Becoming Mexican American: Ethnicity, culture and identity in Chicano Los Angeles, 1900–1945.* New York: Oxford University Press.

Sartori, G. (1969). Politics, ideology and belief systems. *American Political Science Review, 63*, 298–311.

SAS Institute. (1993). *SAS/ETS users guide, version 6* (2nd ed.). Cary, NC: Author.

Savage, W. W., Jr., (1990). *Comic books and America: 1945–1954.* Norman: University of Oklahoma Press.

Scammell, M., & Semetko, H. A. (1995). *Political communications in the 1997 British general election campaign.* Proposal funded by the British Economic and Social Research Council.

Schiffrin, R., & Schneider, W. (1977). Controlled and automatic information processing: II. Perceptual learning, automatic attending, and a general theory. *Psychological Review, 84*, 127–190.

Schlesinger, A. M., Jr. (1958). *Prelude to independence: The newspaper war on Britain, 1764–1776.* New York: Knopf.

Schlesinger, A. M., Jr. (1986). *The cycles of American history.* Boston: Houghton Mifflin.

Schleuder, J., McCombs, M., & Wanta, W. (1991). Inside the agenda-setting process: How political advertising and TV news prime viewers to think about issues and candidates. In F. Biocca (Ed.), *Television and political advertising* (pp. 265–309). Hillsdale, NJ: Lawrence Erlbaum Associates.

Schleuder, J., White, A. V., & Cameron, G. T. (1993). Priming effects of television news bumpers and teasers on attention and memory. *Journal of Broadcasting & Electronic Media, 37*, 437–452.

Schoenbach, K. (1987). The role of mass media in West German election campaigns. *Legislative Studies Quarterly, 12*, 373–394.

Schoenbach, K., & Semetko, H. A. (1992). Agenda-setting, agenda-reinforcing or agenda-deflating? A study of the 1990 German national election. *Journalism Quarterly, 69*, 837–846.

Schudson, M. (1982). The politics of narrative form: The emergence of news conventions in print and television. *Daedalus, 111*, 97–112.

Schulman, N. (1990). A narrative theory approach to understanding news and journalistic form. *Ecquid Novi, 11*, 3–19.

Schutz, A. (1967). *The phenomenology of the social world.* Evanston, IL: Northwestern University Press.

Schwab, P. (1995). Somalia. In *Academic American encyclopedia.* Danbury, CT: Grolier Electronic Publishing, Inc.

Scripps, C. E. (1959). *Economic support of mass communications media 1929–1957: A statistical analysis from Scripps-Howard.* Cincinnati, OH: Scripps-Howard.

Seldes, G. (Ed.). (1967). *The great quotations.* New York: Simon & Schuster.

Semetko, H. A. (1991). Images of Britain's changing party system: TV news and the 1983 and 1987 general election campaigns. *Political Communication and Persuasion, 8*(4), 163–181.

Semetko, H. A. (1996a). The media. In L. LeDuc, R. Niemi, & P. Norris (Eds.), *Comparing democracies* (pp. 51–71). Newbury Park, CA: Sage.

Semetko, H. A. (1996b). Political balance on television: Campaigns in the United States, Britain and Germany. *Harvard International Journal of Press/Politics, 1*(1), 51–71.

Semetko, H. A., Blumler, J. G., Gurevitch, M., & Weaver, D. (1991). *The formation of campaign agendas*. Hillsdale, NJ: Lawrence Erlbaum Associates.

Semetko, H. A., & Borquez, J. (1991). Audiences for election communication. In L. Kaid, J. Gerstle, & K. Sanders (Eds.), *Mediated politics in two cultures: Presidential campaigning in the United States and France* (pp. 223–246). New York: Praeger.

Semetko, H. A., Diez-Nicolas, J., Schoenbach, K., Scammell, M., & Nossiter, T. J. (1994). *Elections and the media in cross-national perspective*. Paper presented at the International Political Science Association, Berlin.

Semetko, H. A., Scammell, M., & Nossiter, T. J. (1994). The media's coverage of the campaign. In A. Heath, R. Jowell, & J. Curtice (Eds.), *Labour's last chance* (pp. 25–42). Aldershot, UK: Dartmouth.

Semetko, H. A., & Schoenbach, K. (1993). The campaign in the media. In R. Dalton (Ed.), *The new Germany votes: Unification and the creation of the new German party system.* (pp. 187–208). Providence, RI: Berg.

Semetko, H. A., & Schoenbach, K. (1994). *Germany's "unity" election: Voters and the media*. Cresskill, NJ: Hampton Press.

Semetko, H. A. & Valkenburg, P. (1996, September). *Political efficacy and media use in the new Germany: Evidence from a three-year panel study*. Paper presented at the American Political Science Association, San Francisco, CA.

Severin, W. J., & Tankard, J. W. (1992). *Communication theories: Origins, methods, and uses in the mass media* (3rd ed.). New York: Longman.

Seymour–Ure, C. (1974). *The political impact of mass media*. London: Constable.

Shabad, G., & Andersen, K. (1979). Candidate evaluations by men and women. *Public Opinion Quarterly, 43*, 18–35.

Shalev, A. (1990). *The intifada: Causes, characteristics and implications*. Tel Aviv: Papyrus.

Shaw, D. L. (1984). *The southern challenge to American cultural union: Newspaper symbols of regional thought 1820–1860*. Unpublished manuscript, University of North Carolina, Chapel Hill.

Shaw, D. L., & Martin. S. E. (1992). The function of mass media agenda setting. *Journalism Quarterly, 69*, 902–920.

Shaw, D. L., & McCombs, M. (Eds.). (1977). *The emergence of American political issues: The agenda setting function of the press*. St. Paul, MN: West.

Sherman, S., Mackie, D. M., & Discoll, D. M. (1990). Priming and the differential use of dimensions in evaluations. *Personality and Social Psychology Bulletin, 16*, 405–418.

Shimizu, I. (1951). *Shakai-shinrigaku* [Social psychology]. Tokyo: Iwanami.

Shoemaker, P. J., & Reese, S. D. (1991). *Mediating the message: Theories of influences on mass media content.* New York: Longman.

Shoemaker, P. J., Wanta, W., & Leggett, D. (1989). Drug coverage and public opinion, 1972–1986. In P. J. Shoemaker (Ed.), *Communication campaigns about drugs: Government, media and the public* (pp. 67–80). Hillsdale, NJ: Lawrence Erlbaum Associates.

Siebert, F. S., Peterson, T. B., & Schramm, W. (1956). *Four theories of the press*. Urbana: University of Illinois Press.

Sigel, R. S. (1964). Effect of partisanship on the perception of political candidates. *Public Opinion Quarterly, 28*, 483–496.

Sims, C. (1972). Money, income, and causality. *American Economic Review, 62*, 540–552.

Singer, J. L. (1980), The power and limitations of television: A cognitive-affective analysis. In P. H. Tannenbaum (Ed.), *The entertainment functions of television* (pp. 31–65). Hillsdale, NJ: Lawrence Erlbaum Associates.

Smith, A. (1979). *Television and political life: Studies in six European countries*. London: Macmillan.

Smith, K. A. (1987). Effects of newspaper coverage on community issue concerns and local government. *Communication Research, 14*, 379–395.

Smith, M. J. (1968). *Mathematical ideas in biology*. New York: Cambridge University Press.

Smith, T. (1980). America's most important problems—A trend analysis, 1946–1976. *Public Opinion Quarterly, 44*, 164–180.

Smith, T. (1990). Liberal and conservative trends in the United States since World War II. *Public Opinion Quarterly, 54*, 479–507.

Smith, T. W. (1985). The polls: America's most important problems. Part 1: National and international. *Public Opinion Quarterly, 49*, 264–274.

Son, J., Reese, S. D., & Davie, W. R. (1987). Effects of visual-verbal redundancy and recaps on television news learning. *Journal of Broadcasting & Electronic Media, 31*, 207–216.

Speer, A. (1970). *Inside the third reich*. New York: Macmillan.

Srull, T. K., & Wyer, R. S. (1979). The role of category accessibility in the interpretation of information about persons: Some determinants and implications. *Journal of Personality and Social Psychology, 37*, 1660–1672.

Srull, T., & Wyer, R. (1980). Category accessability and social perception: Some implication for the study of person memory and interpersonal judgments. *Journal of Personality and Social Psychology, 38*, 841–856.

Stagner, R. (1967). The analysis of conflict. In R. Stagner (Ed.), *The dimensions of human conflict* (pp. 131–167). Detroit, MI: Wayne University Press.

Stein, M. (1994, February 12). Boast of success. *Editor & Publisher*, p. 1.

Stempel, G. H., III, & Westley, B. H. (Eds.). (1989). *Research methods in mass communications* (2nd ed.). Englewood Cliffs, NJ: Prentice-Hall.

Stevenson, R. (1994). The disappearing reader. *Newspaper Research Journal, 15*, 3–22.

Stevenson, R., Gonzenbach, W. J., & Prabu D. (1991, August). *Economic recession and the news*. Paper presented to the Association for Education in Journalism and Mass Communication, Boston.

Stone, G. (1987). *Examining newspapers: What research reveals about America's newspapers*. Newbury Park, CA: Sage.

Stone, G. C., & McCombs, M. E. (1981). Tracing the time lag in agenda-setting. *Journalism Quarterly, 58*, 151–155.

Strack, F., Martin, L. L., & Schwarz, N. (1988). Priming and communication: Social determinants of information use in judgments of life satisfaction. *European Journal of Social Psychology, 18*, 429–442.

Subervi-Vélez, F. (1986). The mass media and ethnic assimilation and pluralism: A review and research proposal with special focus on Hispanics. *Communication Research, 13*(1), 71–96.

Sutherland, M., & Galloway, J. (1981). Role of advertising: Persuasion or agenda setting? *Journal of Advertising Research, 21*, 25–29.

Swanson, D. L. (1988). Feeling the elephant: Some observations on agenda-setting research. In J. A. Anderson (Ed.), *Communication yearbook 11* (pp. 603–619). Newbury Park, CA: Sage.

Swanson, D. L. (1992). Managing theoretical diversity in cross-national studies of political communication. In J. G. Blumler, J. McLeod, & K. E. Rosengren (Eds.), *Comparatively speaking: Communication and culture across space and time*. (pp. 19–34) Newbury Park, CA: Sage.

Swanson, D. L., & Mancini, P. (Eds.). (1996). *Politics, media, and modern democracy: An international study of innovations in electoral campaigning and their consequences.* Westport, CT: Praeger.

Takeshita, T., & Mikami, S. (1995). How did mass media influence the voters' choice in the 1993 general election in Japan? A study of agenda-setting. *Keio Communication Review, 17,* 27–41.

Tankard, J., Hendrickson, L., Silberman, J., Bliss, K. & Ghanem, S. (1991, August). *Media frames: Approaches to conceptualization and measurement.* Paper presented to the Association for Education in Journalism and Mass Communication, Boston.

Tannenbaum, P. H. (1953). The effect of headlines on the interpretation of news stories. *Journalism Quarterly, 30,* 189–197.

Tedrow, L. M., & Mahoney, E. R. (1979). Trends in attitudes toward abortion: 1972–1976. *Public Opinion Quarterly, 43,* 181–189.

Tiffen, R. (1989). *News and power.* Boston: Allen & Unwin.

Tipton, L. P., Haney, R., & Baseheart, J. (1975). Media agenda-setting in city and state election campaigns. *Journalism Quarterly, 52,* 15–22.

Tsuruki, M. (1982). Frame imposing function of the mass media as seen in the Japanese press. *Keio Communication Review, 3,* 27–37.

Tuchman, G. (1978). *Making news: A study in the construction of reality.* New York: The Free Press.

Turk, J. V. (1985). Information subsidies and influence. *Public Relations Review, 11,* 10–25.

Turk, J. V. (1986). Public relations' influence on the news. *Newspaper Research Journal, 7,* 15–27.

Tversky, A., & Kahneman, D. (1981). The framing of decisions and the psychology of choice. *Science, 211,* 453–458.

Tversky, A., & Kahneman, D. (1990) Rational choice and the framing of decisions. In K. S. Cook & M. Levi (Eds.), *The limits of rationality* (pp. 60–89). Chicago: University of Chicago Press.

U.S. Bureau of the Census. (1993). *Current population reports, P23–183, Hispanic Americans today.* Washington, DC: U.S. Government Printing Office.

van der Eijk, C., & van Praag, P. (1987). De strijd om de meerderheid: de verkiezingen van 1986 [The battle for the majority: The 1986 national election]. Amsterdam: CT Press.

Wanta, W., & Hu, Y.(1994). Time-lag differences in the agenda-setting process: An examination of five news media. *International Journal of Public Opinion Research, 6,* 225–240.

Wanta, W., & Roy, M. J. (1995, August). *Memory decay and the agenda-setting effect: An examination of three news media.* Paper presented at the Association for Education in Journalism and Mass Communication, Washington, DC.

Wanta, W., Williams, J., & Hu, Y. (1991, August). *The agenda-setting effects of international news coverage: An examination of differing news frames.* Paper presented to the Association for Education in Journalism and Mass Communication, Boston.

Watt, J. H., Mazza, M., & Snyder, L. B. (1993). Agenda-setting effects of television news coverage and the memory decay curve. *Communication Research, 20,* 408–435.

Watt, J. H., & van den Berg, S. A. (1978). Time series analysis of alternative media effects theories. In B. D. Ruben (Ed.), *Communication yearbook 2* (pp. 215–224). New Brunswick, NJ: Transaction Books.

Watzlawick, P., Weakland, J., & Fisch, R. (1974). *Change: Principles of problem formation and problem resolution.* New York: Norton.

Weaver, D. H. (1977). Political issues and voter need for orientation. In D. L. Shaw & M. E. McCombs (Eds.), *The emergence of American political issues: The agenda-setting function of the press* (pp. 107–119). St. Paul, MN: West.

Weaver, D. H. (1980). Audience need for orientation and media effects. *Communication Research, 7,* 361–376.

Weaver, D. H. (1983). Media agenda-setting and elections: Assumptions and implications. In W. Schulz & K. Schönbach (Eds.), *Massenmedien und Wahlen* (pp. 177–193). Munichü: Öl-schläger Verlag.

Weaver, D. H. (1984). Media agenda-setting and public opinion: Is there a link? In R. N. Bostrom (Ed.), *Communication yearbook 8* (pp. 680–691). Beverly Hills, CA: Sage.

Weaver, D. H. (1987). Media agenda-setting and elections: Assumptions and implications. In D. L. Paletz (Ed.), *Political communication research: Approaches, studies, and assessments* (pp. 176–191). Norwood, NJ: Ablex.

Weaver, D. H. (1991). Issue salience and public opinion: Are there consequences of agenda-setting? *International Journal of Public Opinion Research, 3*, 53–68.

Weaver, D. H., Graber, D. A., McCombs, M. E., & Eyal, C. H. (1981). *Media agenda-setting in a presidential election: Issues, images, and interest.* New York: Praeger.

Weimann, G., & Brosius, H. B. (1994). Is there a two-step flow of agenda-setting? *International Journal of Public Opinion Research, 6*, 323–341.

Weinstein, S., Appel, V., & Weinstein, C. (1980). Brain activity responses to magazine and television advertising. *Journal of Advertising Research, 2*, 57–63.

Wertham, F. (1954). *Seduction of the innocent.* New York: Rinehart.

White, D. M. (1949). The gate-keeper: A case study in the selection of news. *Journalism Quarterly, 27*, 383–390.

Whitney, D. C., & Becker, L. B. (1982). "Keeping the gates" for gatekeepers: The effects of wire news. *Journalism Quarterly, 59*, 60–65.

Wildavsky, A. (1987). Choosing preference by constructing institutions: A cultural theory of preference formation. *American Political Science Review, 81*(3), 3–22.

Willnat, L., & Zhu, J. H. (1996). Newspaper coverage and public opinion in Hong Kong: A time-series analysis of media priming. *Political Communication, 13*(2), 231–246.

Windahl, S. (1981). Uses and gratifications at the cross roads. In G. C. Wilhoit & H. Bock (Eds.), *Mass communication review yearbook 2* (pp. 174–185). Beverly Hills, CA: Sage.

Winship, E. C., & Allport, G. W. (1943). Do rosy headlines sell newspapers? *Public Opinion Quarterly, 7*, 205–210.

Winter, J. (1980). *Differential media-public agenda setting effects for selected issues, 1948–1976.* Unpublished doctoral dissertation, Syracuse University, Syracuse, NY.

Winter, J., & Eyal, C. (1981). Agenda setting for the civil rights issue. *Public Opinion Quarterly, 45*, 376–383..

Wright, C. (1959). *Mass communication.* New York: Random House.

Wu, T. S. (1994). Studying the effect of the prediction model of image voting in Taipei. *Public Opinion Quarterly, 189*, 41–66.

Wyer, R. S., & Hartwick, J. (1980). The role of information retrieval and conditional inference processes in belief formation and change. In L. Berkowitz (Ed.), *Advances in experimental social psychology* (Vol. 13, pp. 241–284). New York: Academic Press.

Wyer, R. S., & Ottati, V. (1992). Political information processing. In S. Iyengar & W. J. McGuire (Eds.), *Explorations in political psychology* (pp. 264–295). Durham, NC: Duke University Press.

Wyer, R. S., & Srull, T. K. (1986). Human cognition in its social context. *Psychological Review, 93*, 322–359.

Wyer, R. S., & Srull, T. K. (1989). *Memory and cognition in its social context.* Hillsdale, NJ: Lawrence Erlbaum Associates.

Yagade, A., & Dozier, D. M. (1990). The media agenda-setting effect of concrete versus abstract issues. *Journalism Quarterly, 67*, 3–10.

Yorke, J., & Li, T. (1975). Period three implies chaos. *American Mathematical Monthly, 82*, 985–992.

Yu, S. L. (1982). *The study of college students' perceptions of rising political figures.* Unpublished masters thesis, The Graduate School of Public Policy, National Chungshin University, Taipei.

Zaller, J. (1992). *The nature and origins of mass opinion.* Cambridge, UK: Cambridge University Press.

Zandpour, F. (1985, May). *1984 presidential candidates, voters' cognitive styles and preferences.* Paper presented at the International Communication Association Convention, Honolulu, HI.

Zhu, J. (1992). Issue competition and attention distraction: A zero-sum theory of agenda-setting. *Journalism Quarterly, 68,* 825–836.

Zhu, J. H., Watt, J. H., Snyder, L. B., Yan, J., & Jiang, Y. (1993). Public issue priority formation: Media agenda-setting and social interaction. *Journal of Communication, 43,* 8–29.

Zucker, H. G. (1978). The variable nature of news media influence. In B. D. Ruben (Ed.), *Communication yearbook 2* (pp. 225–245). New Brunswick, NJ: Transaction Books.

Contributors

Deborah Blood is in the Department of Communication Sciences at the University of Connecticut, Avery Point. She received her PhD from the University of Connecticut, Storrs, where Jian-Hua Zhu was a member of her dissertation committee. She is married to Peter Phillips, co-author of her contribution to this book.

William Boroson, now a graduate student at Syracuse University, was a graduate student in the Department of Communication Studies at the University of Connecticut, Storrs at the time this work was carried out. He was Jian-Hua Zhu's research assistant.

Edward Caudill is at the School of Journalism, University of Tennessee. Caudill received his PhD from the University of North Carolina at Chapel Hill where Donald Shaw chaired his dissertation committee.

Anat First is now teaching at Hebrew University of Jerusalem. She also received her PhD from Hebrew University. During the 1995–1996 academic year First was a visiting scholar at the University of North Carolina at Chapel Hill where she worked with Donald Shaw.

Salma Ghanem is in the Department of Communication, University of Texas–Pan American. Ghanem received her PhD from the University of Texas at Austin where her dissertation committee was chaired by Maxwell McCombs.

William Gonzenbach, who is in the Department of Advertising and Public Relations, University of Alabama, received his PhD from the University of North Carolina at Chapel Hill. Donald Shaw was a member of his dissertation committee.

Bradley J. Hamm is in the Department of Journalism and Communication, Elon College. He received his PhD from the University of North Carolina at Chapel Hill where Donald Shaw chaired his dissertation committee.

Pu-tsung King is in the Department of Journalism at National Chengchi University in Taiwan. King received his PhD from the University of Texas at Austin where his dissertation committee was chaired by Maxwell McCombs.

Dominic Lasorsa is in the Department of Journalism, University of Texas at Austin. Lasorsa received his PhD from Stanford University. He is a faculty colleague of Maxwell McCombs.

Maxwell McCombs holds the Jesse H. Jones Centennial Chair in Communication at the University of Texas at Austin. His PhD is from Stanford University. In 1996 McCombs and Donald Shaw received the Murray Edelman Award of the American Political Science Association in recognition of their 30-year research partnership.

Lee McGavin is in the Department of Speech Communication, University of West Alabama. He received his PhD from the University of Alabama, where William Gonzenbach was a member of his dissertation committee.

Andreina Mandelli is in the Marketing Department at Bocconi University in Milan, Italy. She is a PhD candidate at Indiana University, where David Weaver is chair of her dissertation committee.

Peter C. B. Phillips is Sterling Professor of Economics at Yale University. His PhD is from the London School of Economics, University of London. He is married to Deborah Blood, co-author of his contribution to this book.

Marilyn Roberts is in the Department of Advertising, University of Florida. She received her PhD from the University of Texas at Austin, where Maxwell McCombs was co-chair of her dissertation committee.

America Rodriguez is in the Department of Radio-Television-Film, University of Texas at Austin. Rodriguez received her PhD from the University of California at San Diego. She is a faculty colleague of Maxwell McCombs.

Holli Semetko holds the Chair of Audience Research and Public Opinion at the University of Amsterdam. Her PhD is from the London School of Economics, University of London. David Weaver is a co-author of her book on the formation of campaign agendas in U.S. and British elections. Semetko and Maxwell McCombs were participants in a 1989 summer seminar that visited 14 German journalism and communication programs.

Donald L. Shaw is Kenan Professor in the School of Journalism, University of North Carolina at Chapel Hill. His PhD is from the University of Wisconsin at Madison. In 1996, Shaw and Maxwell McCombs received the Murray Edelman Award of the American Political Science Association in recognition of their 30-year research partnership.

Toshio Takeshita, now in the Department of Political Science, Meiji University in Tokyo, formerly was at the University of Tsukuba. He received his master's degree from the University of Tokyo. A long-standing friend of both Maxwell McCombs and David Weaver, Takeshita prepared the Japanese translation of a longitudinal agenda-setting study of the 1976 U.S. presidential election co-authored by Weaver, McCombs, and their colleagues.

Wayne Wanta is at the School of Journalism and Communication, University of Oregon. Wanta received his PhD from the University of Texas at Austin, where his dissertation committee was chaired by Maxwell McCombs.

David Weaver is the Roy W. Howard Professor in Journalism and Mass Communication research at Indiana University. His PhD is from the University of North Carolina at Chapel Hill, where Donald Shaw chaired his dissertation. He also has co-authored two books on agenda setting and public opinion with Maxwell McCombs.

Lars Willnat is at the School of Media and Public Affairs, George Washington University. He received his PhD from Indiana University, where his dissertation committee was chaired by David Weaver.

Jian-Hua Zhu is in the Department of Communication Sciences, University of Connecticut, Storrs and currently at the City University of Hong Kong. He received his PhD from Indiana University. His dissertation committee was chaired by David Weaver. Zhu has co-authored recent journal articles with both Maxwell McCombs and Lars Willnat.

Author Index

259

Subject Index

A

ABC, 74, 77, 80, 164, 191, 216, 218, 222
Acceleration model of public awareness of issue salience, 122–124
Advertising
  and agenda setting, 85–96
  frames, 23–24
  influence on the news, 91–93
Affective dimension of news, 12–13
Agenda building, 21
Agenda setting, 7–8
  and cognitive priming, 55–56
  cross-national research, 195–207
  cumulative effects, 121–122
  decay of effects, 150–151
  defined, 19–20
  as definition research, 19–21
  differences across news media, 137–143
  and economic news, 97–113
  effects, conditions for, 163–166
  effects, national v. local news, 148–151
  evaluated as a theory, 14
  evidence of positive influence, 104–113
  evolution of research methods, 116–124
  first and second levels contrasted, 3–10
  first level, 4, 29–30, 42, 45–46
  first level as a special dimension, 21–23
  first dimension, 21–23
  as a function of mass media, 161–163
  as historical generalization, 170–173
  historical perspectives, 169–182
  and journalistic paradigm, 19–20
  model of the first and second levels, xi
  object attributes, 3–6
  priming, and political involvement, 58–60
  second dimension, 22–23
  second level, ix–xi, 3–14, 21–24, 29–30, 33–34, 37–38, 41–42, 45–46, 177, 200
    defined, 4–6, 29–30
    effects, 48–50
  study of objects, ix–xi
  as a two-step process, 145–146
  as a useful concept, 20–21
Aggregate analysis of agenda-setting data, 51–53
AIDS, 11, 128, 129
American Institute for Political Communication, 33, 231
American-Statesman, Austin (Texas), 92, 164–166
Ames, Fisher, 214
ANOVA analysis, 39
Arbitron, 189
ARIMA (autoregressive, integrated, moving average), 118, 122
  time-series models, 124–129
  parameters, 125–128